Clare Lighton

The
Concise
Dictionary
of
Foreign Quotations

The
Concise
Dictionary
of
Foreign Quotations

Edited by
Anthony Lejeune

FITZROY DEARBORN PUBLISHERS

CHICAGO • LONDON

The Concise Dictionary of Foreign Quotations

Selection and arrangement © Stacey London 1998

Published in the United Kingdom by
Stacey London
128 Kensington Church Street
London W8 4BH

Published in the United States of America by
Fitzroy Dearborn Publishers
919 North Michigan Avenue
Chicago
Illinois 60611

ISBN 1-57958-341-5 Fitzroy Dearborn

Editor: Anthony Lejeune
Assistant Editor: Kitty Carruthers

Contributing Editors
Latin Section: Anthony Lejeune
French Section: Jessica Hodge
German Section: Clare Haworth-Maden
Italian Section: Alexandra Richardson
Spanish Section: Carmen Suarez

First published in the United States 2001

A Cataloging-in-Publication record for this book is available from the Library of Congress

CONTENTS

ACKNOWLEDGEMENTS

Many people helped in the preparation of this book, making suggestions, providing sources and checking references. Among those to whom we owe special thanks are John Crawley, Professor Sir Henry Swinnerton Dyer, Kyril Fitzlyon, Professor Jasper Griffin, the Reverend Professor Richard Griffiths, J.L.A. Hartley, Frank Johnson, Richard Lamb, Hubert Picarda QC, Professor John White, Nadine Welter and Thérèse Wright.

FOREWORD

by the Publisher

As the compiler of this work, Anthony Lejeune, remarks, any Dictionary of Quotations is a quarry where a reader, dropping in, can browse and inform himself and find constant delight. But one function of this present volume is entirely practical. The press, contemporary literature, documentary and verbal usage are scattered with untranslated and unattributed quotations in foreign languages. How often do we know just what they mean, or where they originated?

They are used for concision and precision. Thus what we offer here is a compendium of clean, sharp expression, fruits of a long tradition of eclectic thought and experience. The user of *The Concise Dictionary of Foreign Quotations* will find herein accuracy and a little light scholarship, and verbal discipline, covering – we trust – just what will be valuable to the speech-maker and the conversationalist and the attentive reader of good prose which from time to time stretches out a hand to the classics or neighbouring languages for felicity, wit, and expression.

May the reader enjoy himself, and benefit.

Tom Stacey

PREFACE

by Anthony Lejeune

"I think," said the Rev. Dr. Folliott, dryly, about one of his companions when they were revisiting Oxford, "he must have finished his education at some very rigid college, where a quotation, or any other overt act showing acquaintance with classical literature, was visited with a severe penalty. For my part, I make it my boast that I was not to be so subdued. I could not be abated of a single quotation by all the bumpers in which I was fined."

Does anyone read Peacock now, let alone quote him? I hope so; he was himself a great quoter and offers a merry maze of scholarly divagations. I stand entirely with Dr. Folliott in that passage from *Crotchet Castle*. He in turn must surely have agreed with Dr. Johnson that "classical quotation is the *parole* of literary men all over the world." By "literary" we do not, of course, mean only (or chiefly or at all) the kind who write unreadable "literary" novels. I would rather say that classical quotation – apt quotation from the classics in any language – is a sure mark of civilised men.

Such quoting has become unfashionable, indeed unusual. Once upon a time, not so very long ago, even Members of Parliament indulged in it, and were not considered pretentious for doing so. Just imagine the response if anyone ventured to make a Latin joke in the House of Commons now! What has been lost, or abandoned, is not only a valuable element in debate and conversation but much personal pleasure and solace. As Gibbon observed, pondering the Emperor Diocletian's almost uniquely contented retirement from a throne to a garden (a market garden – he grew cabbages), busy men of affairs often fail to acquire the art of conversing with themselves. For such inner conversation, too, quotations can play an important role.

A good stock of quotations is therefore a fine thing to possess, and adding to it a lifelong pleasure. The young should be encouraged to keep a commonplace book: few practices will give them more certain satisfaction later. Any Dictionary of Quotations is a kind of commonplace book; a large quarry from which each reader, visiting it however casually, can make his own selection.

Another function for which the present volume was designed is more pragmatic. Even today one quite frequently comes across, in books or newspaper editorials, untranslated and unattributed quotations in some foreign language. Only the most incurious reader will not wish to know what they mean and who uttered them: only the most learned or the most fortunate will invariably recognise them. We have tried here to present as many as possible of the quotations which non-specialist readers are most likely to meet. Our title refers to "foreign" quotations. In practice this means quotations from the commonest European languages which are foreign to an English reader. The effect is to provide a small compendium of European thought, fruits of a single civilisation, with Latin at the base. Ancient Greek should equally be there, but I was reluctantly persuaded that too many modern readers share the view of some mediæval scribes: *"Graecum est. Non potest legi."**

To cover five languages in one modest volume is asking a lot – or, one might say, asking too little of each. A much bigger book would have been easier to make. We could have gone on accumulating quotations indefinitely and enjoyably: but the result, for the reader, would have been less handy. We aimed at a book which would be tractable, portable and therefore relatively concise. So we had to cut.

Immediately, problems of definition arose. Just what is a "quotation"? It must surely be quotable, and, for our purpose, quotable in its original language. This criterion excludes long passages, and passages which an English-speaker is unlikely to quote other than in English (except – there are always exceptions – when reference to the original sheds fresh light on a familiar English version). Excluded on similar grounds are proverbial sayings which occur, without much difference, in all or several European languages. We have tended also to exclude, as not being strictly quotations, mere idioms and phrases – but, again, have allowed in a few marginal cases which we thought might be helpful. Less willingly, we have omitted some undoubted quotations, or what appear to be quotations, because, after much enquiry, we failed to discover their author.

Customary attributions are often wrong. Goering, for example, may have said that when he heard the word "culture" he reached for his gun, but he did not originate this excellent apophthegm**. Marie Antoinette may possibly (though I doubt it) have said "Let them eat cake"† (or even "Let them eat *brioches*") but the anecdote is very much older. I should have liked always to give not only the author but chapter and verse. Limitations of time and space rendered this ideal impracticable, and to pursue it patchily seemed inelegant. But, wherever possible, we have tried to confirm the text.

Even this basic exercise can raise a question, if not of principle, at least of indexing. Many familiar quotations are actually misquotations, and the mis-quotation may well be an improvement on the original, having been smoothed by its passage through the minds and mouths of men. However, a

Book of Quotations can hardly misquote deliberately. We can only trust that a keyword in the index will enable readers to find what they seek. The same hope applies to a reader seeking (as most of us will sometimes need to do) a quotation half-remembered or wrongly remembered.

Translating and sourcing quotations which one might find, italicised, in somebody else's writing is only half the function of this book: it should also be a mine of quotations for use by its readers. For that purpose, familiarity cannot be the sole test. There is much here which will probably be unfamiliar even to readers learned in the language concerned. Stumbling upon new gems is a primary pleasure of turning pages like these. A joy for their editors too. I have included some items which, though not in the least familiar, struck me as irresistible. *"Emax domina"*,†† for example; the reference may be obscure but the meaning is recognisable across two thousand years.

Compiling the Latin section, I was struck anew by the brilliance, clarity and poignancy with which those ancient authors still speak to us. Indeed this whole book illustrates the universality of human experience, of hope and fear and jesting in the dark, of "infinite passion and the pain of finite hearts that yearn." It is, I trust, instructive, perhaps edifying, useful and, I hope, entertaining. At the very least, it should help readers to follow the celebrated advice of Dr. Routh, the venerable President of Magdalen, who, when asked for some wise axiom or precept born of such a long and thoughtful life, replied, "You will find it a very good practice always to verify your references."

AL
London 1998

*	See page 15
**	See page 190
†	See page 109
††	See page 11

HOW TO USE THIS BOOK

Each section is laid out with the quotations in their various languages – Latin, French, German, Italian and Spanish – in the left hand column. Under each quotation, the name of the author (or other source) appears in bold. Beneath that, where appropriate, an explanation of its origin.

The English translation of the quotation appears in italics in the right hand column opposite the original, plus any explanatory remark (such as the literal translation, where a colloquial one is given).

Within each language section, the entries are arranged in alphabetical order of the first word, with the definite and indefinite articles included. For example, *"L'homme"* will be found under *"L"*, *"Der Tag"* under *"D"*. Where there is a definite or indefinite article, the subsequent word appears alphabetically (thus *"L'hypocrisie"* follows *"L'homme"*).

At the end of each section, there is provided an index of entries in that section, listed alphabetically under a keyword (or, in many cases, keywords), and giving the page on which the quotation appears.

At the end of the book is an alphabetical index of English keywords, covering all sections.

Finally, there is an alphabetical index of authors, which includes collective sources such as the Missal, the Vulgate, etc. It should be noted that from Psalm 9, the Vulgate's numbering of the Psalms differs slightly from that of the Book of Common Prayer. BCP numbers are given in brackets.

LATIN

All the charm of all the Muses often flowering in a lonely word.

Tennyson about Virgil

Ab ovo usque ad mala.

Proverb

From egg to apples (referring to the courses of a Roman dinner, or "From soup to nuts.")

Abeunt studia in mores.

Ovid

Things practised become second nature.

Abiit, excessit, evasit, erupit.

Cicero
about Catiline's flight

He has gone, run off, slipped away, flown the coop.

Absit omen.

Latin expression

May it not be an omen.

Actus non facit reum nisi mens sit rea.

Justinian, 3 Inst 107

A guilty intention, not just the act, makes a man guilty.

Addito salis grano.

Pliny the Elder
more commonly "Cum grano salis"

With a grain of salt.

Aegrotat daemon, monachus tunc esse
volebat;
Daemon convaluit, daemon ut ante fuit.

Mediaeval saying

*The devil was sick, the devil a monk would be;
The devil got well, the devil a monk was he.*

Aequam memento rebus in arduis
Servare mentem.

Horace

In difficult times, keep calm.

Aes triplex.

Horace

Triple bronze (i.e. immensely durable).

Aestimes iudicia, non numeres.

Legal principle

You should weigh opinions, not count them.

Afflavit Deus et dissipantur.

Queen Elizabeth's medal
commemorating the destruction of the
Spanish Armada

God blew and they were scattered.

Age iam meorum
Finis amorum.

Horace

Come then, last of my loves.

Agnosco veteris vestigia flammae.

Virgil

I recognise the traces of an old flame.

Agnus Dei, misereri nobis.
The Roman Catholic Missal

Lamb of God, have pity on us.

Agri non omnes frugiferi sunt.
Cicero

Not all fields are fruitful.

Alius quidam veterum poetarum cuius
nomen mihi nunc memoriae non est,
veritatem temporis filiam esse dixit.
Aulus Gellius

Another old poet, whose name I forget, said that truth is the daughter of time.

Alma mater.
Roman expression

The mother who nurtured us.

Amantium irae amoris integratio.
Terence

Lovers' quarrels are the renewal of love.

Amare et sapere vix deo conceditur.
Laberius

To love and be wise is hardly granted even to a god.

Ambo florentes aetatibus, Arcades ambo,
Et cantare pares et respondere parati.
Virgil

They were both in the flower of their youth together, Arcadians both, ready to sing and ready to respond.

Amici, diem perdidi.
The Emperor Titus
having done nothing to help anybody all day

Friends, I have lost a day.

Amicus Plato, amicus Socrates, sed magis
amica veritas.
Cicero

Plato and Socrates are my friends, but truth is a greater friend.

Amphora coepit
Institui; currente rota cur urceus exit?
Horace

It was intended to be a vase. Why does it emerge from the potter's wheel a mere jug?

Anathema sit.
Council of Trent
condemning heresy

May it be accursed.

Anguilla est, elabitur.
Plautus

He's an eel; he slips away.

Animula, vagula, blandula,
Hospes comesque corporis,
Quae nunc abibis in loca,

Little soul of mine, frolicsome, pleasant, guest and comrade of my body, where are you going, pale, cold, unprotected, never again to jest, as

Pallidula, frigida, nudula,
Nec, ut soles, dabis iocos?
                    The dying **Emperor Hadrian**
                        to his soul

you are accustomed to do?

Animum pictura pascit imani.
                    Virgil

He feeds his mind on an empty picture.

Annuncio vobis gaudium magnum.
Habemus Papam.
    The announcement from the Vatican that a
        new Pope has been elected

*I bring you tidings of great joy. We have a
Pope.*

Arbiter elegantiae.
                    Tacitus
                about Petronius

A judge of elegant manners or objects.

Arma virumque cano.
                    Virgil
            first words of the *Aeneid*

Arms and the man I sing.

Ars est celare artem.
                    Roman maxim

Art consists in concealing the art.

Ars longa, vita brevis.
    Roman translation of Hippocrates' aphorism

Life is short, the art so long to learn.

At pulchrum est digito monstrari et dicier,
Hic est.
                    Persius

*It's a sweet thing to be pointed out and have it
said, "That's him."*

At tuba terribili sonitu taratantara dixit.
                    Ennius

*And the trumpet in terrible tones went
taratantara.*

Audacter calumniare, semper aliquid
haeret.
                    Francis Bacon

Spread libel boldly. Some of it always sticks.

Audi alteram partem.
    St Augustine; moral or legal principle

Hear what the other side has to say.

Auream quisquis mediocritatem
Diligit.
                    Horace

Whoever loves the golden mean.

Aut Caesar aut nullus.
Julius Caesar

I will be Caesar or nothing.

Ave, Caesar, morituri te salutant
the gladiators' salute on entering the arena

Hail, Caesar. Those who are about to die salute thee!

Beatus ille, qui procul negotiis,
Ut prisca gens mortalium,
Paterna rura bobus exercet suis,
Solutus omni faenore.
Horace

Happy is he who, far away from business, ploughs ancestral acres, free from financial worries, like the earliest race of men.

Bis dat qui cito dat.
Alciatus

He gives twice who gives quickly.

Brevis esse laboro,
Obscurus fio.
Horace

*I strive to be brief,
I become obscure.*

Brutum fulmen.
Latin expression

Mindless lightning (i.e. a loud but harmless outburst).

Caelo tonantem credimus Iovem regnare.
Horace

When he thunders in the sky we believe that Jupiter reigns.

Caelum non animum mutant qui trans
mare currunt.
Horace

They change their skies but not their minds who rush across the sea.

Candida me capiet, capiet me flava puella.
Ovid

I shall fall for the ash-blonde – and the tawny haired girl too.

Cantabit vacuus coram latrone viator.
Juvenal

The penniless traveller will sing in the presence of a robber.

Cantate Domino
The Vulgate, 97th Psalm (BCP 98th)

Sing unto the Lord.

Cato mirari se aiebat quod non rideret
haruspex haruspicem cum videret.
Cicero

Cato used to say that he was amazed one soothsayer could keep a straight face when he met another.

Catus amat pisces sed non vult tingere
plantas.
Mediaeval adage

The cat loves fish but doesn't want to get his feet wet.

Cave canem.
Petronius Arbiter
describing a notice beside the door

Beware of the dog.

Caveat emptor.
Legal maxim

Let the buyer beware.

Certum est quia impossibile.
Tertullian
about the resurrection

Assuredly true because it seems impossible.

Cetera desunt.
Copyists' or scholars' expression

The rest is missing.

Ceteris paribus.
Latin expression

Other things being equal.

Chimaera bombinans in vacuo.
Rabelais

An imaginary monster buzzing in empty space.

Chommoda dicebat si quando commoda
vellet
Dicere et insidias Arrius hinsidias.
Catullus

Arrius, if he wanted to say "amenities" would say hamenities, and instead of "ambushes" hambushes.

Civis Romanus sum.
Cicero

I am a Roman citizen.

Cogito, ergo sum.
Descartes

I think, therefore I am.

Consuetudo vicit: quae cum omnium
domina rerum, tum maxime verborum est.
Aulus Gellius

Usage won: usage which rules all things and especially language.

Corruptio optimi pessima.
Latin saying

The best when corrupted becomes the worst.

Corruptissima in republica plurimae leges.
Tacitus

The most corrupt state will have the most laws.

Cras amet qui nunquam amavit quique
amavit cras amet.
Pervigilium Veneris

Tomorrow he shall love who has never loved before, and he who has loved shall love tomorrow.

Credite posteri.
Horace

Believe it, posterity.

Credo ut intelligam.
St Ambrose

I believe in order that I may understand.

Cucullus non facit monachum.
Mediaeval saying

The cowl does not make the monk.

Cui bono?
Principle of legal enquiry, quoted by **Cicero**

To whose advantage?

Cuius est solum, eius est usque ad caelum et ad inferos.
Sir Edward Coke; legal maxim

Whoever owns the land owns everything above it, even to the sky.

Cum aliquos numquam soluturos significare vult, "ad Kalendas Graecas soluturos" ait.
Suetonius

When he [Augustus] *wanted to suggest that a debt would never be paid he used to say, "it will be paid on the Greek calends"* (i.e. never).

Cum dignitate otium.
Cicero

Leisure with honour.

Cum grano salis.
Roman expression

With a grain of salt. (Because we'd need salt to help us swallow it.)

Curiosa felicitas.
Petronius Arbiter
referring to Horace

Studied felicity (of style).

Currente calamo.
Roman expression

With a flowing pen.

Da mihi castitatem et continentiam, sed noli modo.
St Augustine

Give me chastity and continence – but not yet!

Damnosa hereditas.
Gaius, *Inst;* legal term

A ruinous inheritance.

De gustibus non disputandum.
Mediaeval scholiasts' saying

There's no arguing about tastes.

De minimis non curat lex.
Sir George Croke

The law doesn't concern itself with trifles.

De mortuis nil nisi bonum.
Latin saying
adapted from the Greek sage Chilon

One should speak only good of the dead.

De nihilo nihil, in nihilum nil posse reverti.

Persius

Nothing comes from nothing, and nothing which exists can become nothing.

Decus et tutamen.

Virgil
inscribed on British £1 coin

Handsome and secure.

Delenda est Carthago.

Cato the Elder
who added at the end of every speech
"Ceterum censeo Carthaginem delendam esse"

Carthage must be destroyed.

Deo optimo maximo.

Roman Catholic slogan
usually just DOM

To God, the sum of all goodness, the sum of all greatness.

De profundis clamavi ad te, Domine; Domine, exaudi vocem meam.
The Vulgate, 129th Psalm (BCP 130th)

Up from the depths I have cried to thee, Lord; Lord, hear my voice.

Deo volente.

Latin expression
often just DV

God willing.

Deus ex machina.

Latin expression

A god from the machine. Referring (lit.) to the god who, in some classical plays, descends, with special effects, to solve the problem.

Dicebamus hesterno die...

Fray Luis de León

We were saying yesterday... (on resuming his lectures after five years in prison).

Dictum sapienti sat est.

Plautus and **Terence**

A word to the wise is enough.

Dies irae, dies illa,
Solvet saeclum in favilla
Teste David cum Sybilla

Mediaeval hymn
attributed to the friar Thomas of Celano

Day of wrath, that day which shall dissolve the world into ashes, as both David and the Sybil testify.

Dis aliter visum.

Virgil

The gods decided otherwise.

Dilige et quod vis fac.

St Augustine

Love and do what you will.

Disce, puer, virtutem ex me, verumque laborem,
Fortunam ex aliis.

Virgil

Learn from me, boy, courage and exertion, good fortune from others.

Divide et impera.

Roman maxim

Divide and rule.

Dominus vobiscum.

The Roman Catholic Missal

The Lord be with you.

Dulce et decorum est pro patria mori.

Horace

It is sweet and seemly to die for one's country.

Dulce ridentem Lalagen amabo,
Dulce loquentem.

Horace

I will love Lalage, sweetly smiling, sweetly talking.

Dulcis moriens reminiscitur Argos.

Virgil

Dying, he remembers his dear Argos.

Dum deliberamus quando incipiendum est, incipere iam serum est.

Quintilian

While we debate when a start should be made, it is already too late to start.

Dum lego, assentior.

Cicero
on reading Plato's argument for the immortality of the soul

While I'm reading I agree.

Dum se bene gesserit.

Legal expression
for example, specifying the tenure of judges

So long as he conducts himself properly.

Dum spiro, spero.

Motto

While I breathe, I hope.

Dum vivimus, vivamus.

From an ancient inscription

While we live, let us live.

Durum! Sed levius fit patientia
Quicquid corrigere est nefas.

Horace

It's hard! But what cannot be mended becomes lighter with patience.

Dux femina facti.

Virgil

The leader of this enterprise was a woman.

E pluribus unum.

St Augustine
and motto of the U.S.A.

Several become one.

Ecce homo!

Pontius Pilate
John XIX.5; often used as title for pictures of
Jesus wearing the crown of thorns

Behold the man.

Ego et rex meus.

Cardinal Wolsey
wrongly thought to be arrogant but in fact
the correct Latin word order

I and my king.

Eheu! Fugaces, Postume, Postume,
Labuntur anni; nec pietas moram
Rugis et instanti senectae
Afferet indomitaeque morti.

Horace

*Alas, Postumus, the fleeting years slip by, nor
can piety delay the coming of wrinkles or
approaching old age or unconquerable death.*

Emax domina.

Ovid

The lady is addicted to shopping.

Entia non sunt multiplicanda praeter
necessitatem.

William of Occam's "razor"

Entities [i.e. philosophic or economic
concepts] *should not be multiplied
unnecessarily.*

Epicuri de grege porcum.

Horace
about himself

A pig from Epicurus's herd.

Ergo necesse est devenire ad aliquod
primum movens, quod a nullo movetur; et
hoc omnes intelligunt Deum.

St Thomas Aquinas

*Necessarily, therefore, one comes to a prime
mover which has not itself been moved; and
this everyone understands to be God.*

Errare humanum est.

Melchior de Polignac

To err is human.

Esse oportet ut vivas, non vivere ut edas.

Cicero

*You should eat in order to live, not live in
order to eat.*

Esto peccator et pecca fortiter, sed fortius
fide et gaude in Christo.

Martin Luther

*Be a sinner and sin strongly, but more
strongly have faith and rejoice in Christ.*

Esto perpetua.
Father Paul Sarpi
dying words about his native Venice

May you last forever.

Et ego in Arcadia *or* Et in Arcadia ego.
Latin phrase

Either *"I too have lived in Arcady,"* or (usually of death) *"Even in Arcady there am I."*

Et hoc genus omne.
Horace

And everything [or everyone] *of that kind.*

Et tu, Brute!
Latin version of Caesar's cry at his assassination, uttered in Greek

Even you, Brutus!

Ex Africa semper aliquid novi.
Pliny the Younger
slightly misquoted; actually "Vulgare Graeciae dictum, Semper Africam aliquid novi afferre." The common Greek saying that there is always something new out of Africa

There's always something new from Africa.

Ex nihilo nihil fit.
Lucretius

Nothing comes of nothing.

Ex pede Herculem.
Latin saying

You can tell the size of Hercules from his footprint. (6'7", according to Pythagoras, who worked it out from the Olympic stadium which had supposedly been measured by the hero's foot.)

Exegi monumentum aere perennius.
Horace
of his poetry

I have built a monument more enduring than brass.

Exeunt omnes.
Stage direction

They all go out.

Expedit esse deos, et, ut expedit esse, putemus.
Ovid

It is expedient that there should be gods, and, since it is expedient, let us assume that there are.

Facilis descensus Averno,
Sed revocare gradus superasque evadere
ad auras
Hic opus, hic labor est.
Virgil

Easy is the descent to hell, but retracing one's steps and regaining the open air, that's very hard work.

Favete linguis.
Horace
a phrase which introduced sacred
ceremonies

Speak propitiously (or maintain a holy
silence).

Fecisti nos ad te et inquietum est cor
nostrum donec requiescat in te.
St Augustine

*Thou has made us for thyself and our heart is
restless until it rests in thee.*

Felix qui potuit rerum cognoscere causas
Atque metus omnes et inexorabile fatum
Subiecit pedibus strepitumque Acherontis
avari.
Virgil (of Lucretius)

*Happy is he who has been able to understand
the cause of things, and to tread beneath his
feet all fear and unyielding fate and the noise
of death's greedy stream.*

Festina lente.
A favourite saying of both **Augustus** and
Titus

Hasten slowly.

Fiat experimentum in corpore vili.
Latin saying

*Let the experiment be made on a worthless
body.*

Fiat iustitia, ruat coelum.
Sir James Dyer, CJCP; legal maxim

Let justice be done though the heavens fall.

Fiat lux.
The Vulgate, Genesis 1.3

Let there be light.

Fidei Defensor.
Ecclesiastical title
used mainly by British Sovereigns since
Henry VIII was given it by the Pope

Defender of the Faith.

Fidus Achates.
Virgil
referring to the companion of Aeneas, but
used now of any close friend

Faithful Achates.

Finis coronat opus.
Proverb

The end crowns the work.

Floreat Etona.
Eton College motto

May Eton flourish.

Fons et origo.
Latin expression

The fountain and source.

Forsan et haec olim meminisse iuvabit.
Virgil

Perhaps one day even these things will be a pleasure to recall.

Fortes fortuna adiuvat.
Terence

Fortune favours the brave.

Fortuna vitrea est: tum cum splendet frangitur.
Publilius Syrus

Fortune is like glass: as it shines, it shatters.

Frustra fit per plura quod potest fieri per pauciora.
William of Occam

It is wasteful to use more things for what can be done with fewer.

Fuit Ilium.
Virgil

Troy was (i.e. and is no more).

Functus officio.
Latin expression
of an official whose task has been completed

Having discharged his duties.

Galeatum sero duelli paenitet.
Juvenal

Once you've got your helmet on it's too late to regret the battle.

Gallia est omnis divisa in partes tres.
Julius Caesar

The whole of Gaul is divided into three parts.

Gaudeamus igitur
Iuvenes dum sumus.
Post iucundam iuventutem,
Post molestam senectutem,
Nos habebit humus.
Mediaeval students' song

Then let us rejoice while we are young. After sweet youth, after burdensome age, the earth will hold us.

Genius loci.
Latin expression

The genius [presiding spirit] of the place.

Genus immortale manet, multosque per annos
Stat fortuna domus, et avi numerantur avorum.
Virgil

The race dies not; through many years the fortunes of the house stand firm, and its children's children multiply.

Gradus ad Parnassum.
Horace
traditional name for a Latin verse textbook

The path to Parnassus.

14

Graecum est. Non potest legi.
Mediaeval scribes

This is Greek. Impossible to read.

Gratis anhelans, multa agendo nihil agens.
Phaedrus

Puffing pointlessly, very busy doing nothing.

Habeas corpus.
Legal term

You are to present the body (e.g. when a person is, allegedly, being wrongly held in prison).

Habent sua fata libelli.
Terentianus Maurus

Books have their own destiny.

Hae tibi erunt artes, pacique imponere
morem,
Parcere subiectis et debellare superbos.
Virgil

These shall be thine arts – to impose civilisation after peace, to spare the conquered and subdue the proud.

Heu pietas! Heu prisca fides!
Virgil

Alas for piety! Alas for old time faith!

Heu quotiens fidem
Mutatosque deos flebit et aspera
Nigris aequora ventis
Emirabitur insolens,
Qui nunc te fruitur credulus aurea,
Qui semper vacuam, semper amabilem
Sperat, nescius aurae
Fallacis.
Horace

Alas, how often shall he weep for faith and gods so changed, and, from lack of experience, marvel at the waters rough beneath the darkening gales, who now enjoys you, naïvely thinking you pure gold, hoping that you will always be free of heart, always lovable – little he knows of the treacherous wind.

Hi motus animorum atque haec certamina
tanta
Pulveris exigui iactu compressa quiescunt.
Virgil
about the bees

These turbulent hearts and these mighty battles are stilled by the throwing of a little dust.

Hic amor, haec patria est.
Virgil

Here is my love, here is my native land.

Hinc illae lacrimae.
Terence and **Horace**

Hence (i.e. consequently) *those tears.*

Homo proponit, sed Deus disponit.
Thomas à Kempis

Man proposes but God disposes.

Homo sum; humani nil a me alienum puto.

Terence

I am a man; everything human is of concern to me. (St Augustine says that, when these words were spoken in the theatre, the audience applauded thunderously.)

Horas non numero nisi serenas.

Inscription on sundials

I count only the sunny hours.

Horresco referens.

Virgil

I shudder to recall it.

Iacta alea est.

Roman expression
used most famously by Julius Caesar
when he crossed the Rubicon

The die is cast.

Ignorantia elenchi.

Logicians' term

Missing the point of the argument.

Ignotum per ignotius.

Latin expression

To explain something not understood by something even less understood.

Ille terrarum mihi praeter omnes
Angulus ridet.

Horace

That little corner of the world charms me beyond all others.

Illi robur et aes triplex
Circa pectus erat, qui fragilem truci
Commisit pelago ratem
Primus.

Horace

He must have had a heart of oak encircled with threefold bronze who first launched a frail bark upon the raging sea.

Imperium Traiani, rara temporum felicitate, ubi sentire quae velis et quae sentias dicere licet.

Tacitus

The reign of Trajan, a rare and happy time when one might think what one pleased and say what one thought.

Imprimatur.

A censor's permission
especially in the Catholic Church

It may be printed.

In eburna vagina plumbeus gladius.

Diogenes
deriding a showy shallow man

A leaden sword in an ivory sheath.

In flagranti delicto.
Legal term

In the very act of crime.

In forma pauperis.
Legal term

As a pauper (and therefore entitled to free legal aid).

In hoc signo vinces.
words seen by the Emperor Constantine, accompanying a cross in the sky

By this sign shalt thou conquer.

In loco parentis.
Latin phrase, often of schoolteachers

In place of a parent.

In magnis et voluisse sat est.
Propertius

In great endeavours the intention is enough.

In medio tutissimus ibis.
Ovid

The middle is the safest course.

In partibus infidelium.
Ecclesiastical expression
as of a bishop without a see in Christendom

In the lands of the infidel.

In pectore.
Roman Catholic ecclesiastical term
referring to cardinals whose names the Pope does not publish

Hidden in his breast.

In perpetuum, frater, ave atque vale.
Catullus

Brother, hail and farewell forever.

Inauditi atque indefensi, tamquam inno-centes perierant.
Tacitus

They were condemned unheard and undefended, just as though they were innocent.

In statu pupillari.
University statutes
describing undergraduates

In the rank or condition of a pupil.

In te, Domine, speravi: non confundar in aeternum.
The Vulgate, 70th Psalm (BCP 71st) and the last verse of the Te Deum

In thee, Lord, have I placed my hope: let me never be confounded.

In vino veritas.
Proverb

Under the influence of wine, the truth emerges.

Incipe, parve puer, risu cognoscere matrem. **Virgil**	*Begin, baby boy, to recognise your mother with a smile.*
Indignor quandoque bonus dormitat Homerus. **Horace**	*I am censorious when great Homer nods.*
Infandum, regina, iubes renovare dolorem. **Virgil**	*Unspeakable, O queen, is the grief which you ask me to renew.*
Infra dignitatem. **Latin phrase,** usually just "Infra dig"	*Beneath one's dignity.*
INRI, *standing for* Iesus Nazarenus Rex Iudaeorum. **The inscription above the cross**	*Jesus of Nazareth, King of the Jews.*
Integer vitae scelerisque purus non eget Mauris iaculis neque arcu nec venenatis gravida sagittis, Fusce, pharetra. **Horace**	*A man of upright life, unstained by guilt, needs no Moorish javelins, Fuscus, nor bow nor quiver laden with poisoned arrows.*
Inter alia. **Latin expression**	*Among other things.*
Inter pocula. **Latin expression**	*Between drinks.*
Inter silvas Academi quaerere verum. **Horace**	*To seek the truth amid the groves of Academus.*
Interdum stultus bene loquitur. **Proverb**	*Occasionally a fool says something sensible.*
Intoleranda Romanis vox, Vae victis! **Livy** recalling Brennus the Gaul's insult	*"Woe to the conquered!", a saying intolerable to Romans.*
Intuta quae indecora. **Tacitus**	*What is unseemly is unsafe.*
Ipsa scientia potestas est. **Francis Bacon**	*Knowledge is power.*
Ipsissima verba. **Latin expression**	*The actual words.*

Isne tibi melius suadet, qui "rem facias, rem,
si possis, recte, si non, quocumque modo,
rem"?
Horace

Does he advise you better who tells you,
"Wealth, acquire wealth; honestly if you can; if
not, by any means available"?

Ite, missa est.
The Roman Catholic Missal

Go, the Mass is ended.

Iudicium parium aut leges terrae.
Magna Carta

The judgement of his peers or the laws of the
land. (Only by these may an Englishman
be convicted.)

Iuppiter ex alto periuria ridet amantum.
Ovid

Jupiter smiles from on high at lovers' lies.

Iuravi lingua, mentem iniuratam gero.
Cicero
from Euripides

With my tongue I have sworn, but my mind is
unsworn.

Iure sit gloriatus marmoream se relinquere
quam latericiam accepisset.
Suetonius
about Augustus

He could rightly boast that he found a city of
brick and left a city of marble.

Ius primae noctis.
Mediaeval expression
of a feudal lord's supposed entitlement

A claim to the first night (with a newly
married bride).

Iustitiae tanta vis est ut ne illi quidem qui
maleficio et scelere pascuntur possint sine
ulla particula iustitiae vivere.
Cicero

So powerful is the idea of justice that not even
those who thrive on crime and wrongdoing can
live without some touch of it.

Iustum et tenacem propositi virum
Non civium ardor prava iubentium,
Non voltus instantis tyranni,
Mente quatit solida.
Horace

The just man, firm of purpose, is not moved
from his resolution either by his fellow citizens
urging iniquity or by the tyrant's threatening
countenance.

Laborare est orare.
Proverb

To work is to pray.

Lapsus calami.
Latin phrase

A slip of the pen.

Lares et penates.
Roman phrase

Household gods, guardians of hearth and
home.

Latrante uno, latrat statim et alter canis.
Latin proverb

When one dog barks another immediately barks too.

Laudator temporis acti.
Horace

A praiser of past times.

Lex talionis.
Legal phrase

The law of retaliation.

Literae humaniores.
Academic phrase
at Oxford the study of the classics, ancient history and philosophy

Humane letters, the humanities.

Locus paenitentiae.
Legal phrase

An opportunity to change one's mind.

Locum tenens.
Latin phrase
a deputy; e.g. a doctor standing in for another

Occupying his place.

Locus standi.
Legal phrase

A standing place (i.e. the right to be in court or on a committee).

Lucus a non lucendo.
Quintilian
ridiculing etymological guesswork

Lit: *A grove because there is no light there;* "lucus", a grove, being supposedly derived from "lucere", to shine.

Lugete, O Veneres Cupidinesque,
Et quantum est hominum venustiorum.
Passer mortuus est meae puellae,
Passer, deliciae meae puellae.
Catullus

Mourn, O Loves and Cupids and all people of heart. Dead is my lady's sparrow, the sparrow that was my lady's joy.

Macte virtute.
Virgil

Be strong in virtue.

Magna civitas, magna solitudo.
Latin translation of a line from Greek comedy

A great city, a great loneliness.

Magna est veritas et praevalet.
The Vulgate, III Edras 4,41

The truth is great and it prevails.

Magnas inter opes inops.

Horace

Poverty amidst great wealth. Palmerston's reply to Kentish hop-growers who complained that their crop had suffered more from bad weather than crops in surrounding districts.

Magni nominis umbra.

Lucan

The shadow of a great name.

Magnus ab integro saeclorum nascitur ordo.
Iam redit et Virgo, redeunt Saturnia regna,
Iam nova progenies caelo demittitur alto.

Virgil

From the cycle of years a great age is born. Now returns the virgin godess, now returns the reign of Saturn, now descends a newborn race from heaven above.

Malo cum Platone errare quam cum istis
vera sentire.

Cicero

I would rather be wrong with Plato than right with those people.

Malo malo malo malo.

Schoolboy joke
playing on the different meanings of what
looks like the same word

*Malo, I would rather be,
Malo, in an apple tree,
Malo, than a naughty boy,
Malo, in adversity.*

Malo me Galatea petit, lasciva puella,
Et fugit ad salices et se cupit ante videri.

Virgil

Galatea, mischievous girl, throws an apple at me, and flees into the willows and wants me to see where she goes.

Malum vas non frangitur.

Proverb

A worthless vase doesn't get broken.

Malum in se. Malum prohibitum.

Contrasted legal phrases

Something inherently wrong as distinct from something wrong because there is a law against it.

Mandamus.

Legal term
a writ ordering someone to do something

We order.

Manet alta mente repostum
Iudicium Paridis spretaeque iniuria formae.

Virgil

Deep in her heart lie the judgement of Paris and the insult of her slighted beauty.

Manibus date lilia plenis.

Virgil

Give me lilies by the armful.

Mansuetae naturae.

Legal phrase generally of domestic as
opposed to wild animals ("ferae naturae")

Of a gentle disposition.

Manus manum lavat.
Seneca

One hand washes the other.

Maximum remedium irae mora est.
Cicero

Time is the best cure for anger.

Me iudice.
Latin expression

In my opinion.

Mea culpa, mea maxima culpa.
Christian liturgical phrase

My fault, my very great fault.

Medio de fonte leporum
Surgit amari aliquid quod in ipsis floribus
angat.
Lucretius

From amidst the fountain of delight something bitter springs to trouble us even among the flowers.

Memento mori.
Philosophic or theological injunction
represented by a sobering object or warning

Remember thou wilt die.

Memoriae proditur Tiberium, quotiens
curia egrederetur, Graecis verbis in hunc
modum eloqui solitum: "O homines ad
servitutem paratos!"
Tacitus

Tradition says that Tiberius, whenever he left the Senate House, used to exclaim in Greek, "How ready these men are to be slaves!"

Mens sana in corpore sano.
Juvenal

A healthy mind in a healthy body.

Mentis gratissimus error.
Horace

A most delightful wandering of the mind.

Meos tam suspicione quam crimine
iudico carere oportere.
Julius Caesar

I consider that my own family should be not only guiltless but above suspicion.

Meum est propositum in taberna mori.
Walter Mapes
a mediaeval drinking song

I mean to die in a pub.

Militavi non sine gloria.
Horace
about the battles of love

I have fought not without glory.

Mirabile dictu.
Virgil

Wondrous to relate.

Misce stultitiam consiliis brevem:
Dulce est desipere in loco.
Horace

*Blend a little foolishness with your wisdom:
it's nice to be silly at the right moment.*

Misere est tacere cogi quod copias loqui.
Publilius Syrus

*It's wretched being forced to keep quiet about
something one's bursting to tell.*

Miseri, quibus
Intentata nites.
Horace
about a fickle girl

Unhappy are they for whom you shine untested.

Mobilium turba Quiritium.
Horace
originating our phrase "the mob"

A crowd of inconstant citizens.

Modus vivendi.
Latin expression
especially of adverse parties learning to
live together

A way of living.

Monstrum, horrendum, informe, ingens.
Virgil
of the Cyclops Polyphemus

A monster, horrible, misshapen, huge.

More maiorum.
Latin phrase

In the manner of our fathers.

Multum in parvo.
Latin expression

Much contained in a small compass.

Mutato nomine de te
Fabula narratur.
Horace

Change the name, and the story is about you.

Natis in usum laetitiae scyphis
Pugnare Thracum est; tollite barbarum
Morem.
Horace

*Fighting over one's cups, which were made for
pleasure, is a Thracian habit; away with such
barbarous doings.*

Natura abhorrat vacuum.
Descartes

Nature abhores a vacuum.

Narratur et prisci Catonis
Saepe mero caluisse virtus.

Horace

They say that even old Cato's stern disposition was often warmed by wine.

Naturam expelles furca, tamen usque recurret.

Horace

You may drive nature out with a pitchfork but she will always return.

Ne sutor ultra crepidam.

Apelles

Let the cobbler stick to his last. (Rebuke to a shoemaker who, having justly pointed out an error in the painting of a slipper, went on to more general criticism.)

Nec audiendi qui solent dicere, Vox populi, vox Dei, quum tumultuositas vulgi semper insaniae proxima sit.

Alcuin

They should not be listened to who keep saying that "The voice of the people is the voice of God", since the turbulence of the crowd is always very near to madness.

Nec gemino bellum Troianum orditur ab ovo.

Horace

Nor does he start the Trojan war from the twin eggs (i.e. from Helen's birth).

Nemo fit fato nocens.

Seneca

No one is driven to crime by fate.

Nemo me impune lacessit.

Latin motto
the motto in the Royal Arms for Scotland, used by the Order of the Thistle

No one provokes me unpunished.

Neque semper arcum
Tendit Apollo.

Horace

Nor is Apollo always bending his bow.

Nequeo monstrare, et sentio tantum.

Juvenal

I can't demonstrate it; I just feel it.

Nescio quid curtae semper abest rei.

Horace

No state of affairs is ever perfect.

Nescire quod antea quam natus sis acciderit, id est semper esse puerum; quid enim est aetas hominis nisi memoria rerum nostrarum cum superiorum aetate contexerit?

Cicero

To be ignorant of what occurred before one's birth is to be always a child, for what is adult life unless memory enables us to compare the events of our own time with those of earlier periods?

Nescis, mi fili, quantula sapientia guberne-
tur mundus?

Count Oxenstierna
writing to his son

*Do you not know, my son, with how little
wisdom the world is governed?*

Nescit vox missa reverti.

Horace

A word once uttered cannot be recalled.

Nihil aeque gratum est adeptis quam
concupescentibus.

Pliny the Younger

*Nothing is as pleasing when one has obtained
it as when one desired it.*

Nihil est ab omni
Parte beatum.

Horace

Nothing is entirely good.

Nihil simile est idem.

Latin proposition

Things similar are not identical.

Nil actum credens dum quid superesset
agendum.

Lucan
of Julius Caesar

*Considering nothing done while anything
remained to be done.*

Nil desperandum Teucro duce et auspice
Teucro.

Horace

*We must not despair while Teucer is our leader
and we are under Teucer's banner.*

Nisi caste, saltem caute.

Proverb

If not chastely, at least cautiously.

Nobis cum semel occidit brevis lux,
Nox est perpetua una dormienda.

Catullus

*When our brief day is done, we must sleep
through a single endless night.*

Nocturna versate manu, versate diurna.

Horace

*Turn these things over by night, turn them
over all day long.*

Noli me tangere.

The Vulgate, John 20, 17

Touch me not.

Nolle prosequi.

Legal expression

Unwillingness to prosecute.

Nolo episcopari.

Ecclesiastical expression
implying a suitable modesty

I don't want to be made a bishop.

Non amo te, Sabidi, nec possum dicere
                quare;
Hoc tantum possum dicere, non amo te.
Martial

I don't like you, Sabidius, but I can't say why;
all I can say is that I don't like you.
(Famously applied by Tom Brown, when
an undergraduate, to the Dean of Christ
Church: I do not love thee, Doctor Fell,/
The reason why I cannot tell;/But this I
know, and know full well,/I do not love
thee, Doctor Fell.)

Non Angli sed angeli.

Pope Gregory the Great,
on seeing some handsome English boys
in the marketplace

Not Angles but angels.

Non cuivis homini contingit adire
Corinthum.
Horace

It's not given to everybody to visit Corinth (a
luxurious holiday spot).

Non compos mentis.

Latin phrase

Off his head (i.e. mad).

Non ego hoc ferrem, calidus iuventa,
Consule Planco.
Horace

I wouldn't have put up with such treatment in
my hot-blooded youth when Plancus was
consul.

Non ego ventosae venor suffragia plebis.
Horace

I don't pursue the votes of the fickle masses.

Non id videndum, coniugum ut bonis bona
At ut ingenium congruat et mores moribus;
Probitas pudorque virgini dos optima est.
Terence

What matters is not that a married couple
should be equal in wealth but that their minds
and manners should be compatible; integrity
and modesty are a girl's best dowry.

Non nobis, Domine.
The Vulgate, 113th Psalm, 2nd part
(BCP 115th)

Not unto us, O Lord (...but unto thy name
give glory).

Non omnis moriar; multaque pars mei
Vitabit Libitinam.
Horace

I shall not wholly die; a great part of me will
escape Libitina [the goddess of funerals].

Non olet. | *It doesn't smell.*

Vespasian
about a coin charged for the use of public
lavatories

Non scribit, cuius carmina nemo legit. | *A man whose work nobody reads isn't a writer.*

Martial

Non sum qualis eram bonae sub regno | *I'm not the man I used to be when sweet*
Cynarae. | *Cynara ruled my heart.*

Horace

Non tamen intus | *You should not put upon the stage things*
Digna geri promes in scenam. | *which would occur more suitably behind the*

Horace | *scenes.*

Non tali auxilio nec defensoribus istis. | *This is not the kind of help nor are those the*

Virgil | *champions that we need.*

Nonumque prematur in annum. | *Let it be kept back for nine years.*

Horace
of a literary work

Nondum amabam et amare amabam... | *I did not yet love, but I was in love with*
quaerebam quid amarem, amans amare. | *love...I sought what I might love, loving to*

St Augustine | *love.*

Novus homo. | *A new man (i.e. an upstart).*

Roman expression

Nulla fere causa est in qua non femina | *There are hardly any legal disputes which*
litem moverit. | *weren't started by a woman.*

Juvenal

Nulla salus bello. | *There's no safety in war.*

Virgil

Nulli negabimus, nulli deferemus iustitiam. | *To no man will we deny, to no man will we*
Magna Carta | *delay, justice.*

Nullius addictus iurare in verba magistri. | *Not bound to swear by the words of any*
Horace | *master.*

Nullum quod tetigit non ornavit. | *He touched nothing which he did not adorn.*
Dr Johnson
epitaph on Oliver Goldsmith

Numeros memini, si verba tenerem.
Virgil

I'd remember the tune if only I could get the words.

Numquam se minus otiosum esse quam cum otiosus, nec minus solum quam cum solus esset.
Cicero

(Scipio used to say of himself) Never less idle than when he was at leisure, never less lonely than when alone.

Nunc dimittis.
The Vulgate, Luke 2, 29

Now lettest thou [thy servant] *depart.*

Nunc est bibendum, nunc pede libero Pulsanda tellus.
Horace

Now is the time for drinking, now let the ground shake beneath a lively dance.

O fons Bandusiae, splendidior vitro.
Horace

O spring of Bandusia, brighter than glass.

O fortunatam natam, me consule, Romam!
Cicero's attempt at poetry

O fortunate Rome, born when I was consul!

O fortunati nimium, sua si bona norint, Agricolae.
Virgil

O happy farmers, if only they recognised their own good fortune!

O mihi praeteritos referat si Iuppiter annos!
Virgil

Oh that Jupiter would give me back the years that are past!

O noctes cenaeque deum.
Horace

O nights and feasts of the gods.

O passi graviora, dabit deus his quoque finem!
Virgil

O you who have suffered worse, God will bring an end to this too.

O quanta qualia sunt illa sabbata Quae semper celebrat superna curia.
Peter Abelard

O what sabbaths, and how many, are those which the company of heaven perpetually enjoys.

O quanta species cerebrum non habet!
Phaedrus

O that such beauty should be brainless!

O sancta simplicitas!
John Huss
when, as he was burnt at the stake, he saw an old peasant bringing extra faggots

What holy simplicity!

O Sancte Pater, sic transit gloria mundi.
  reminder to the Popes during their enthrone-
    ment, accompanied by the burning of flax

Holy Father, thus passes away the glory of this world.

O si sic omnia! *or* O si sic omnes!
    Juvenal

Oh that all things [or all men] *were like this!*

O tempora! O mores! Senatus haec intelle-
git, consul videt; hic tamen vivit.
    Cicero

Oh, what times! What manners! The Senate is aware of these things, the consul sees them; and yet this man is still alive.

O testimonium animae naturaliter
Christianae!
    Tertullian

O evidence of a mind naturally Christian! (i.e. the belief in a supreme being, without benefit of Christian revelation).

O Tite tute Tati tibi tanta tyranne tulisti!
    Ennius

O tyrant Titus Tatius, what a lot you brought upon yourself!

Obiter dictum.
    Latin phrase

Something said incidentally.

Obsequium amicos, veritas odium parit.
    Terence

Obsequiousness begets friends, truth begets hatred.

Obstupui, steteruntque comae et vox fau-
cibus haesit.
    Virgil

I was astounded, my hair stood on end and my voice stuck in my throat.

Occidit miseros crambe repetita
magistros.
    Juvenal
  about schoolmasters

Re-cooked cabbage is the death of these unhappy teachers.

Oderint dum metuant.
  Cicero, Suetonius, and frequently said by
    Caligula

Let them hate me, provided they fear me.

Odi et amo. Quare id faciam fortasse
                requiris.
Nescio: sed fieri sentio, et excrucior.
    Catullus

I hate and I love. Why, you may ask, do I behave in this way? I don't know; I just know that this is how I feel, and I am in torment.

Odi profanum vulgus et arceo.
    Horace

I hate and spurn the common crowd.

Odium scholasticum *or* Odium theologicum.
Mediaeval expression

Hatred between scholars or between theologians.

Olet lucernam.
Proverb
about some literary work

It smells of the lamp.

Omina sunt aliquid.
Ovid

There is something in omens.

Omne animal post coitum triste.
Proverb

After making love all creatures are sad.

Omne ignotum pro magnifico.
Tacitus

The unknown is always taken to be grand.

Omnia vincit amor, nos et cedamus amori.
Virgil

Love conquers all; let us yield to love.

Omnis ars imitatio est naturae.
Seneca

All art is an imitation of nature.

Omnium consensu capax imperii nisi imperasset.
Tacitus
about the Emperor Galba

Universally judged fit to rule – until he ruled.

Ovis ovem sequitur.
Proverb

One sheep follows another.

Paene insularum, Sirmio, insularumque Ocelle.
Catullus

Sirmio, bright eye of islands and of almost islands.

Palinodum canere.
Stesichorus
recanting in a new poem an earlier one in which he had slighted Helen

To sing a palinode.

Pallida mors aequo pulsat pede pauperum tabernas
Regumque turres. O beate Sesti,
Vitae summa brevis spem nos vetat incohare longam.
Horace

Pale death knocks with impartial foot on the hovels of the poor and the palaces of kings. Oh happy Sestus, life's brief sum forbids us to form any long-term hope.

Panem et circenses.

Juvenal
saying that this was all the decadent
Roman people cared about

Bread and circuses.

Parcus deorum cultor et infrequens
Insanientis dum sapientiae
Consultus erro; nunc retrorsum
Vela dare atque iterare cursus
Cogor relictos.

Horace

A grudging and infrequent worshipper of the
gods while I wandered professing a wisdom
which was no wisdom, I am forced now to
re-set my sails and follow again the course I
had abandoned.

Parturiunt montes, nascetur ridiculus mus.

Horace

The mountains are in labour, and a silly mouse
will be born.

Pax vobiscum.

The Roman Catholic Missal

Peace be with you.

Penitus toto divisos orbe Britannos.

Virgil

Britons, virtually separated from the whole
world.

Per ardua ad astra.

Motto of the Royal Air Force

With endurance to the stars.

Per varios casus, per tot discrimina rerum,
Tendimus in Latium.

Virgil

Through many chances and changes of fortune
we press on towards Latium.

Pereant illi qui ante nos nostra dixerunt.

St Jerome
quoting Aelius Donatus

May they perish who have made our own good
remarks before us.

Persicos odi, puer, apparatus.

Horace

I hate, my boy, those Persian fripperies.

Petitio principii.

Logical fallacy
assuming as a premise the conclusion to
be proved

Begging the question.

Pirata est hostis humani generis.

Sir Edward Coke

A pirate is the enemy of all mankind.

Pollice verso.
signal given in the arena when one
gladiator was at the mercy of another

Thumbs down.

Pone seram, cohibe; sed quis custodiet ipsos
Custodes?

Juvenal

*Shoot the bolt, close the door; but who is to
guard the guardians?*

Pons asinorum.
proverbially the Fifth Proposition of **Euclid**

The asses' bridge.

Populus me sibilat: at mihi plaudo.

Horace

The people hiss me: but I applaud myself.

Populus vult decipi. Decipiatur.
attributed to **Cardinal Caraffa** but
probably older

*The people wish to be deceived. Let them be
deceived.*

Posse comitatus.
Mediaeval Latin for the assembly
summoned to help the sheriff

A posse.

Possunt quia posse videntur.

Virgil

They can because it's thought they can.

Post bellum auxilium.

Proverb

Help – after the war.

Post equitem sedet atra cura.

Horace

Black care sits behind the rider.

Post hoc, ergo propter hoc.

Logical fallacy

After this, therefore because of this.

Primo avulso non deficit alter
Aureus, et simili frondescit virga metallo.

Virgil

*When a bough is torn away, another golden
bough grows with leaves of the same metal.*

Primus inter pares.

Latin phrase
e.g. the Prime Minister's position in the
Cabinet

First among equals.

Procul, o procul este, profani.

Virgil

Away, away, ye profane.

Proprium humani ingenii est odisse quem
laeseris.

Tacitus

*It is human nature to hate someone you have
injured.*

Prospectandum vetulo latrante.
Proverb

When an old dog barks, look out.

Pulvis et umbra sumus.
Horace

We are dust and shadow.

Purpureus late qui splendeat unus et alter
Assuitur pannus.
Horace

One or two brightly shining purple patches are sewn on.

Quadrupedante putrem sonitu quatit
ungula campum.
Virgil
an example of onomatopoeia

With four-footed pulse the hoof shakes the dusty plain.

Qualis artifex pereo.
Nero
just before his death

What an artist dies in me.

Quamquam ridentem dicere verum
Quid vetat?
Horace

Nevertheless, what prevents us from telling the truth cheerfully?

Quantum meruit.
Legal phrase
quantifying money due for a service

As much as it was worth.

Quantum sufficit.
Medical term
often simply "quant.suff."

As much as necessary.

Quem deus vult perdere prius dementat.
Proverb
adapted from Publilius Syrus

Whom God wishes to destroy he first makes mad.

Quem di diligunt adolescens moritur.
Plautus

Whom the gods love dies young.

Quem si puellarum insereres choro,
Mire sagaces falleret hospites
Discrimen obscurum, solutis
Crinibus ambiguoque vultu.
Horace

If you were to place him in a throng of girls, the most discerning strangers could hardly tell the difference, with his flowing locks and his androgynous face.

Qui amant ipsi sibi somnia fingunt.
Virgil

Lovers construct their own dreams.

Qui desiderat pacem praeparet bellum.
Flavius Vegetius Renatus

Whoever desires peace should prepare for war.

Qui me amat, amat et canem meum.
Proverb
quoted by St Bernard

Who loves me loves my dog too.

Quid est ergo tempus? Si nemo ex me quaerat, scio; si quarenti explicare velim, nescio.
St Augustine

What then is time? If no one asks me, I know; if I want to explain it to someone who asks me, I don't know.

Quidquid agis, prudenter agis et respice finem.
Gesta Romanorum

Whatever you do, do prudently and look to the end.

Quieta non moveri.
Proverb

Leave well alone.

Quis desiderio sit pudor aut modus
Tam cari capitis?
Horace

What shame should there be or limit in our longing for one so dear?

Quo vadis?
Christ
appearing to St Peter as he fled from Rome

Where are you going?

Quod erat demonstrandum.
Geometry book
usually just "QED"

Which was to be demonstrated.

Quod licet Iovi non licet bovi.
Proverb

What is permissable for Jove is not permissible for an ox.

Quod ubique, quod semper, quod ab omnibus creditum est.
St Vincent of Lerins

What has everywhere, always and by everyone been believed.

Quot homines tot sententiae.
Terence

As many opinions as there are people.

Rara avis in terris, nigroque simillima cygno.
Ovid
but "rara avis" occurs also in Horace and Juvenal

A bird rarely seen on earth, very like a black swan.

Rari nantes in gurgite vasto
Virgil

Scattered swimmers in the huge sea.

Reductio ad absurdum.
Logicians' phrase
demonstrating, by carrying it to extremes,
the absurdity of an opponent's position

Reduction to absurdity.

Regum aequabat opes animis; seraque
revertens
Nocte domum, dapibus mensas onerabat
inemptis.
Virgil
about a happy old man who cultivates his
garden

In his heart he equalled the wealth of kings;
returning home at night, he loaded his table
with unbought feasts.

Relata refero.
Latin phrase

I tell what I've been told.

Relicta non bene parmula.
Horace
confessing that he ran away from the
battle at Philippi

My little shield ingloriously discarded.

Religentem esse oportet, religiosum nefas.
Aulus Gellius
quoting an old poem

One should be religious but not too religious.

Rem acu tetigisti.
Plautus
quoted by Jeeves in P. G. Wodehouse

You've touched the thing with a needle (i.e. hit
the spot).

Requiem aeternam dona eis, Domine.
beginning of the **Roman Catholic Mass**
for the Dead

Give them eternal rest, O Lord.

Requiescat in pace.
often simply RIP on tombstones

May he rest in peace.

Res ipsa loquitur.
Latin, especially legal, expression

The thing speaks for itself.

Res iudicata.
Legal expression

A matter which has been settled.

Res nullius.

Latin, especially legal, phrase

A thing which belongs to no-one.

Roma locuta est, causa finita est.

St Augustine

Rome has spoken. The matter is settled.

Rus in urbe.

Martial

A bit of country in the town.

Saeva indignatio.

Jonathan Swift's epitaph
(Ubi saeva indignatio ulterius cor
lacerare nequit.)

Fierce indignation.

Sal Atticum.

Roman expression

Attic salt (i.e. wit).

Salus extra ecclesiam non est.

St Augustine

There is no salvation outside the Church.

Sardonius risus.

Roman expression

A sardonic smile. (Referring to a bitter herb
which grew in Sardinia and contorted the
features of those who tasted it.)

Securus iudicat orbis terrarum bonos non
esse qui se dividunt ab orbe terrarum in qua-
cunque parte terrarum.

St Augustine

*It is the calm judgement of the world that those
men cannot be good who in any part of the
world cut themselves off from the world.*

Sed fugit interea, fugit inreparabile
tempus.

Virgil

But time flies, irretrievable time.

Semel emissum volat irrevocabile verbum.

Horace

A word once spoken flies beyond recall.

Semper ad eventum festinat et in medias
res non secus ad notas auditorem rapit.

Horace

*He always hurries to the outcome and plunges
his listener into the middle of things as though
they were already familiar with them.*

Sero te amavi, pulchritudo tam antiqua et
tam nova, sero te amavi! et ecce intus eras
et ego foris et ibi te quaerebam.

St Augustine

*Late have I loved thee, beauty so ancient and so
new, late have I loved thee! And, lo, thou wert
within me, and I was without and sought thee
there.*

Servata semper lege et ratione loquendi.
Juvenal

Always keep to the rules and logic of language.

Sesquipedelia verba.
Horace

Words a foot and a half long.

Si fractus inlabatur orbis, impavidum
ferient ruinae.
Horace

*If the world were to break and fall upon him,
he would be unafraid as the wreckage struck.*

Si monumentum requiris, circumspice.
Sir Christopher Wren's
memorial in St Paul's Cathedral

If you seek his monument, look around you.

Si natura negat, facit indignatio versum.
Juvenal

If talent fails, anger prompts a verse.

Si parva licet componere magnis.
Virgil

If one may compare small things with great.

Si volet usus,
Quem penes arbitrium est et ius et norma
loquendi.
Horace

*If usage sanctions it – this is the criterion, the
law and the practice of language.*

Sic itur ad astra.
Virgil

This is the way to the stars.

Sic me servavit Apollo.
Horace
on being rescued from the attentions of a
garrulous fellow

Thus Apollo saved me.

Sic semper tyrannis.
attributed to Brutus as he killed Caesar, and
exclaimed by John Wilkes Booth at the
assassination of Lincoln

May this always be the fate of tyrants.

Silent leges inter arma.
Cicero

The laws fall silent when swords are drawn.

Simplex munditiis.
Horace

Simple in her neatness.

Sine Cerere et Libero friget venus.
Terence

Without food and wine love grows cold.

Sine die.
Legal or administrative phrase

Without a fixed day (i.e. for reassembly; indefinitely).

Sine qua non.
Latin expression

Without which, not (i.e. indispensable).

Solamen miseris socios habuisse doloris.
Mephosophilis in Marlowe's *Dr Faustus*

Having companions in sorrow is a comfort to the wretched.

Solitudinem faciunt, pacem appellant.
Tacitus

They make a desert and call it peace.

Solvitur ambulando.
Philosophers' phrase

The question is solved as we proceed.

Sortes Virgilianae.
Latin phrase

The Virgilian lottery (i.e. opening Virgil at random, as some Christians open the Bible, seeking an oracle).

Spatio brevi
Spem longam reseces. Dum loquimur
fugerit invida
Aetas. Carpe diem, quam minimum
credula postero.
Horace

Confine your hopes to a short space. While we talk, envious time has been flying. Seize today, trust as little as possible to the morrow.

Spectatum veniunt, veniunt spectentur ut ipsae.
Ovid

The women come to see the show, and they come to be seen.

Splendide mendax.
Horace

Gloriously false.

SPQR: Senatus Populusque Romanus.
Initials inscribed on military standards

The Senate and the People of Rome.

Stabat Mater dolorosa.
Jacapone da Todi

There stood the Mother [the Virgin Mary] *in her sorrow.*

Stare super antiquas vias, et videre quaeam sit via recta et bona, et ambulare in ea.
The Vulgate
Jeremiah, 6.16, quoted in Bacon's essay *"Of Innovations"*

To stand upon the old ways, and to see which is the straight and good road, and to walk in it.

Stat sua cuique dies; breve et irreparabile
tempus
Omnibus est vitae; sed famam extendere
facti,
Hoc virtutis opus.

Virgil

Every man has his appointed day; to all men a short and unalterable span of life; but by deeds to extend our fame, this is virtue's task.

Status quo ante bellum.

Latin phrase
used mainly about international affairs

The situation before war began (e.g. to restore it).

Stet.

Instruction to printers

Let it stand (i.e. ignore deletion or correction).

Stomachor omnia.

Cicero
growing old

I get cross about everything.

Suave mari magno turbantibus aequora
ventis
E terra magnum alterius spectare laborem.

Lucretius

It is agreeable, when out at sea the winds are whipping up the waves, to watch from shore another's trouble.

Suaviter in modo, fortiter in re.

Latin motto, adopted by the Jesuits

Gentle in manner, strong in practice.

Sub judice.

Legal expression

Currently the subject of legal action.

Sub rosa.

Latin expression

Under the rose (i.e. under a seal of silence). Because Cupid once bribed Harpocrates, the god of Silence, with a rose not to divulge the amours of Venus, a rose hanging above the table became a symbol of discretion.

Sub specie aeternitatis.

Theological expression
used by Spinoza

In the sight of eternity.

Sublimi feriam sidera vertice.

Horace

In exaltation I shall smite the stars.

Suggestio falsi, suppressio veri.

Latin phrases
for statements which, though not actually
untruthful, are deliberately misleading

False implications, suppression of the truth.

Sui generis.

Latin phrase

Of its own special kind, unique.

Summum bonum.

Cicero; philosophers' phrase

The ultimate good.

Summum ius summa iniuria.

Cicero

More law, less justice.

Sunt geminae Somni portae, quarum
altera fertur
Cornea, qua veris facilis datur exitus
umbris,
Altera candenti perfecta nitens elephanto,
Sed falsa ad caelum mittunt insomnia
Manes.

Virgil

There are twin gates of Sleep, one said to be of horn through which true ghosts may readily pass, the other wrought of shining ivory but through it the spirits send false dreams up to the world.

Sunt lacrimae rerum et mentem mortalia
tangunt.

Virgil

Tears are due and the fate of mortal man touches the heart.

Sursum corda.

The Missal

Lift up your hearts.

Tabula rasa.

Latin phrase

A blank sheet.

Tacitum vivit sub pectore vulnus.

Virgil

The wound festers silently within his breast.

Taedium vitae.

Latin phrase

Weariness of life.

Tantae molis erat Romanam condere gentem.

Virgil

So huge was the effort to found the Roman race.

Tantum bona valent quantum vendi
possunt.

Sir Edward Coke
quoting Justinian

Things are worth precisely what they can be sold for.

Te Deum laudamus.

Hymn
said to have been improvised by St Ambrose
while baptising St Augustine

We praise thee, O Lord.

Tecum vivere amem, tecum obeam libens.
Horace

With thee I would love to live, with thee I would gladly die.

Tempora mutantur, nos et mutamur in illis.
Attributed to the **Emperor Lothar I**

Times change and we change with them.

Tempus edax rerum.
Horace

Time that devours all things.

Tendebantque manus ripae ulterioris amore.
Virgil

They stretched out their hands in longing for the further shore.

Tenet insanabile multos
Scribendi cacoethes.
Juvenal

An incurable itch for writing seizes many people.

Teres atque rotundus.
Horace

A man smooth and plump.

Terminus a quo, terminus ad quem.
Latin phrases

Starting point, finishing point.

Terra antiqua, potens armis atque ubere glebae.
Virgil

An ancient land, strong in arms and in the richness of the soil.

Terra incognita.
Latin phrase

Unknown territory.

Tertium quid.
Latin expression
often about negotiations

A third possibility or participant.

Timeo Danaos et dona ferentes.
Virgil

I fear the Greeks, even [or especially] *when they bear gifts.*

Timeo hominem unius libri.
St Augustine

I fear a man who knows only one book.

Timor mortis conturbat me.
William Dunbar

The fear of death troubles me.

Tityre, tu patulae recubans sub tegmine fagi
Silvestrem tenui Musam meditaris avena.
Virgil

Tityrus, lying beneath a roof of spreading beech, you practice a woodland Muse upon your slim reed.

Tolle lege, tolle lege.

St Augustine
hearing a voice from outside, in the manner
of a child's game

Take them and read them, take them and read them (i.e. the Sacred Scriptures - he opened them at Rom.13,13).

Tu quoque.

Latin phrase

You too.

Tuba mirum spargens sonum.

a line from the **Dies irae**

The trumpet sending forth its marvellous sound.

Tuta timens.

Virgil

Frightened even when there is no danger.

Uberrima fides.

Legal expression

Fullest good faith (e.g. as a term of contract).

Ubi mel ibi apes.

Plautus

Where there is honey there will be bees.

Ultima ratio regum.

Inscription on Louis XIV's cannon

The final argument of kings.

Ultima Thule.

Virgil

Furthest Thule (i.e. the utmost corner of the world).

Ululas Athenas portas.

Proverb

You are taking owls to Athens (i.e. coals to Newcastle).

Una salus victis nullam sperare salutem.

Virgil

The only safety for the conquered is to have no hope of safety.

Unus homo nobis cunctando restituit rem;
Non ponebat enim rumores ante salutem.

Ennius
about Fabius Cunctator, who, for a long
while, avoided battle with Hannibal

By delay one man saved everything for us; he cared more about the safety of the state than about public opinion.

Urbi et orbi.

Papal benediction

To the city and the world.

Usque ad aras.

Roman phrase

Even to the altars (i.e. to the last extremity).

Uti possidetis.

Latin phrase, mainly diplomatic

Keep what you hold.

Utinam populus Romanus unam cervicem haberet.

Caligula

Would that the Roman people had only one neck.

Vade mecum.

Latin phrase
generally of a companionable book

Go with me.

Vade retro, Satana.

The Vulgate, *Luke 4.8*

Get thee behind me, Satan.

Vae! Puto deus fio.

Vespasian
when dying

Alas, I think I am becoming a god.

Vanitas vanitatum. Omnia vanitas.

The Vulgate, *Ecclesiastes 1.2*

Vanity of vanities. All is vanity.

Vare, redde legiones!

Augustus
lamenting that a Roman army under Quintilius Varus had been wiped out by the German chieftain, Arminius

Varus, give me back my legions!

Varium et mutabile semper Femina.

Virgil

Woman, always fickle and changeable.

Velut inter ignes Luna minores.

Horace

Like the moon among the lesser lights.

Veni Gotham, ubi multos Si non omnes vidi stultos.

Drunken Barnaby's Journal
"the Wise Men of Gotham" being proverbial in the Middle Ages for their stupidity

I came to Gotham, where most of those I saw, if not all, were stupid.

Veni, vidi, vici.

Julius Caesar,
reporting to the Senate his victory over Pharnaces

I came, I saw, I conquered.

Verbum sapienti sat est.

Proverb

A word is enough for the wise.

Vestigia terrent
Omnia in adversum spectantia, nulla
                retrorsum.
              Horace

The tracks frighten me, all going towards you but none returning. (Said by the wily fox to the lion at the entrance to his den.)

Vice versa.
              Latin phrase

Changed around.

Vicisti Galilaee.
        Julian the Apostate

Thou has conquered, O Galilean.

Victrix causa deis placuit sed victa Catoni.
              Lucan

The gods favoured the triumphant cause, Cato the lost cause.

Vide licet.
            Latin phrase,
abbreviated in English to "viz"

You may see (i.e. "namely" or "that is to say'").

Video meliora proboque;
Deteriora sequor
            Ovid

I see and approve what is better, but I follow the worse.

Vides ut alta stet nive candidum
Soracte, nec iam sustineant onus
Silvae laborantes.
          Horace

You see how Soracte stands white in deep snow and the burdened woods can no longer bear the weight.

Vires acquirit eundo.
           Virgil
about rumour

She acquires strength as she goes.

Vita hominum altos recessus magnasque
latebras habet.
      Pliny the Younger

A man's life contains hidden depths and large secret areas.

Vivamus, mea Lesbia, atque amemus,
Rumoresque senum severiorum
Omnes unius aestimemus assis.
         Catullus

Let us live, my Lesbia, and let us love, and let us value all the mutterings of grumpy old men at just a farthing.

Vixere fortes ante Agamemnona
Multi; sed omnes illacrimabiles
Urgentur ignotique longa
Nocte, carent quia vate sacro.
          Horace

Many brave men lived before Agamemnon but, unlamented and unknown, they are all swallowed up in long darkness, because they found no holy poet.

Vixit.
Roman announcement of a death

He has lived.

Volenti non fit iniuria.
Legal maxim

No wrong is done to one who submitted to it willingly.

Vos valete et plaudite.
Terence
one of the customary invitations to applaud
at the end of a Roman comedy

Farewell – and applaud!

Vox et praeterea nihil.
Latin phrase
adapted from the Greek, about the
nightingale

A voice and nothing more.

LATIN INDEX

FRENCH

Petrus Ronsardus iacet hic: si caetera nescis,
Nescis quid Phoebus, Musa, Minerva, Charis.

Epitaph by Pontus de Tyard

Ronsard lies here: and if a question follow,
Ye know not Muses, Graces and Apollo.

A la bonne et sincère amour est crainte perpétuellement annexée.

Rabelais
Gargantua et Pantagruel

Good and sincere love always brings fear.

A la guerre, les trois quarts sont des affaires morales, la balance des forces réelles n'est que pour un autre quart.

Napoléon I

In war, three-quarters turns on morale; the balance of manpower and materials counts only for the remaining quarter.

A la recherche du temps perdu.

Marcel Proust
title of novel

In search of lost time.

A l'oeuvre on connaît l'artisan.

La Fontaine
Les Frelons et les Mouches à Miel

A craftsman is recognized by his work.

A quoi que ce soit que l'homme s'applique, la nature l'y destinait.

Denis Diderot
Le Neveu de Rameau

Whatever man turns to, nature destined him for.

A vaincre sans péril, on triomphe sans gloire.

Pierre Corneille
Le Cid

To win without danger is to triumph without glory.

Adieu, chers compagnons! adieu, mes chers amis!
Je m'en vais le premier vous préparer la place.

Pierre de Ronsard
Derniers Vers

Farewell, dear companions, farewell, my dear friends. I am leaving first to prepare a place for you.

Adieu tristesse
Bonjour tristesse
Tu es inscrite dans les lignes du plafond.

Paul Eluard
A peine défigurée

Farewell sadness
Good morning sadness
You are inscribed in the lines of the ceiling.

Ah, je le répète sans cesse, il n'y a qu'un malheur, celui d'être né!

Mme du Deffand

I keep on repeating again and again that there is only one misfortune, being born.

Ah, la belle pleine lune,
Grosse comme une fortune!

Laforgue
Complainte de la Lune en Provence

Ah, the beautiful full moon, as fat as a fortune.

Ah! je suis leur chef, il fallait bien les
suivre.

Alexandre August Ledru-Rollin

Ah well! I am their leader, I really had to
follow them!

Aime la vérité, mais pardonne l'erreur.

Voltaire
Deuxième Discours, de la Liberté

Love truth, but forgive error.

Ainsi va le monde; on travaille, on projette,
on arrange d'un côté; la fortune accomplit
l'autre.

Beaumarchais
Le Mariage de Figaro

That's the way of the world; we work, we plan,
we manoeuvre one way; fate ends it in another.

Allez dire à votre maître que nous sommes
ici par la volonté du peuple et qu'on ne
nous en arrachera que par la puissance des
baïonnettes.

Mirabeau

Go and tell your master that we are here by the
will of the people and we will be moved only by
the power of bayonets.

Allons, enfants de la Patrie,
Le jour de gloire est arrivé!...
Aux armes, citoyens!
Formez vos bataillons!

Rouget de Lisle
'La Marseillaise'

Come, children of our country, the day of glory
has arrived!... To arms, citizens! Form your
battalions!

Alors, c'est l'enfer. Je ne l'aurais jamais
cru.... Vous vous rappelez: le souffre, le
bûcher, le gril... Ah quelle plaisanterie.
Pas besoin de gril, l'enfer, c'est les
Autres.

Jean-Paul Sartre
Huit Clos

So, that is what hell is. I would never have
believed it. You remember, the sulphur, the
funeral-pyre, the gridiron. Ah, what a joke. No
need of a gridiron, hell is other people.

Amour, amour, quand tu nous tiens,
On peut bien dire: Adieu, prudence!

La Fontaine
Le Lion Amoureux

Love, when we are in your grip, we may well
say, Farewell, caution.

"Anne, ma soeur Anne, ne vois-tu rien venir?" Et sa soeur Anne lui répondit, "Je ne vois rien que le soleil qui poudroye, et l'herbe qui verdoye."

Charles Perrault
"Bluebeard" from *Histoire et contes du temps passé*

"Anne, sister Anne, do you see nothing coming?" And her sister Anne replied, "I see nothing but the sun making dust and the green grass growing."

Après nous le déluge.

Mme Pompadour

After us the deluge.

Au clair de la lune,
Mon ami Pierrot,
Prête-moi ta plume
Que j'écrive un mot.
Ma chandelle est morte,
Je n'ai plus de feu;
Ouvre-moi ta porte,
Pour l'amour de Dieu.

Folksong

In the moonlight, Pierrot my friend, lend me your pen so that I can write a note. My candle has gone out and I have no more light. Open your door, for the love of God.

Aucun chemin de fleurs ne conduit à la gloire.

La Fontaine
Les Deux Aventuriers et le Talisman

The road to glory is not strewn with flowers.

Autre temps, autres mœurs.

Proverb

Other days, other ways.

Aux faux soupçons la nature est sujette,
Et c'est souvent à mal que le bien
s'interprète.

Molière
Le Tartuffe

Human nature is a prey to false suspicion, and good is often interpreted as evil.

Belle tête mais de cervelle point.

Proverb

A fine head, but no brains.

Bonjour Tristesse.

Françoise Sagan
title of novel

Good morning, sadness.

C'est brutal, mais ça marche!

René Panhard
on the car gearbox he had invented

It's rough but it works!

C'est Dieu qui le veut.

Victor Hugo
Réponse à un Acte d'Accusation

It is God's will.

C'est double plaisir de tromper le trompeur.

La Fontaine
L'Enfouisseur et son Compère

It is doubly pleasing to deceive the deceiver.

C'est hasarder notre vengeance que de la reculer.

Molière
Don Juan

It is risking our vengeance to postpone it.

C'est la sagesse! Aimer le vin,
La beauté, le printemps divin,
Cela suffit. Le reste est vain.

Théodore de Banville
Adolphe Gaïffe

Here is wisdom: to love wine, beauty and the divine Spring. That is enough, the rest is worthless.

C'est le coeur qui fait tout.

Molière
Mélicerte

It is the heart which does everything.

C'est le commencement de la fin.

Talleyrand
on the Hundred Days

It is the beginning of the end.

C'est magnifique, mais ce n'est pas la guerre.

Maréchal Bosquet
about the charge of the Light Brigade

It's magnificent, but it is not war.

C'est moi seul qui fait la politique, et sous ma seule responsabilité. Moi seul ai le pouvoir de décision.

Charles de Gaulle

I alone make policy, and I alone am responsible. I alone have the power of decision.

C'est pire qu'un crime, c'est une faute.

Boulay de la Meurthe
about the execution of the Duc d'Enghien

It is worse than a crime, it is a mistake.

C'est un fossé qui sera franchi lorsqu'on aura l'audace de le tenter.

Napoléon I

It [the Channel] is a mere ditch, and will be crossed as soon as someone has the courage to attempt it.

C'est un malheur de n'être point aimée; mais c'est un affront de ne l'être plus.

Montesquieu
Lettres

It is unfortunate not to be loved at all; but it is insulting to be loved no longer.

C'est un vin pur et généreux; mais nous avons bu trop du nôtre.

Hyppolyte Taine
Lettres

[Equality] is a pure and noble wine, but we have drunk too much of ours.

C'est une belle langue que l'anglais; il en faut peu pour aller loin.

Beaumarchais
Le Mariage de Figaro

English is a fine language; a little goes a long way.

C'est une étrange entreprise que celle de faire rire les honnêtes gens.

Molière
La Critique de l'Ecole des Femmes

It is a strange business making decent people laugh.

C'était, dans la nuit brune,
Sur le clocher jauni,
La lune
Comme un point sur un i.

Alfred de Musset
Ballade à la Lune

At dusk, over the yellowing bell tower, it was the moon, like the dot on an "i".

Ça ira.

French revolutionary song

Things will work out. (A phrase perhaps borrowed from Benjamin Franklin.)

Car sache que, dans les Enfers, il n'est d'autre châtiment que de recommencer toujours le geste inachevé de la vie.

André Gide

You must know that in hell there is no other punishment than to start again and again the *unfinished business of life.*

Ce corps qui s'appelle encore le saint empire romain n'était en aucune manière ni saint, ni romain, ni empire.

Voltaire

This entity which was called and still calls itself the Holy Roman Empire was in no way holy nor Roman nor an empire.

Ce n'est pas ce qui est criminel qui coûte le plus à dire; c'est ce qui est ridicule et honteux.

Jean-Jacques Rousseau
Les Confessions

It is not criminal admissions which are hardest to make, but those which are ridiculous and shameful.

Ce n'est pas toujours en allant de mal en pis que l'on tombe en révolution... Le régime qu'une révolution détruit vaut presque toujours mieux que celui qui l'avait immédiatement précédé, et l'expérience apprend que le moment le plus dangereux pour un mauvais gouvernement est d'ordinaire celui où il commence à se réformer.

Alexis de Tocqueville
L'Ancien régime

It is not always by going from bad to worse that a society falls into revolution... The social order destroyed by a revolution is almost always better than that which immediately preceded it, and experience shows that the most dangerous moment for a bad government is generally that in which it sets about reform.

Ce n'est pas victoire, si elle ne met fin à la guerre.

Montaigne
Essais

A victory is not a victory if it does not put an end to the war.

Ce n'est plus une ardeur dans mes veines cachée,
C'est Vénus toute entière à sa proie attachée.

Jean Racine
Phèdre

This is no longer a passion hidden in my heart, it is Venus herself seized of her prey.

Ce n'est point le temps qui manque, c'est nous qui lui manquons.

Claudel
Le Partage de Midi

It is not time that is short but we who waste it.

Ce qu'il nous faut, c'est la haine. D'elle naîtront nos idées.

Jean Genet
Les Nègres

Hatred is essential to us; our ideas will be born of it.

Ce que peut la vertu d'un homme ne se doit mesurer par ses efforts, mais par son ordinaire.

Blaise Pascal
Pensées

A man's worth should be measured by his normal actions not by his special efforts.

Ce qui n'est pas clair n'est pas français.
Antoine de Rivarol
Discours sur l'Universalité de la Langue Française

What is not clear is not French.

Certains ouvrages sont créés par leur public.
Certains autres créent leur public.

Valéry
Choses Tues

Some works are created by their public, others create their public.

Cet animal est très méchant.
Quand on l'attaque, il se défend.

originally from a comic song

This animal is very naughty. When attacked, it defends itself.

Cette cloison qui nous sépare du mystère des choses et que nous appelons la vie.

Victor Hugo
Les Misérables

This barrier which separates us from the mystery of things and which we call life.

Chacun a son défaut où toujours il revient.
Honte ni peur n'y remédie.

La Fontaine
L'Ivrogne et sa Femme

Everyone has recurring faults; neither shame nor fear can remedy them.

Chacun à son goût.

Proverb

Each to his own [taste].

Chacun le sien, ce n'est pas trop.

Molière
Le Malade Imaginaire

Each to his own, that's not too much to expect.

Chacun passe sa vie à jeter des petites pincées de poudre dans l'oeil de son voisin.

Labiche et Martin
La Poudre aux Yeux

Everyone spends his life throwing sand in his neighbour's eye.

Cherche à qui le crime profite.

Proverb

Look for the beneficiary of a crime.

Cherchez la femme.

Alexandre Dumas
Les Mohicans de Paris
attrib. Joseph Fouché

Look for the woman.

Chevalier sans peur et sans reproche.

description of Pierre Bayard in the old chronicles

A knight fearless and blameless.

Citoyens, vouliez-vous une révolution
sans révolution?

Robespierre
addressing the National Assembly, 1792

Citizens, would you want a revolution without revolution?

Coeur tu n'est qu'un théâtre,
Mais on y joue
Dans les décors de plâtre
Un drame fou.

Charles Péguy
Quatrains

Heart, you are only a theatre, but a mad drama is played there amid the plaster decorations.

Comme il n'y a pas de fumée sans feu...il
n'y a pas de feu sans allumage!

Georges Feydeau
La Dame de Chez Maxim's

Just as there is no smoke without fire, there is no fire without a spark.

Comme quelqu'un pourrait dire de moi
que j'ai seulement fait ici un amas de
fleurs étrangères, n'y ayant fourni du mien
que le filet à les lier.

Montaigne

It might be said of me that what I have made here is only a bunch of other men's flowers, supplying of my own just the string which ties them together.

Comment pourrais-je gouverner autrui,
qui moi-même gouverner ne saurais?

Rabelais
Gargantua et Pantagruel

How should I rule anyone else, who do not know how to rule myself?

Comment voulez-vous gouverner un pays
qui a deux cent quarante-six variétés de
fromage?

Charles de Gaulle

How can you govern a country which has 246 varieties of cheese?

Comparer, c'est comprendre.

Proverb

To compare is to understand.

Cueillez, cueillez votre jeunesse:
Comme à cette fleur, la vieillesse
Fera ternir votre beauté.

Pierre de Ronsard
Odes

Gather your youth: like that flower, old age will tarnish your beauty.

Cueillez dès aujourd'hui les roses de la vie.

Pierre de Ronsard
Sonnet pour Hélène

Gather ye rosebuds while ye may. (Lit. gather today the roses of life.)

D'où vient que l'on rit si librement au théâtre, et que l'on a honte d'y pleurer?
La Bruyère
Des Ouvrages de L'Esprit

How is it that we laugh so freely at the theatre but are embarrassed to weep there?

Dame dynamite, que l'on danse vite...
Dansons et chansons et dynamitons!
French anarchist song of the 1880s

*Dame Dynamite, quick, let's dance...
Let's dance and sing and blow everything up!*

Dans ce meilleur des mondes possibles... tout est au mieux.
Voltaire
Candide

All is for the best in this best of all possible worlds.

Dans ce pays-ci il est bon de tuer de temps en temps un amiral pour encourager les autres.
Voltaire
Candide

In this country, it is good to kill an admiral from time to time, to encourage the rest.
(About England, referring to the execution of Admiral Byng.)

Dans l'adversité de nos meilleurs amis, nous trouvons toujours quelque chose qui ne nous deplaît pas.
La Rochefoucauld
Réflexions ou Maximes Morales

In the misfortune of our best friends, we always find something which is not displeasing to us.

Dans le domaine des sentiments, le réel ne se distingue pas de l'imaginaire.
André Gide

In the realm of emotions, we cannot distinguish the real from the imaginary.

Dans le tumulte des hommes et des événements, la solitude était ma tentation. Maintenant, elle est mon amie. De quelle autre se contenter quand on a rencontré l'Histoire?
Charles de Gaulle
Le Salut

In the tumult of men and events, solitude was my temptation. Now it is my friend. What else is adequate when one has encountered history?

Dans les champs de l'observation le hasard ne favorise que les esprits préparés.
Louis Pasteur

Where observation is concerned, chance favours only the prepared mind.

Dans toute magistrature, il faut compenser la grandeur de la puissance par la brièveté de sa durance.

Montesquieu
Lettres

With any office, one has to balance the greatness of the power with the brevity of its duration.

De l'audace, et encore de l'audace, et toujours de l'audace.

Georges Jacques Danton

Boldness, and again boldness, always boldness.

De loin c'est quelque chose, et de près ce n'est rien.

La Fontaine
Le Chameau et les Bâtons Flottants

What seems important from a distance may prove insignificant close to.

De tout inconnu le sage se méfie.

La Fontaine
Le Renard, le Loup et le Cheval

The wise man distrusts everything unknown.

Deux excès: exclure la raison, n'admettre que la raison.

Blaise Pascal
Pensées

Two forms of excess: to exclude reason, and to admit only reason.

Dieu a donc oublié tout ce que j'ai fait pour lui!

Louis XlV
after losing the battle of Ramillies to the English, 1706

So God has forgotten all that I have done for him.

Dieu a recommandé le pardon des injures, il n'a point recommandé celui des bienfaits.

Nicholas-Sébastien Chamfort
Caractères et Anecdotes

God has enjoined that we pardon injuries, but not that we pardon kindnesses.

Dieu bénit l'homme. Non pour avoir trouvé, mais pour avoir cherché.

Victor Hugo
Les Contemplations

God blesses man, not for having found but for having sought.

Dieu et mon droit.

Richard I
password at the battle of Gisors; now the motto of English sovereigns

God and the right.

Dieu fait bien ce qu'il fait.

La Fontaine
Le Gland et la Citrouille

What God does he does well.

Dieu m'a donné du bien, et je me suis donné du superflu.

Montesquieu
Cahiers

God gave me wealth, and I have given myself a bit extra.

Dieu me pardonnera; c'est son métier.

Heinrich Heine

God will pardon me. It's his business.

Dieu, que le son du cor est triste au fond des bois!

Vigny
Le Cor

God, how melancholy is the sound of the horn deep in the woods.

Dis-moi ce que tu manges, je te dirai ce que tu es.

Anthelme Brillat-Savarin
Physiologie du Goût

Tell me what you eat and I will tell you what you are.

Du reste, continua Mme de Cambremer, j'ai horreur des couchers de soleil, c'est romantique, c'est opéra.

Marcel Proust
Sodome et Gomorrhe

"Anyhow,"Mme de Cambremer went on, "I have a horror of sunsets, they're so romantic, so operatic."

Du sublime au ridicule il n'y a qu'un pas.
Napoléon I
after his retreat from Moscow in 1812

It's only a step from the sublime to the ridiculous.

Elle a tout vu, elle a tout lu, elle sait tout.
Naudé
letter, about Queen Christina of Sweden, 1652

She has seen everything, read everything, knows everything.

Eminence grise.

Expression
originally of Cardinal Richelieu's private secretary, Père Joseph

Grey eminence. (A person who exercises power or influence without holding office.)

En Amérique l'homme n'obéit jamais à l'homme, mais à la justice ou à la loi.

Alexis de Tocqueville
De la Démocratie en Amérique

In America man never obeys man, but justice or the law.

En fait d'amour, vois-tu, trop n'est pas
même assez!

Beaumarchais
Le Mariage de Figaro

*With love, you see, even too much is not
enough.*

En fait de religion, les plus proches sont
les plus grandes ennemies.

Montesquieu
Lettres

*When it comes to religion, the worst enemies
are the nearest.*

En France, on étudie les hommes, en
Allemagne, les livres.

Mme de Staël
De l'Allemagne

In France they study men, in Germany books.

En mariage, comme ailleurs, contentement
passe richesse.

Molière
Le Médecin malgré lui

*In marriage, as elsewhere, contentment
surpasses wealth.*

En toute chose il faut considérer la fin.

La Fontaine
Le Renard et le Bouc

Consider the outcome of every action.

En toutes compagnies il y a plus de fous
que de sages, et la plus grand partie sur-
monte toujours la meilleure.

Rabelais

*In every company there are more fools than wise
men, and the bigger faction always overcomes
the better.*

En vieillissant on devient plus fou et plus
sage.

La Rochefoucauld
Réflexions

*As we age, we become both wiser and more
foolish.*

En vin saveur, en drap couleur, en fille
pudeur.

Lebon
Adages Français

*Wine should have flavour, cloth colour, and a
girl modesty.*

Entre nos ennemis, les plus à craindre sont
souvent les plus petits.

La Fontaine
Le Lion et le Moucheron

The enemy to fear most is often the smallest.

Et Jeanne, la bonne Louraine,
Qu'Anglais brûlèrent à Rouen?
Où sont-ils, où, Vierge souveraine?
Mais où sont les neiges d'antan?

François Villon
Ballade des Dames du Temps Jadis

And the good Joan of Lorraine, whom the English burned at Rouen? Where are they, where, queenly Virgin? But where are the snows of yesteryear.

Et l'on voit de la flamme aux yeux des
jeunes gens,
Mais dans l'oeil du vieillard on voit de la
lumière.

Victor Hugo
Boöz Endormi

In the eyes of youth we see a flame, but in the eyes of the old we see light.

Et maintenant elle est commes les autres.

Charles de Gaulle
on the death of his daughter, who suffered
from Down's Syndrome

And now she is like everyone else.

Et pour cet art de connaître les hommes, qui
vous sera si important... Je vous dirai, mon
fils, qu'il se peut apprendre, mais qu'il ne se
peut enseigner.

Louis XlV
*Mémoires Historiques et Instructions
pour le Dauphin*

And as to this skill of knowing men, which will be so important to you... I will say this, my son, that it can be learned but not taught.

Et tout d'un coup le souvenir m'est apparu.
Ce goût c'était celui du petit morceau de
madeleine que le dimanche matin à Combray
ma tante Léonie m'offrait après l'avoir trem-
pé dans son infusion de thé ou de tilleul.

Marcel Proust
Du côté de chez Swann

And suddenly the memory revealed itself. The taste was that of the little piece of madeleine which on Sunday mornings at Combray...my aunt Léonie used to give me, dipping it first in her own cup of tea or tisane.

Etonne-moi.

Sergei Diaghilev
to Cocteau

Astonish me.

Fais comme moi: vis du monde éloignée...
résignée.

Victor Hugo
A Ma Fille

Do as I do: live detached from the world, resigned.

Faites vos devoirs, et laissez faire aux dieux.
Pierre Corneille
Horace

Do your duty and leave the rest to the gods.

Familles, je vous hais! foyers clos; portes
refermées; possessions jalouses du bonheur.
André Gide
Les Nourritures Terrestres

Families, I hate you: cold hearths, closed doors,
possessions more valued than happiness.

Fay ce que voudras.
Rabelais

Do what thou wilt.

Fortune aveugle suit aveugle hardiesse.
La Fontaine
Les Deux Aventuriers et le Talisman

Blind luck follows blind audacity.

France, mère des arts, des armes et des lois.
Joachim du Bellay

France, mother of arts, arms and law.

Géronte: Il me semble que vous les placez
autrement qu'ils ne sont: que le coeur est
du côté gauche, et le foie du côté droit.
Sganarelle: Oui, cela était autrefois ainsi,
mais nous avons changé tout cela, et nous
faisons maintenant la médecine d'une
méthode toute nouvelle.
Molière
Le Médecin malgré lui

Géronte: *It seems to me that you've got things*
in the wrong place; that the heart is on the left
and liver on the right.
Sganarelle: *Yes, that's how they were once,*
but we've changed all that. We now practise a
totally new sort of medicine.

Hé! Dieu, si j'eusse étudié
Au temps de ma jeunesse folle
Et à bonnes moeurs dédié,
J'eusse maison et couche molle.
François Villon
Le Grand Testament

Ah, God, if I had studied in my wild youth,
and cultivated good habits, I should have a
home and a soft bed.

Heureux qui comme Ulysse a fait un beau
voyage
Ou comme celui-là qui conquit la toison,
Et puis est retourné, plein d'usage et
raison,
Vivre entre ses parents le reste de son âge.
Joachim du Bellay

Happy is he who, like Ulysses, has journeyed
well, or like him who found the golden fleece,
and returned, full of experience and wisdom, to
dwell among his fathers for the rest of his life.

Honi soit qui mal y pense.
Motto of the Order of the Garter

Shame on him who evil thinks.

Hypocrite lecteur – mon semblable – mon frère!

Charles Baudelaire
Les Fleurs du Mal

Hypocritical reader – my fellow – my brother!

Il a été permis de craindre que la Révolution, comme Saturne, dévorât successivement tous ses enfants.

Pierre Vergniaud

There was reason to fear that the Revolution, like Saturn, might devour in turn each one of her children.

Il est bien difficile enfin d'être fidèle
A de certains maris faits d'un certain
modèle.
Molière
Tartuffe

It is very difficult to be faithful to certain husbands of a certain type.

Il est bon d'être charitable; Mais envers qui, c'est là le point.

La Fontaine
Le Villageois et le Serpent

It is good to be charitable; but to whom, that's the point.

Il est dangereux de dire au peuple que les lois ne sont pas justes, car il n'y obéit qu'à cause qu'il les croit justes.

Blaise Pascal
Pensées

It is dangerous to tell people that the laws are unjust, for they obey them only because they believe them to be just.

Il est interdit d'interdire.
slogan of the 1968 student revolt

Forbidding is forbidden.

Il est plus facile de faire la guerre que la paix.

Georges Clemenceau
speech at Verdun, July 1919

It is easier to make war than peace.

Il est plus honteux de se défier de ses amis que d'en être trompé.

La Rochefoucauld
Réflexions

It is more shameful to distrust one's friends than to be deceived by them.

Il faut ce qu'il faut.

Proverb

What must be must be.

Il faut cultiver notre jardin.

Voltaire
Candide

We must cultivate our garden.

Il faut dans les lois une certaine candeur.
Faites pour punir la méchanceté des
hommes, elles doivent avoir elles-mêmes
la plus grande innocence.

Montesquieu
De l'Esprit des Lois

Laws should have a certain candour. Made to
punish the wickedness of men, they themselves
must retain the greatest innocence.

Il faut de plus grandes vertus pour
soutenir la bonne fortune que la mauvaise.
La Rochefoucauld
Réflextions

It takes greater qualities to sustain good luck
than bad luck.

Il faut écouter beaucoup et parler peu
pour bien agir au gouvernement d'un
Etat.

Richelieu
Maximes d'Etat

You have to listen much and speak little to
govern a country well.

Il faut entrer en soi-même armé jusqu'aux
dents.

Valéry
Quelques Pensées de Monsieur Teste

To enter into your own mind you must go
armed to the teeth.

Il faut épater les bourgeois.
Charles Baudelaire

One must shock the bourgeoisie.

Il faut être toujours botté et prêt à partir.
Montaigne

One should always be booted and ready to
leave.

Il n'appartient qu'aux grands hommes
d'avoir de grands défauts.
La Rochefoucauld
Réflexions

Great men are apt to have great faults.

Il n'est point de diable plus insupportable
qu'une dame bien aimée et qui ne veut
point aimer.
Marguerite de Navarre
Heptaméron

There is no more unbearable anguish [lit.
devil] *than a much loved woman who is not
interested in loving.*

Il n'existe pas de sciences appliquées, mais
seulement des applications de la science.
Louis Pasteur

There are no such things as applied sciences,
only applications of science.

Il n'y a chose si innocente oû les hommes ne puissent porter de crime.

Molière
Tartuffe

There is nothing so innocent that man cannot introduce crime.

Il n'y a pas de grands esprits sans un grain de folie.

Proverb

There are no great souls without a touch of folly.

Il n'y a point de héros pour son valet de chambre.

Mme Cornuel

No man is a hero to his valet.

Il n'y a pour l'homme que trois événements: naître, vivre et mourir. Il ne se sent pas naître, il souffre à mourir, et il oublie de vivre.

La Bruyère
Les Caractères

There are only three events for man: birth, life and death. He is not aware of his birth, suffers at death, and forgets to live.

Il n'y a qu'un seul vice dont on ne voie personne se vanter, c'est l'ingratitude!

Gérard de Nerval
Paradoxe et Vérité

There is only one vice of which no one boasts — ingratitude.

Il ne faut pas être plus royaliste que le roi.
phrase dating from the time of Louis XVI

One should not be more royalist than the king.

Il ne faut pas mettre les étoupes trop près du feu.

Proverb

Don't put a fuse too near the fire.

Il ne sert de rien d'être jeune sans être belle, ni d'être belle sans être jeune.

La Rochefoucauld
Réflexions

It is no use being young without being beautiful, nor beautiful without being young.

Il pleut dans mon coeur
Comme il pleut sur la ville;
Quelle est cette langueur
Qui pénètre mon coeur?

Paul Verlaine
Ariettes Oubliées

It rains in my heart, just as it rains on the town; what is this melancholy that pierces my heart?

Il réussit, celui que Dieu protège.
La Chanson de Roland

He succeeds whom God protects.

Il se faut réserver une arrière-boutique, toute nôtre, toute franche, en laquelle nous établissions notre vraie liberté en principale retraite et solitude.

Montaigne

One should always keep a little back shop, entirely our own and uninhabited, where we can experience the true liberty of solitude.

Il vaut mieux mourir selon les règles que de réchapper contre les règles.

Molière
L'Amour Médecin

It is better to die according to the rules than to recover in spite of them.

Il vaut mieux pour moi, n'avoir que peu
Mais l'avoir seul.

André Gide
Le Roi Candaule

I prefer to have little but enjoy it alone.

Il y a dans les hommes plus de choses à admirer que de choses à mépriser.

Albert Camus
La Peste

There are more things to admire than to scorn in man.

Il y a de bon mariages, mais il n'y a point de délicieux.

La Rochefoucauld
Maximes

There are good marriages, but no delightful ones.

Il y a des héros en mal comme en bien.
La Rochefoucauld
Réflexions

There are heroes of evil as well as of good.

Il y a malgré vous quelque chose
Que j'emporte, et ce soir, quand j'entrerai
                                        chez Dieu,
Mon salut balayera largement le seuil bleu,
Quelque chose que sans un pli, sans une
                                        tache,
J'emporte, malgré vous....et c'est ...mon
                                        panache!
Edmond Rostand
Cyrano de Bergerac

There is, in spite of you, one thing that I take with me, and tonight, when I enter God's house, sweeping a salute on its blue threshold, I shall take with me something without crease or stain, in spite of you... and it is... my panache!

Il y a plus de quarante ans que je dis de la prose sans que j'en susse rien.

Molière
Le Bourgeois Gentilhomme

For more than forty years I've been speaking prose without knowing it.

Il y a toujours un qui baise, et l'autre qui tend la joue.

Proverb

There is always one who kisses and one who offers a cheek.

Il y a une mélancholie qui tient à la grandeur de l'esprit.

Nicholas-Sébastien Chamfort
Maximes et Pensées

There is a melancholy that comes from greatness of mind.

Ils ne passeront pas.

French army slogan
during the defence of Verdun

They shall not pass.

Ils ne se servent de la pensée que pour autoriser leurs injustices, et n'emploient les paroles que pour déguiser leurs pensées.

Voltaire

They use thought only to justify their bad behaviour and words only to disguise their thoughts.

J'accuse.

Emile Zola
heading his letter about Dreyfus

I accuse.

J'ai conclu que le repos, l'amitié et la pensée étaient les seuls biens qui convinssent à un homme qui a passé l'âge de la folie.

Nicholas-Sébastien Chamfort
Caractères et Anecdotes

I concluded that rest, friendship and thought were the only suitable pleasures for a man who has passed the age of folly.

J'ai eu 10,000 femmes depuis l'age de 13 ans et demi. Ce n'était pas du tout un vice. Je n'ai aucun vice sexuel, mais j'avais besoin de communiquer.

Georges Simenon

I have had intercourse with 10,000 women since I was 13 $\frac{1}{2}$. This was in no way a vice. I have no sexual vices, but I had a need to communicate.

J'ai failli attendre.

Louis XIV

I was nearly kept waiting.

J'ai vécu pour ma gloire autant qu'il fallait vivre,
Et laisse un grand exemple à qui pourra me suivre.

Pierre Corneille
Suréna

I have lived as I should for my glory, and leave a great example for any who can follow.

J'ai vécu.
The Abbé Sieyès
when asked what he did during the French
Revolution

I survived.

J'ai violé l'histoire, mais je lui ai fait des
enfants!
Alexandre Dumas

I raped history, but at least I gave her children.

J'aime, et je veux pâlir; j'aime et je veux
souffrir;
J'aime, et pour un baiser je donne mon
génie.
Alfred de Musset
La Nuit d'Août

*I am in love and I want to grow pale; I am in
love and I want to suffer; I am in love, and I
give away my genius in exchange for a kiss.*

J'aime la majesté des souffrances
humaines.
Vigny
La Maison du Berger

I love the majesty of human suffering.

J'enrage de bon coeur d'avoir tort, lorsque
j'ai raison.
Molière
Georges Dandin

It infuriates me to be wrong when I am right.

J'y suis, j'y reste.
Marshal MacMahon
when urged to abandon the newly
captured Malakoff Tower

Here I am, here I stay.

Jamais l'homme, tant qu'il meure,
Ne demeure
Fortuné parfaitement,
Toujours avec la liesse,
La tristesse
Se mêle secrètement.
Pierre de Ronsard
Les Bacchanales

*Man is never, as long as he lives, perfectly
fortunate; there is always sorrow secretly
mingled with felicity.*

Je l'ai trop aimé pour ne le point haïr!
Jean Racine
Andromaque

I loved him too much not to hate him at all!

Je me presse de rire de tout, de peur d'être obligé d'en pleurer.

Beaumarchais
Le Barbier de Seville

I make myself laugh at everything, for fear of having to weep at it.

Je meurs de soif auprès de la fontaine, Tremblant de froid au feu des amoureux.

Charles d'Orléans
Ballades

I die of thirst at the fountain, trembling with cold in the grip of lovers' fire.

Je n'ai fait celle-ci plus longue que parce que je n'ai pas eu le loisir de la faire plus courte.

Blaise Pascal
Lettres Provinciales

I have made this [letter] *longer than usual, only because I have not had the time to make it shorter.*

Je n'ai pas succédé à Louis XIV mais à Charlemagne.

Napoléon I
Letter to Pope Pius VII, 1804

I have succeeded, not Louis XIV, but Charlemagne.

Je n'ai rien contre les drogues: simplement l'alcool me suffit et le reste me fait peur.

Françoise Sagan
La Garde du Coeur

I have nothing against drugs, but alcohol suits me and the rest frightens me.

Je n'aime pas dormir quand ta figure
                                    habite,
La nuit, contre mon cou;
Car je pense à la mort laquelle vient si vite
Nous endormir beaucoup.

Jean Cocteau
Plain-Chant

I do not like to sleep when your body lies against mine at night, for I think of death which comes so quickly to put us thoroughly to sleep.

Je ne suis pas ni le courtisan, ni le modéra-teur, ni le tribun, ni le défenseur de peu-ple, je suis peuple moi-même.

Robespierre
speech at the Jacobin Club, 27 April 1792

I am not a courtier nor a moderator, nor a tribune, nor a defender of the people: I am myself the people.

Je parle. Il le faut bien. L'action met les ardeurs en oeuvre. Mais c'est la parole qui les suscite.

Charles de Gaulle
La France Combattante

I talk. It is necessary. Action puts the passions to work, but it is speech that arouses them.

Je parvins à faire s'évanouir dans mon esprit toute l'espérance humaine.

Arthur Rimbaud
Une Saison en Enfer

I have succeeded in emptying my mind of all human hope.

Je pense donc je suis

René Descartes
Discours de la Méthode

I think therefore I am.

Je puis en un quart d'heure faire vingt ducs et pairs; il faut des siècles pour faire un Mansart.

Louis XlV
to the architect Mansart, telling him to keep his head covered in the king's presence for fear of the sun

I can make twenty dukes and peers in a quarter of an hour, but it takes centuries to produce a Mansart.

Je respecte mon Dieu, mais j'aime l'univers.

Voltaire
Poème sur le Désastre de Lisbonne

I respect my God, but I love the world.

Je serai grand, et toi riche,
Puisque nous nous aimerons.

Victor Hugo
Un Peu de Musique

I shall be great and you rich, because we love each other.

Je suis celui au coeur vêtu de noir.

Charles d'Orléans
Ballades

I am he whose heart is clothed in black.

Je suis comme un milieu entre Dieu et le néant.

René Descartes
Discours de la Méthode

I am a kind of medium between God and nothing.

Je suis le Ténébreux – le Veuf – l'Inconsolé,
Le Prince d'Aquitaine à la Tour abolie:
Ma seule Etoile est morte – et mon luth
constellé
Porte le soleil noir de la Mélancholie.

Gérard de Nerval
Je Suis Le Ténébreux

I am the mysterious one, the widower, the disconsolate, the Prince of Aquitaine of the shattered tower: my only star is dead, and my star-spangled lute bears the black sun of melancholy.

Je suis Marxist – tendance Groucho.

graffiti in Paris, 1968

I am a Marxist – of the Groucho variety.

Je suis une brave poule de guerre –
Je mange peu et produis beaucoup.
World War 1 poster
showing a hen with a large number of eggs

*I am a fine wartime hen –
I eat little and produce a lot.*

Je t'aime plus qu'hier, moins que demain.
Edmond Rostand
Les Musardises

*I love you more than yesterday, less than
tomorrow.*

Je te salue, heureuse et profitable Mort!
Pierre de Ronsard

I salute thee, happy and profitable Death!

Je vais quérir un grand Peut-être... Tirez le
rideau, la farce est jouée.
Rabelais
when dying, but the attribution is disputed

*I go to seek a great Perhaps... Let the
curtain fall, the farce is ended.*

Je veux montrer à mes semblables un
homme dans toute la vérité de la nature; et
cet homme, ce sera moi.
Jean-Jacques Rousseau
Les Confessions

*I want to show my fellow-men a man in all the
honesty of nature; and that man will be me.*

Je veux qu'il n'est si pauvre paysan en
mon royaume qu'il n'ait tous les dimanch-
es sa poule au pot.
Henri IV
Histoire de Henry le Grand

*I want there to be no peasant in my kingdom
so poor that he is unable to have a chicken in
his pot every Sunday.*

Je voudrais, et ce sera le dernier et le plus
ardent de mes souhaits, je voudrais que le
dernier des rois fût étranglé avec les boyaux du dernier prêtre.
Jean Messelier
in his Will

*I wish, and this will be the last and most ardent
of my desires, I wish that the last king might be
strangled with the guts of the last priest.*

Jeunesse dorée.
Feuron
about the Dandies of 1714

Gilded youth.

Jeunesse oiseuse, vieillesse disetteuse.
Meurier
Trésor des Sentences

Prodigal youth, needy old age.

L'Abbé Guyot Desfontaines: Il faut que je vive.
D'Argenson: Je n'en vois pas la nécessité.
quoted by **Voltaire**

Desfontaines: *I must live.*
D'Argenson: *I don't see why.*

L'absence diminue les médiocres passions et augmente les grandes, comme le vent éteint les bougies et allume le feu.
La Rochefoucauld
Réflexions

Absence lessens mild passions and increases great ones, just as the wind blows out candles but brightens the fire.

L'ambition prend aux petites âmes plus facilement qu'aux grandes, comme le feu prend plus aisément à la paille des chaumières qu'aux palais.
Nicholas-Sébastien Chamfort
Maximes et Pensées

Ambition seizes small minds more readily than great, just as thatched cottages catch fire more easily than palaces.

L'amour est aveugle: l'amitié ferme les yeux.
Proverb

Love is blind: friendship shuts its eyes.

L'amour est un sot qui ne sait ce qu'il dit.
Molière
Le Dépit Amoureux

Love is a fool who does not know what he says.

L'amour et l'amitié s'excluent l'un l'autre.
La Bruyère
Les Caractères

Love and friendship are incompatible.

L'amour n'est pas un feu que l'on tient dans la main.
Marguerite de Navarre
Heptaméron

Love is not a light that one holds in the hand.

L'Angleterre est un empire, l'Allemagne un pays, une race, la France est une personne.
Jules Michelet
Histoire de France

England is an empire, Germany is a country, a race, France is an individual.

L'Angleterre est une nation de marchands.
Napoléon I
while exiled on St Helena, quoting Paoli but perhaps ultimately from Adam Smith

England is a nation of shopkeepers.

L'appétit vient en mangeant.

Rabelais

Appetite grows with eating.

L'argent qu'on possède est l'instrument de la liberté; celui qu'on pourchasse est celui de la servitude.

Jean-Jacques Rousseau
Les Confessions

The money we have is the means to liberty; that which we pursue is the means to slavery.

L'art est bête.

Arthur Rimbaud

Art is stupid.

L'art est long et le temps est court.

Charles Baudelaire
Le Guignon

Art is long and time is short.

L'avarice perd tout en voulant tout gagner.

La Fontaine
La Poule aux Oeufs d'Or

Avarice loses all in trying to win all.

L'éducation de l'homme commence à sa naissance; avant de parler, avant d'entendre, il s'instruit déjà.

Jean-Jacques Rousseau
Emile, ou de l'Education

Man's education begins at birth; before he can speak or hear, he is already learning.

L'embarras de richesses.

Abbé d'Allainval
title of comedy

An embarrassment of riches.

L'enthousiasme est une maladie qui gagne.

Voltaire
Lettres Philosophiques

Fanaticism is a sickness that spreads.

L'espérance et la crainte sont inséparables, et il n'y a point de crainte sans espérance, ni d'espérance sans crainte.

La Rochefoucauld
Réflexions

Hope and fear are inseparable; you never have fear without hope, or hope without fear.

L'esprit d'escalier.

Denis Diderot

The witticism you think of only when it's too late. (Lit. when going downstairs.)

L'esprit de nouveauté est capable d'abattre les édifices les plus solides.

Servin
Les Réguliers

The spirit of change is capable of overthrowing the most solid edifice.

L'esprit français est de ne pas vouloir de *supérieur*. L'esprit anglais est de vouloir des *inférieurs*. Le Français lève les yeux sans cesse au-dessus de lui avec inquiétude. L'Anglais les baisse au-dessous de lui avec complaisance. C'est de part et d'autre de l'orgueil, mais entendu de manière différente.

Alexis de Tocqueville
Voyage en Angleterre et en Irlande de 1835

The French want no-one to be their superior. *The English want* inferiors. *The Frenchman constantly raises his eyes above him with anxiety. The Englishman lowers his beneath him with satisfaction. On either side it is pride, but understood in a different way.*

L'Etat c'est moi.

Louix XIV

I am the State.

L'Europe des états.

Charles de Gaulle
explaining his vision of a united Europe (often misquoted as "L'Europe des patries")

A Europe of separate nations.

L'exactitute est la politesse des rois.

Louis XVIII

Punctuality is the politeness of kings.

L'existentialisme est un humanisme

Jean-Paul Sartre
title of lecture

Existentialism is a form of humanism.

L'habit ne fait point le moine.

Rabelais

Fine clothes don't make a gentleman. (Lit. the habit does not make the monk).

L'histoire des hommes se reflète dans l'histoire des cloaques.

Victor Hugo
Les Misérables

The history of men is reflected in the history of sewers.

L'homme absurde est celui qui ne change jamais.

Georges Clemenceau
Discours de Guerre

The absurd man is he who never changes.

L'homme arrive novice à chaque âge de la vie.

Nicholas-Sébastien Chamfort
Caractères et Anecdotes

Man enters each stage of life as a novice.

L'homme est né libre et partout il est dans les fers.

Jean-Jacques Rousseau
Du Contrat Social

Man is born free, and everywhere he is in chains.

L'homme n'est ni ange ni bête.

Blaise Pascal
Pensées

Man is neither angel nor beast.

L'homme n'est qu'un roseau, le plus faible de la nature; mais c'est un roseau pensant.

Blaise Pascal
Pensées

Man is just a reed, the weakest thing in nature, but he is a thinking reed.

L'homme n'est rien qu'un jonc qui tremble au vent.

Victor Hugo
A Villequier

Man is just a rush trembling in the wind.

L'homme qui a le plus vécu n'est pas celui qui a compté le plus d'années, mais celui qui a le plus senti la vie.

Jean-Jacques Rousseau
Emile ou de l'Education

The man who has lived most fully is not the one who has survived the most years, but the one who has been most aware of life.

L'homme, sans plaisir,
Vivrait comme un sot
Et mourrait bientôt.

Beaumarchais
Le Barbier de Séville

Without pleasure, man would live like a fool and die early.

L'hypocrisie est un hommage que le vice rend à la vertu.

La Rochefoucauld
Réflexions

Hypocrisy is the homage that vice offers to virtue.

L'hypocrisie est un vice à la mode, et tous les vices à la mode passent pour vertus.

Molière
Don Juan

Hypocrisy is a fashionable vice, and all fashionable vices pass for virtues.

L'important dans ces olympiades, c'est moins d'y gagner que d'y prendre part.
Baron Pierre de Coubertin

The important thing about the Olympics is not so much winning as taking part.

L'ingratitude est une variété de l'orgueil.
Labiche & Martin
Le Voyage de M. Perrichon

Ingratitude is a form of pride.

L'irrésolution me semble le plus commun et apparent vice de notre nature.
Montaigne
Essais

Indecision seems to me to be the commonest and most obvious vice of human nature.

L'obéissance est un métier bien rude.
Pierre Corneille
Nicomède

Obedience is a hard trade.

L'oiseau cache son nid, nous cachons nos amours.
Victor Hugo
Les Contemplations: L'Hirondelle

The bird hides its nest, we hide our loves.

L'on voit des hommes tomber d'une haute fortune par les mêmes défauts qui les y avaient fait monter.
La Bruyère
Les Caractères

Men can be seen to fall from high estate through the same failings that caused them to rise.

L'univers est vrai pour nous tous et dissemblable pour chacun.
Marcel Proust
La Prisonnière

The universe is true for all of us and dissimilar for each of us.

La beauté n'est que vent, la beauté n'est pas bien:
Les beautés en un jour s'en vont comme les roses.
Pierre de Ronsard
Sonnet

Beauty is but air, beauty is worth nothing; beauties fade in a day like roses.

La carrière ouverte aux talents.
Napoléon I

The career open to talent.

La célébrité est le châtiment du mérite et la punition du talent.
Nicholas-Sébastien Chamfort
Maximes et Pensées

Fame is the chastisement of merit and the punishment of talent.

La colère est bonne à rien.

Beaumarchais
Le Mariage de Figaro

Anger will get you nowhere.

La condition humaine.

André Malraux
title of a book

The human condition.

La conscience règne et ne gouverne pas.

Paul Valéry
Mauvaises Pensées

Conscience reigns and does not govern.

La constance n'est bonne que pour des ridicules.

Molière
Don Juan

Constancy is good only for ridicule.

La conversation est un jeu de sécateur, où chacun taille la voix du voisin aussitôt qu'elle pousse.

Jules Renard
Journal

Conversation is a game of secateurs, where each prunes the next person's voice as soon as possible.

La clémence des princes n'est souvent qu'une politique pour gagner l'affection des peuples.

La Rochefoucauld
Réflexions

The clemency of princes is often just a ruse to gain the people's affection.

La clémence est, au fait, un moyen comme un autre.

Victor Hugo
Cromwell

In the end clemency is just another means to an end.

La distance n'y fait rien; il n'y a que le premier pas qui coûte.

Mme du Deffand
about the legend that St Denis walked two leagues, carrying his head in his hands

The distance is nothing; it is only the first step that counts.

La duration de nos passions ne dépend pas plus de nous que la durée de notre vie.

La Rochefoucauld
Réflexions

The duration of our emotions no more depends on us than the duration of our lives.

La façon de donner vaut mieux que ce qu'on donne.

Proverb

The manner of giving is worth more than the gift.

La félicité est dans le goût et non pas dans les choses.

La Rochefoucauld
Réflexions

Happiness is a matter of taste, and not of possessions.

La femme ne voit jamais ce que l'on fait pour elle, elle ne voit que ce qu'on ne fait pas.

Georges Courteline
La Paix Chez Soi

Women never notice what is done for them, only what is not done.

La flatterie est une fausse monnaie qui n'a de cours que par notre vanité.

Le Rochefoucauld
Réflexions

Flattery is counterfeit coin that only gains currency through our vanity.

La foi qui n'agit point, est-ce une foi sincère?
Jean Racine
Athalie

A faith that does not act, is it a sincere faith?

La force est la reine du monde, est non pas l'opinion. Mais l'opinion est celle qui use de la force. C'est la force qui fait l'opinion.
Blaise Pascal
Pensées

Force, and not opinion, is queen of the world. But opinion makes use of force; and force makes opinion.

La forêt façonne l'arbre.

Proverb

The forest shapes the tree.

La foule met toujours, de ses mains
                      dégradées,
Quelque chose de vil sur les grandes idées.
Victor Hugo
Cromwell

The crowd, with their filthy hands, will always tarnish great ideas.

La France a plus besoin de moi que je n'ai besoin de la France.

Napoléon I
to a deputation of the legislature, 1813

France needs me more than I need France.

La générosité n'est que la pitié des âmes nobles.

Nicholas-Sébastien Chamfort
Maximes et Pensées

Generosity is just the pity of noble spirits.

La géométrie est aux arts plastiques ce que la grammaire est à l'art de l'écrivain.

Guillaume Apollinaire
Les Peintres Cubistes

Geometry is to the plastic arts what grammar is to the art of the writer.

La gloire est une espèce de maladie que l'on prend pour avoir couché avec sa pensée.

Paul Valéry
Choses Tues

Glory is a kind of sickness that we catch from sleeping with the thought of it.

La gloire expose à la calomnie.

Proverb

Glory exposes us to calumny.

La Guarde muert, mais ne se rend pas.

Pierre, Baron de Cambronne
attrib. when called upon to surrender at Waterloo, but later denied by him

The Guards die but do not surrender.

La guerre, c'est une chose trop grave pour la confier à des militaires.

Georges Clemenceau

War is too serious a matter to entrust to military men.

La jalousie n'est qu'un sot enfant de l'orgueil.

Beaumarchais
Le Mariage de Figaro

Jealousy is just a foolish child of pride.

La liberté est le droit de faire ce que les lois permettent.

Montesquieu
Réflexions et Pensées

Liberty is the right to do what the law allows.

La loi, en général, est la raison humaine, en tant qu'elle gouverne tous les peuples de la terre.

Montesquieu
Lettres

On the whole law reflects human reason, in so far as reason governs all the nations on earth.

La main à plume vaut la main à charrue.
Arthur Rimbaud
Mauvais Sang

The hand that holds the pen is as important as the hand that guides the plough.

La mer est anglaise par inclination; elle n'aime pas la France; elle brise nos vaisseaux; elle ensable nos ports.
Jules Michelet
Histoire de France

The sea is English by inclination; it does not like France; it wrecks our ships and silts up our ports.

La monarchie est le meilleur ou le pire des gouvernements.
Voltaire
Brutus

Monarchy is the best or the worst of governments.

La mort, c'est tellement obligatoire que c'est presqu'une formalité.
Marcel Pagnol
César

So much is death obligatory that it is almost a formality.

La mort entrait comme un voleur.
Victor Hugo
Le Revenant

Death entered like a thief.

La mort ne surprend point le sage;
Il est toujours prêt à partir.
La Fontaine
La Mort et le Mourant

Death does not surprise the wise man; he is always ready to go.

La mort nous parle d'une voix profonde pour ne rien dire.
Paul Valéry
Mauvaises Pensées

Death speaks to us in a profound voice to say nothing.

La nuit est bonne conseillère.
Proverb

Sleep on it. (Lit. night is a good counsellor.)

La paix est un mot vide de sens; c'est une paix glorieuse qu'il nous faut.
Napoléon I to his brother Joseph, 1805

Peace is a meaningless word; what we must have is a glorious peace.

La parfaite valeur est de faire sans témoins ce qu'on serait capable de faire devant tout le monde.
La Rochefoucauld
Réflexions

Perfect courage lies in behaving without witnesses as we would be capable of behaving in full view.

La patrie est où l'on vit heureux.

Voltaire
Le Siècle de Louis XIV

Our own country is where we live content.

La pensée fait la grandeur de l'homme.

Blaise Pascal
Pensées

Thought is the source of the greatness of mankind.

La plus ancienne de toutes les sociétés, et la seule naturelle, est celle de la famille.

Jean-Jacques Rousseau
Du Contrat Social

The oldest of all social groups, and the only natural one, is the family.

La plus grande bassesse de l'homme est la recherche de la gloire.

Blaise Pascal
Pensées

Man stoops lowest in his pursuit of glory.

La plus perdue de toutes les journées est celle où l'on n'a pas ri.

Nicholas-Sébastien Chamfort
Maximes et Pensées

The days most wasted are those during which we have not laughed.

La poésie est semblable à l'amandier; ses fleurs sont parfumées et ses fruits sont amers.

Louis Bertrand
Gaspard de la Nuit

Poetry resembles an almond tree; its blossom is perfumed but its fruit is bitter.

La politique et le sort des hommes sont formés par des hommes sans idéal et sans grandeur. Ceux qui ont une grandeur en eux ne font pas de politique.

Albert Camus
Carnets

Politics and the fate of mankind are decided by men without ideals or greatness. Those who have greatness in them do not take part in politics.

La profession d'hypocrite a de merveilleux avantages!

Molière
Don Juan

The occupation of hypocrite has great advantages.

La propriété c'est le vol.

Pierre-Joseph Proudhon

Property is theft.

La puissance qui vient de l'amour des peuples est sans doute la plus grande.

Jean-Jacques Rousseau
Du Contrat Social

Power that stems from popular affection is undoubtedly the greatest.

La république des lettres.

Molière
Le mariage forcé

The republic of letters.

La reconnaissance de la plupart des hommes n'est qu'une secrète envie de recevoir de plus grands bienfaits.

La Rochefoucauld
Maximes

In most of mankind gratitude is merely a secret hope of greater favours.

La révolution est la guerre de la liberté contre ses enemies, la constitution est le régime de la liberté victorieuse et paisable.

Robespierre
addressing the National Convention, 1793

Revolution is the war of liberty against her enemies; the constitution is the rule of liberty victorious and at peace.

La Révolution? Je suis un homme d'affaires. La Révolution est une affaire comme les autres.

Audiberti
La Poupée

The Revolution? I am a businessman. Revolution is a business like any other.

La rose naît du mal qu'a le rosier
Mais elle est la rose.

Louis Aragon
Le Roman Inachevé

The rose is born of the rosebush's pain, but it is still a rose.

La saturation, il y a un moment où cela vient dans ce repas qu'on appelle la vie; il ne faut qu'une goutte alors pour faire déborder la coupe de dégoût.

Sainte-Beuve
Causeries du Lundi

There is a moment in this meal we call life when saturation is reached; it needs only one drop more for the cup of disgust to overflow.

La seule philosophie est peut-être après tout de tenir bon longtemps.

Stéphane Mallarmé
Lettres

In the end the only philosophy is perhaps to keep well as long as possible.

La soirée n'est jamais plus belle pour moi que quand je suis content avec ma matinée!

Denis Diderot
Le Neveu de Rameau

The evening is never more lovely for me than when I am satisfied with my morning.

La trahison des clercs.
Julien Benda (title of book)

The treachery of the intellectuals.

La véritable éloquence consiste à dire tout
ce qu'il faut, et à ne dire que ce qu'il faut.
La Rochefoucauld
Réflexions

*True eloquence is saying all that is necessary
and nothing else.*

La vie contemplative est souvent misérable.
Il faut agir davantage, penser moins, et ne
pas se regarder vivre.
Nicholas-Sébastien Chamfort
Maximes et Pensées

*The contemplative life is often miserable. We
should do more, think less, and not watch
ourselves living.*

La vie est brève,
Un peu d'amour,
Un peu de rêve,
Et puis, Bonjour.
La vie est vaine,
Un peu d'espoir,
Un peu de haine,
Et puis, Bonsoir.

Alfred de Musset

*Life is short, a little love, a little dream, and
then Good Day. Life is vain, a little hope, a
little hate, and then Goodnight.*

La vipère engendre la vipère.
Victor Hugo
Cromwell

Vipers breed vipers.

La voix de la conscience et de l'honneur
est bien faible, lorsque les boyaux crient.
Denis Diderot
Le Neveu de Rameau

*The voice of conscience and honour is pretty
weak when the stomach complains.*

La volonté générale gouverne la société
comme la volonté particulière gouverne
chaque individu isolé.
Robespierre
Lettres à ses commettans

*The general will rules in society as the private
will governs each separate individual.*

La vraie morale se moque de la morale.
Blaise Pascal
Pensées

True morality laughs at morals.

Lafayette, nous voilà!
Charles Stanton
at Lafayette's tomb in Paris, 4 July, 1917

Lafayette, we [the American army] *are here!*

Laisser-faire.

Marquis d'Argenson

No interference.

Laissons les jolies femmes aux hommes sans imagination.

Marcel Proust
Albertine Disparue

Let us leave pretty women to men without imagination.

Le bien de la fortune est un bien périssable;
Quand on bâtit sur elle, on bâtit sur le
sable.

Racan
Stances sur la Retraite

The benefits of chance are perishable; if you build on them, you build on sand.

Le bien nous faisons; le mal, c'est la Fortune.

La Fontaine
L'Ingratitude and l'Injustice des Hommes envers la Fortune

We claim responsibility for our successes and blame fortune for our failures.

Le bonheur a ses tempêtes.

Marceau
En de Secrètes Noces

Happiness has its storms.

Le chemin est long du projet à la chose.

Molière
Tartuffe

It is a long way from idea to fulfilment.

Le ciel fut son désir, la mer sa sépulture: Est-il plus beau dessin, ou plus riche tombeau?

Desportes
Icare

The heavens were his aim, the sea his sepulchre: could there be a finer aim or a richer tomb?

Le client n'a jamais tort.

César Ritz

The customer is never wrong.

Le coeur a ses raisons que la raison ne connaît point.

Blaise Pascal
Pensées

The heart has its reasons which reason knows not.

Le coeur de l'homme est un grand fripon!

Marivaux
La Fausse Suivante

Man's heart is a great rascal.

Le combat cessa faute de combattants.
Pierre Corneille
Le Cid

Battle ceased for want of combattants.

Le commencement et le déclin de l'amour se font sentir par l'embarras où l'on est de se trouver seuls.
La Bruyère
Les Characteres ou les moeurs de ce siècle

The onset and the waning of love make themselves felt in the uneasiness experienced at being alone together.

Le communisme passera. Mais la France ne passera pas.
Charles de Gaulle
La France Combattante

Communism will pass but France will not.

Le congrès ne marche pas, il danse.
Charles-Joseph, Prince de Ligne
about the Congress of Vienna

The Congress makes no progress; it dances.

Le coût fait perdre le goût.
Proverb

The cost destroys the appetite.

Le crime fait la honte, et non pas l'échafaud.
Pierre Corneille
Le Comte d'Essex

It is the crime which shames, not the scaffold.

Le Diable
Fait toujours bien ce qu'il fait.
Charles Baudelaire
L'Irrémédiable

The devil always does everything well.

Le Dieu du Monde
C'est le Plaisir.

Gérard de Nerval
Chanson Gothique

Pleasure is the god of the people.

Le dix-neuvième siècle est grand mais le vingtième sera heureux.
Victor Hugo
Les Misérables

The nineteenth century is great but the twentieth will be happy.

Le droit de premier occupant, si faible dans l'état de nature, est respectable à tout homme civil.
Jean-Jacques Rousseau
Du Contrat Social

The right of the first occupant, so weak in the natural world, is accepted by every civilised man.

Le flambeau de l'amour s'allume à la cuisine.

Proverb

The torch of love is lit by the kitchen stove.

Le fruit des guerres civiles à Rome a été l'esclavage, et celui des troubles d'Angleterre la liberté.

Voltaire
Lettres Philosophiques

In Rome the product of civil war was slavery, in England it was liberty.

Le génie n'est qu'une plus grande aptitude à la patience.

Comte de Buffon
Voyage à Montbar

Genius is only a greater aptitude for patience.

Le gouvernement est comme toutes les choses du monde; pour le conserver, il faut l'aimer.

Montesquieu
Lettres

Government is like anything else; to keep it, you have to like it.

Le grand Pan est mort.

Blaise Pascal
Pensées

Great Pan is dead (i.e. the Golden Age is past; the reference being to the re-telling by Rabelais of a story in Plutarch).

Le mal que nous faisons ne nous attire pas tant de persécution et de haine que nos bonnes qualités.

La Rochefoucauld
Réflexions

The evil we do does not earn us as much persecution and hatred as our good qualities.

Le malheur succède au bonheur le plus doux.

Pierre Corneille
Horace

Misfortune follows the sweetest happiness.

Le mieux ext l'ennemi du bien.

Voltaire

The best is the enemy of the good.

Le monarque prudent et sage
De ses moindres sujets sait tirer quelque usage.

La Fontaine
Le Lion s'en Allant en Guerre

A wise and prudent king knows how to make use of even the least of his subjects.

Le monde en marchant n'a pas beaucoup plus de souci de ce qu'il écrase que le char de l'idole de Jagarnata.

Ernest Renan
in the *Revue des Deux Mondes*, 1876

The world in its progress has little more care for what it crushes than the chariot of the Juggernaut.

Le monde n'a jamais manqué de charlatans.

La Fontaine
Le Charlatan

The world has never lacked for charlatans.

Le monde récompense plus souvent les apparences du mérite que le mérite même.

La Rochefoucauld
Réflexions

The world rewards the appearances of merit more often than merit itself.

Le mort n'entend sonner les cloches.

Diderot
Le Neveu de Rameau

The dead do not hear the funeral bells.

Le nez de Cléopâtre; s'il eût été plus court, toute la face de la terre aurait changé.

Blaise Pascal
Pensées

If Cleopatra's nose had been shorter, the whole history of the world would have been different.

Le peuple anglais pense être libre, il se trompe fort; il ne le'est que durant l'election des membres du parliament. Sitot qui'ils sont elus, il est escalve, il n'est rien.

Jean-Jacques Rousseau

The English believe themselves free, but they are quite wrong; they are free only during the election of members of parliament. Once the election is over, they are enslaved, they are nothing.

Le pire n'est pas toujours sûr, il est seulement bien probable!

Proverb

The worst is not always certain, it is just very likely.

Le plus beau patrimoine est un nom révéré.

Victor Hugo
Odes et Ballades

The best inheritance is a respected name.

Le plus grand danger de la bombe est dans l'explosion de bêtise qu'elle provoque.

Mirbeau
Oeuvres

The greatest danger of the bomb is the explosion of stupidity it provokes.

Le poète est semblable au Prince des Nuées, Qui hante le ciel et rit de l'archer;

The poet is like the Prince of Clouds, who lives in the sky and laughs at the archer; exiled on

Exilé sur le sol au milieu des huées,
Ses ailes de géant l'empêchent de marcher.
Charles Baudelaire
L'Albatros

*earth and surrounded by jeers, his giant's
wings prevent him from walking.*

Le premier précepte était de ne recevoir
jamais aucune chose pour vraie que je ne
la connusse évidement être telle.
René Descartes
Discours de la Méthode

*The first rule was never to accept anything as
true which I did not manifestly know to be
such.*

Le profit de l'un est le dommage de l'autre.
Montaigne
Essais

One man's profit is another's loss.

Le riche parle bien des richesses, le roi
parle froidement d'un grand don qu'il
vient de faire, et Dieu parle bien de Dieu.
Blaise Pascal
Pensées

*The rich man speaks approvingly of wealth, the
king speaks loftily of a great gift he has just
conferred, and God speaks well of God.*

Le rire est un refus de penser.
Paul Valéry
Lust

Laughter is a refusal to think.

Le roi le veut.
formula of royal assent

The king wishes it.

Le savoir a son prix.
La Fontaine
L'Avantage de la Science

Knowledge has its price.

Le scandale du monde est ce qui fait
l'offense,
Et ce n'est pas pécher que pécher en silence.
Molière
Tartuffe

*Public scandal is what offends us, and a silent
sin is no sin.*

Le scandale est souvent pire que le péché.
Marguerite de Navarre
Heptaméron

The scandal is often worse than the offence.

Le seul rêve intéresse,
Vivre sans rêve, qu'est-ce?
Et j'aime la Princesse Lointaine.
Edmond Rostand
La Princesse Lointaine

*The dream, alone, is of interest. What is life,
without a dream? And I love the Distant
Princess.*

Le silence des peuples est la leçon des rois.
Mirabeau
Discours à l'Assemblée

The silence of the people is the tutor of kings.

Le silence éternel de ces espaces infinis m'effraie.

Blaise Pascal
Pensées

The eternal silence of these infinite spaces terrifies me.

Le style est l'homme même.
George-Louis Leclerc de Buffon
Discours sur le Style

A man's style is the man himself.

Le temps ne s'arrête pour admirer la gloire; il s'en sert and passe outre.
Chateaubriand
Les Quatre Stuarts

Time does not stop to admire glory; it uses it and passes on.

Le temps, qui fortifie les amitiés, affaiblit l'amour.
La Bruyère
Les Caractères

Time, which strengthens friendships, weakens love.

Le temps s'en va, le temps s'en va, ma dame. Las! le temps non, mais nous, nous en allons.
Pierre de Ronsard

Time passes, time passes, my lady.
Alas, it is not time but we who pass.

Le trop d'attention qu'on a pour le danger Fait le plus souvent qu'on y tombe.
La Fontaine
Le Renard et les Poulets d'Inde

The more aware you are of danger, the more likely you are to meet it.

Le vent qui éteint une lumière allume un brasier.

Beaumarchais
Le Barbier de Séville

The wind can blow out a light and light a brazier.

Le vice, c'est le mal qu'on fait sans plaisir.
Colette
Claudine en Ménage

Vice is the evil we do without pleasure.

Le vin est tiré, il faut le boire.
Empress Eugénie of France
to Napoléon lll's surgeon, who told him he was too ill to lead his army

The wine is poured, we must drink it.

Le vrai est trop simple, il faut y arriver toujours par le compliqué.

Georges Sand
Lettres

Truth is too simple, we always have to get there via the complicated.

Les absents ont toujours tort.

Destouches

The absent are always in the wrong.

Les Anglais n'ont point de mot pour désigner l'ennui.

Holbach
Apologie de l'Ennui et des Ennuyeux

The English have no word for ennui.

Les Anglais s'amusent tristement selon l'usage de leur pays.

Maximilien de Béthune

The English take their pleasures sadly after the fashion of their country.

Les Anglais sont occupés; ils n'ont pas le temps d'être polis.

Montesquieu
Pensées et fragments inédits

The English are busy; they don't have time to be polite.

Les arbres tardifs sont ceux qui portent les meilleurs fruits.

Molière
Le Malade Imaginaire

Slow-growing trees bear better fruit.

Les armes n'ont pas d'opinion.

Audiberti
La Poupée

Arms have no [political] view.

Les bêtes sont au bon Dieu,
Mais la bêtise est à l'homme.

Victor Hugo
La Coccinelle

The beasts belong to God, but beastliness to man.

Les choses existent, nous n'avons pas à les créer.

Stéphane Mallarmé
Réponses à des Enquêtes sur l'Evolution Littéraire

Things exist – we don't have to create them.

Les Chrétiens ont droit, les Païens ont tort.

La Chanson de Roland

Christians are right, pagans are wrong.

Les courtisans qui l'entourent n'ont rien oublié et n'ont rien appris.

Maréchal Dumouriez
about Louis XVIII; (also attributed to Talleyrand)

The courtiers who surround him have forgotten nothing and learned nothing.

Les dieux eux-mêmes meurent,
Mais les vers souverains
Demeurent
Plus forts que les airains.

Théophile Gautier
L'Art Poétique

The gods themselves die but the best poems remain, stronger than bronzes.

Les enfants terribles.

Paul Gavarni
title of a series of prints

The little terrors.

Les erreurs de langage sont des crimes.

Margueritte Duras
Les Petits Chevaux de Tarquinia

Errors of language are crimes.

Les femmes d'aujourd'hui sont en train de détrôner le mythe de la féminité.

Simone de Beauvoir
Le Deuxième Sexe

Women of today are overthrowing the myth of feminity.

Les femmes libres ne sont pas des femmes.

Colette
Claudine à Paris

Free women are not women.

Les flûtes sauvages du malheur.

Perse
Vents

The wild flutes of misfortune.

Les gens qui prient perdent du temps.

Gustave Courbet
Manuscrit

People who pray waste time.

Les gouvernements périssent ordinairement par impuissance ou par tyrannie.
Dans le premier cas, le pouvoir leur
échappe; on le leur arrache dans l'autre.

Alexis de Tocqueville
De la Démocratie en Amérique

Governments usually fall through impotence or tyranny. In the first case power eludes them; in the second it is taken from them.

Les hommes de génie sont des météores
destinés à brûler pour éclairer leur siècle.

Napoléon I
Discours de Lyon

*Men of genius are meteors destined to burn in
order to illuminate their century.*

Les hommes ne peuvent engendrer de
nouvelles forces, mais seulement unir et
diriger celles qui existent.

Jean-Jacques Rousseau
Du Contrat Social

*Man cannot generate new forces, only combine
and control existing ones.*

Les hommes prennent souvent leur imagination pour leur coeur.

Blaise Pascal
Pensées

*Men often mistake their imagination for their
heart.*

Les homosexuels seraient les meilleurs
maris du monde s'ils ne jouaient pas la
comédie d'aimer les femmes.

Marcel Proust
Albertine Disparue

*Homosexuals would be the best husbands in
the world if they did not play at being in love
with women.*

Les maladies suspendent nos vertus et nos
vices.

Marquis de Vauvenargues
Réflexions et Maximes

Illness suspends our virtues and our vices.

Les moments de crise produisent un
redoublement de vie chez les hommes.

Chateaubriand
Mémoires d'Outre-Tombe

*Moments of crisis produce a redoubling of life
in man.*

Les peuples heureux n'ont pas d'histoire.
L'histoire est la science du
malheur des hommes.

Raymond Queneau
Une Histoire Modèle

*Happy nations have no history. History is the
study of man's bad luck.*

Les philosophes savent que les poètes ne
pensent pas.

Anatole France
Les Torts de l'Histoire

Philosophers know that poets don't think.

Les pierres parlaient pour lui.

Baillet

The stones spoke for him.

Les récits vrais traitent de la faim, et les récits imaginaires de l'amour.

Raymond Queneau
Une Histoire Modèle

True stories tell of hunger, imaginary ones of love.

Les références qu'on ne vérifie pas sont les bonnes.

Charles Péguy
Victor-Marie Comte Hugo

References which one does not verify are the good ones.

Les ruines d'une maison
Se peuvent réparer: que n'est cet avantage
Pour les ruines du visage!

La Fontaine
La Fille

A house in ruins can be restored: no such advantage for the ruins of a face!

Les sages qui veulent parler au vulgaire leur langage au lieu du sien n'en sauraient être entendus.

Jean-Jacques Rousseau
Du Contrat Social

Wise men who try to speak in a vulgar tongue instead of their own will not be understood.

Les sanglots longs
Des violons
De l'automne
Blessent mon coeur
D'une langueur
Monotone.

Paul Verlaine
Chanson d'Automne

The long-drawn sobs of the violins of autumn wound my heart with a monotonous languor.

Les vers viennent de Dieu.

Pierre de Ronsard

Poetry comes from God.

Les visages souvent sont de doux imposteurs.

Pierre Corneille
Le Menteur

Faces are often sweet imposters.

Leur ventre leur est pour dieu, la cuisine pour religion.

Jean Calvin
Institution de la Religion Chrétienne

Their stomach serves them as a god, food as a religion.

Lever matin n'est point bonheur,
Boire matin est le meilleur.

*Getting up in the morning is no pleasure;
drinking in the morning is better.*

Rabelais
Gargantua et Pantagruel

Liberté! Egalité! Fraternité!
Motto of the French Revolution

Liberty! Equality! Brotherhood!

Longtemps, je me suis couché de bonne
heure.

For a long time I used to go to bed early.

Marcel Proust
Du côté de chez Swann

Louis XVI: C'est une révolte?
La Rochefoucauld-Liancourt: Non, Sire, c'est
une révolution.

Louix XVI: *Is it a revolt?*
Rochefoucauld-Liancourt: *No, Sire, it is a
revolution.*

La Rochefoucauld-Liancourt
after the fall of the Bastille

Mon centre cède, ma droite recule, situation excellente, j'attaque.

*My centre gives way, my right retreats,
situation excellent, I attack.*

Marshall Foch
during the first Battle of the Marne

Madame, si c'est possible, c'est fait; impossible? cela se fera.

*Madam, if a thing is possible, consider it done;
the impossible? that will be done.* (Better
known as the US Armed Forces's slogan:
"The difficult we do immediately; the
impossible takes a little longer.")

Charles Alexandre de Calonne

Mais qu'est-ce donc que je suis? Une chose
qui pense. Qu'est-ce qu'une chose qui
pense?

*But what is it then that I am? A thing that
thinks. What is a thing that thinks?*

René Descartes
Discours de la Méthode

Mariage est un état de si longue durée
qu'il ne doit être commencé légèrement, ni
sans l'opinion de nos meilleurs amis et
parents.

*Marriage is such a long-lasting condition that
it should not be undertaken lightly, nor
without the appproval of our closest friends
and relations.*

Marguerite de Navarre
Heptaméron

Marquis: Mettez un canard sur un lac au
milieu des cygnes, vous verrez qu'il regret-
tera sa mare et finira par y retourner.

Marquis: *Put a duck on a lake in the midst of
swans, and you'll see he misses his pond and
will eventually return to it.*

Montrichard: La nostalgie de la boue!
Emile Augier
Le Mariage d'Olympe

Montrichard: Longing to be back in the mud!

Mauvaise herbe croît toujours.
Erasmus
Adages

Weeds always flourish.

Méfie-toi de celui qui rit avant de parler!
Alphonse Daudet
Tartarin sur les Alpes

Beware of him who laughs before speaking.

Mieux est de ris que de larmes écrire,
Pour ce que rire est le propre de l'homme.
Rabelais
Gargantua et Pantagruel

Best to write of laughter, not tears, because laughter is man's particular attribute.

Moi, je serai autocrate: c'est mon métier. Et le bon Dieu me pardonnera: c'est son métier.
Catherine the Great

I shall be autocratic: that's my business. And God will forgive me: that's his business.

Mon amour est écrit sur les murs d'Edimbourg.
Etienne Gilson
Le Chant du Triste Communal

My love is written on the walls of Edinburgh.

Mon métier et mon art, c'est vivre.
Montaigne

Life is my calling and my art.

Mon prix n'est pas dans ma couronne.
Anne of Austria, wife of Louis Xlll

My value does not lie in my crown.

Monsieur Wagner a de beaux moments, mais de mauvais quart d'heures.
Gioacchino Rossini

Wagner has some beautiful moments, but some bad quarters of an hour.

Morbleu! Faut-il que je vous aime?
Molière
Le Misanthrope

God! Must I love you?

Mort soudaine seule à craindre.
Blaise Pascal
Pensées

Sudden death is the only thing to fear.

Morte la bête, mort le venin.
Proverb

Dead men tell no tales. (Lit. once the beast is dead, the poison dies.)

Mourir pour le pays n'est pas un triste sort:
C'est s'immortaliser par une belle mort.

Pierre Corneille
Le Cid

To die for your country is not a sad fate: a fine death brings you immortality.

Mourrant sans déshonneur, je mourrais
sans regret.

Pierre Corneille
Le Cid

Dying without dishonour, I die without regret.

Muet, aveugle et sourd au cri des créatures,
Si le ciel nous laissa comme un monde
avorté,
Le juste opposera le dédain à l'absence
Et ne répondra plus que par un froid silence
Au silence éternel de la Divinité.

Vigny
Le Mont des Oliviers

If heaven, dumb, blind, and deaf to the cry of creatures, has abandoned us as an aborted world, the just man will meet its absence with disdain, and respond with a cold silence to the eternal silence of the deity.

N'espérez pas un parfait bonheur; il n'y en
a point sur la terre, et, s'il y en avait, il ne
serait pas à la cour.

Mme de Maintenon

Do not hope for perfect happiness; there is no such thing on earth, and if there were, it would not be found at court.

Ne cessez point d'être aimable, puisque
vous êtes aimé.

Mme de Sévigné
Lettres

Do not stop being lovable just because you are loved.

Ne clochez pas devant les boiteux.

Rabelais
Gargantua et Pantagruel

Don't limp in front of the lame.

Ne me laisse jamais seul avec la Nature,
Car je la connais trop pour n'en avoir pas
peur.

Vigny
La Maison du Berger

Do not ever leave me alone with nature, for I know her too well not to fear her.

Ne plaisantez pas avec l'humeur,
L'humeur c'est sérieux!

Jacques Prévert
Définir l'Humeur

Don't joke about humour – humour is serious.

Ne soyez pas un vaincu!

Arthur Rimbaud
L'Impossible

Never admit defeat!

Ne vaut pas le détour.
Michelin guidebooks

Not worth the trouble. (Lit. not worth the detour.)

Noblesse oblige.
Duc de Lévis
Maximes et Réflexions

Nobility has its obligations.

Notre nature est dans le mouvement; le repos entier est la mort.
Blaise Pascal
Pensées

Our being lies in movement; total rest is death.

Nourri dans le sérail, j'en connais tous les détours.
Jean Racine
Bajazet

Brought up in the harem, I know all its byways.

Nous avons sur les bras un homme malade – un homme gravement malade.
Emperor Nicholas I of Russia

We have a sick man on our hands – a very sick man (i.e. Turkey, the sick man of Europe).

Nous avons tous assez de force pour supporter les maux d'autrui.
La Rochefoucauld
Maximes

We are all strong enough to bear the misfortunes of others.

Nous doit aussi souvenir que Satan a ses miracles.
Jean Calvin
Institution de la Religion Chrétienne

We must also bear in mind that Satan has his miracles.

Nous entreprenons toujours choses défendues et convoîtons ce que nous est dénié.
Rabelais
Gargantua et Pantagruel

We always undertake forbidden things and desire what is denied us.

Nous mourrons de la correction!
Couteli
Remarks

We are dying of accuracy!

Nous n'éprouvons pas des sentiments qui nous transforment, mais des sentiments qui nous suggèrent l'idée de transformation.
Albert Camus
Carnets

We do not experience feelings that transform us, but feelings that suggest the idea of transformation to us.

Nous n'irons plus aux bois, les lauriers sont coupés.

Théodore de Banville
from an old nursery rhyme

We will go no more to the woods, the laurels are all cut down.

Nous ne saurions aller plus avant que les anciens.

La Fontaine

We cannot improve on the classics.

Nous vivons contrefaits, plutôt que de ne pas ressembler au portrait que nous avons tracé de nous d'abord.

André Gide
Les Caves du Vatican

We live in disguise, rather than depart from the picture we first had of ourselves.

O bienheureux le siècle où le peuple sauvage
Vivait par les forêts de glands et de fruitage.

Pierre de Ronsard
Elégie au Seigneur Baillon

Happy the age when the savage people lived on acorns and fruits of the forest.

O combien le péril enrichirait les dieux,
si nous nous souvenions des voeux qu'il nous fait faire.

La Fontaine
Jupiter et le Passager

How danger would enrich the gods if we remembered the vows we made when we were exposed to it.

O Français! Serez-vous donc toujours des enfants?

Jean Paul Marat
L'Ami du Peuple

Oh Frenchmen, will you always be children?

O liberté! O liberté! que de crimes on commet en ton nom!

Mme. Roland

O liberty, liberty, what crimes are committed in thy name!

O paroles, que de crimes on commet en votre nom!

Eugène Ionesco
Jacques ou la Soumission

O, words, what crimes are committed in your name!

O patrie! O patrie, ineffable mystère! Mot sublime et terrible! inconcevable amour!

Alfred de Musset
Retour, Le Havre

Fatherland, ineffable mystery! Sublime and awful word, inconceivable love!

O triste, triste était mon âme
A cause, à cause d'une femme.

Paul Verlaine
Ariettes Oubliées

Oh sad, sad was my heart, because of a woman.

On a souvent besoin d'un plus petit que soi.

La Fontaine
Le Lion et le Rat

We often need someone smaller than ourselves.

On aime toujours ce qui est beau ou ce qu'on trouve tel; mais c'est sur ce jugement qu'on se trompe.

Jean-Jacques Rousseau
Du Contrat Social

We always love what is good, or what we find good; it is in judging this that we make mistakes.

On appréhende plus de blesser ceux dont l'affection est plus utile et l'aversion plus dangereuse.

Blaise Pascal
Pensées

We are more afraid of injuring those whose friendship is useful and whose dislike is dangerous.

On devient moral dès qu'on est malheureux.

Marcel Proust
A l'Ombre des Jeunes Filles en Fleurs

We become ethical as soon as we are unhappy.

On dit bien vrai qu'un honnête homme c'est un homme mêlé.

Montaigne
Essais

It is truly said that an honest man is a busy man.

On dit que Dieu est toujours pour les gros bataillons.

Voltaire

God is said always to be on the side of the big battalions.

On est gai le matin, on est pendu le soir.

Voltaire
Charlot

Gay in the morning, hanged in the evening.

On est souvent ferme par faiblesse, et audacieux par timidité.

La Rochefoucauld
Réflexions

We are often firm through weakness and audacious through timidity.

On hasarde de perdre en voulant trop gagner.

La Fontaine
Le Héron

We risk losing all in trying to win too much.

On meurt deux fois, je le vois bien;
Cesser d'aimer et d'être aimable,
C'est une insupportable mort;
Cesser de vivre, ce n'est rien.

Voltaire
Stances

We die twice, I see clearly; ceasing to love and be loved is an unbearable death; ceasing to live is nothing.

On n'aime point à voir ceux à qui l'on doit tout.

Pierre Corneille
Nicomède

We do not like to see those to whom we owe everything.

On n'écrit pas un roman d'amour pendant qu'on fait l'amour.

Colette
Lettres au Petit Corsaire

One does not write a love story while making love.

On ne badine pas avec l'amour.

Proverb
also title of a play by Alfred de Musset

One does not fool with love.

On ne donne de louanges que pour en profiter.

La Rochefoucauld
Réflexions

We only praise in order to profit from it.

On ne donne rien si libéralement que ses conseils.

La Rochefoucauld
Réflexions

Nothing is so freely offered as advice.

On ne guérit pas de Paris.

Proverb

No one wearies of Paris.

On ne peut trop louer trois sortes de
personnes:
Les dieux, sa maîtresse, et son roi.

La Fontaine
Simonide Préservé par les Dieux

There are three kinds of people we cannot praise too much: the gods, our mistress and our king.

On ne voit bien qu'avec le coeur.
Antoine de Saint-Exupéry
Le Petit Prince

We only see clearly with our hearts.

On nous apprend à vivre quand la vie est passée.
Montaigne
Essais

We learn how to live once life is over.

On passe souvent de l'amour à l'ambition, mais on ne revient guère de l'ambition à l'amour.
La Rochefoucauld
Réflexions

We often pass from love to ambition, but rarely return from ambition to love.

On peut être pendu sans corde.
Cyrano de Bergerac
Poésies

One can be hanged without a rope.

On rencontre sa destinée souvent par des chemins qu'on prend pour l'éviter.
La Fontaine
l'Horoscope

We often meet our fate by the routes we take to avoid it.

On risque autant à croire trop qu'à croire trop peu.
Denis Diderot
Etrennes des Esprits Forts

It is as dangerous to believe too much as to believe too little.

On sait que le propre du génie est de fournir des idées aux crétins une vingtaine d'années plus tard.
Louis Aragon
Traité du Style

We know that the peculiar function of genius is to provide cretins with ideas twenty years later.

On trouve son semblable
Beau, bien fait, et surtout aimable.
La Fontaine,
L'Aigle et le Hibou

Those who resemble us we find good-looking, well set up, and above all charming.

Ordinairement la grandeur de caractère résulte de la balance naturelle de plusieurs qualités opposées.
Denis Diderot
Le Neveu de Rameau

Greatness of character is usually due to an innate balance of opposing qualities.

Où l'hôtesse est belle, le vin est bon.
Lebon
Adages Français

Where the hostess is beautiful the wine is good.

Où la valeur, la courtoisie.
Jean Baïf
Mimes, Enseignements et Proverbes

Where there is valour there is courtesy.

Oui, c'est l'Europe, depuis l'Atlantique jusqu' à l'Oural, c'est toute l'Europe, qui decidera du destin du monde.
Charles de Gaulle

Yes, it is Europe, from the Atlantic to the Urals, it is the whole of Europe, which will decide the destiny of the world.

Pâli comme un vieux livre.
Stéphane Mallarmé
Hérodiade

Faded like an old book

Paradis peint, où sont harpes et luz.
François Villon

Painted paradise, with harps and lutes.

Paris vaut bien une messe.
Henri IV
on his conversion to Catholicism;
alternatively attributed to his minister Sully,
during conversation

Paris is well worth a mass.

Partons, dans un baiser, pour un monde inconnu.
Alfred de Musset
La Nuit de Mai

Let us leave, with a kiss, for an unknown world.

Pends-toi, brave Crillon, nous avons combattu à Arques et tu n'y étais pas.
Henri IV

Hang yourselve, brave Crillon; we fought at Arques and you were not there.

Peu de chose nous console parce que peu de chose nous afflige.
Blaise Pascal
Pensées

Small things console us because small things distress us.

Peuples libres, souvenez-vous de cette maxime: on peut acquérir la liberté; mais on ne la recouvre jamais.
Jean-Jacques Rousseau
Du Contrat Social

Free nations, remember this maxim: one can gain liberty, but never recover it.

Philosopher, c'est douter.

Montaigne
Essais

To be a philosopher is to doubt.

Plaisir d'amour ne dure qu'un moment,
Chagrin d'amour dure toute la vie.

Jean-Piere Claris de Florian
Celestine

The joy of love lasts only a moment, the pain of love lasts a lifetime.

Plus ça change, plus c'est la même chose.

Alphonse Karr
Les Guêpes

The more things change, the more they are the same.

Plus le visage est sérieux, plus le sourire est beau.

Chateaubriand
Mémoires d'Outre-Tombe

The more serious the face, the more beautiful the smile.

Plus on apprend à connaître l'homme, plus on apprend à estimer le chien.

A. Toussenel
L'Esprit des bêtes

The more one gets to know of men, the more one values dogs.

Plutôt ce qu'ils font que ce qu'ils ont été.

Jean Racine
Andromaque

What they are doing matters more than what they have been.

Pour chaque indigent qui pâlit de faim, il y a un riche qui pâlit de peur.

Jean Blanc
Organisation du Travail

For each beggar, pale with hunger, there is a rich man, pale with fear.

Pour mon honneur et celui de ma nation, je choisirai plutôt honnête prison que honteuse fuite.

Francois l, King of France

For the sake of my own honour and that of my country, I shall choose honourable imprisonment rather than shameful flight.

Pour un plaisir, mille douleurs.

François Villon
Ballade des Dames des Temps Jadis

For one pleasure, a million pains.

Pourquoi demander au rossignol ce que signifie son chant?

Mme de Staël
Corinne ou l'Italie

Why ask the nightingale what its song means?

Prélude à l'après-midi d'un faune.
Stéphane Mallarmé
title of a poem

Prelude to the afternoon of a fawn.

Prendre conscience de ce qui est atroce et en rire, c'est devenir maître de ce qui est atroce.
Ionesco
La Démystification par l'Humeur Noire

To take note of the atrocity and to laugh at it is to overcome atrocity.

Prêter de l'argent fait perdre la mémoire.
Proverb

To lend money to someone makes him lose his memory.

Prouver que j'ai raison serait accorder que je puis avoir tort.
Beaumarchais
Le Mariage de Figaro

To prove that I am right would mean agreeing that I could be wrong.

Qu'est-ce que l'avenir? Qu'est-ce que le passé? Qu'est-ce que nous? Quel fluide magique nous environne et nous cache les choses qu'il nous importe le plus de connaître? Nous naissons, nous vivons, nous mourons au milieu du merveilleux.
Napoléon I
letter to Josephine

What is the future? What is the past? What are we? What magic fluid envelops us and hides from us the things we most need to know? We are born, we live, we die amid marvels.

Qu'il est difficile d'être content de quelqu'un!
La Bruyère
Les Caractères, Du Coeur

How difficult it is to be satisfied with someone.

Qu'il est difficile de proposer une chose au jugement d'un autre sans corrompre son jugement par la manière de lui proposer.
Blaise Pascal
Pensées

How hard it is to ask someone's advice without influencing his judgement by the way we present our problem.

Qu'il fût né d'un grand Roi, moi d'un
simple Pasteur,
Son sang auprès du mien est-il d'autre
couleur?
Cyrano de Bergerac
La Mort d'Agrippine

Though his father was a great king and mine a simple shepherd, is his blood a different colour from mine?

Qu'il y a loin de la connaissance de Dieu à l'aimer!

Blaise Pascal
Pensées

How far it is between knowing God and loving him!

Qu'ils mangent de la brioche.

attrib. Marie-Antoinette
but certainly much older

Let them eat cake.

Quand il fait sombre, les plus beaux chats sont gris.

Proverb

Even the handsomest cats are grey in the dark.

Quand le gouvernement viole les droits du peuple, l'insurrection est pour le peuple le plus sacré et le plus indispensable des devoirs.

Robespierre
addressing the National Convention, 1794

When the government violates the rights of the people, insurrection is the people's most sacred and indispensable duty.

Quand on cède à la peur du mal, on ressent déjà le mal de la peur.

Beaumarchais
Le Barbier de Séville

When we yield to the fear of evil, we already feel the evil of fear.

Quand on met son coeur avec son argent, la malédiction de Dieu est dans la maison.

Comtesse de Ségur
Un Bon Petit Diable

When the heart is set on money, the curse of God is on the house.

Quand vous serez bien vieille, au soir, à la chandelle
Assise auprès du feu, dévidant et filant,
Direz, chantant mes vers, en vous émerveillant,
Ronsard me célébrait du temps que j'éstois belle.

Pierre de Ronsard
Sonnets pour Hélène

When you are very old, in the evening, by candlelight, seated by the fire, spinning, you will say, reciting my poems and marvelling in your heart, "Ronsard sang my praises in the days when I was beautiful."

Quant au courage moral, il avait trouvé fort rare, disait-il, celui de deux heures après minuit; c'est-à-dire le courage de l'improviste.

Napoléon I

As to moral courage, I have very rarely met with two o'clock in the morning courage: I mean unprepared-for courage.

Que diable allait-il faire dans cette galère?
Molière
Les Fourberies de Scapin

Why the devil did he have to come aboard this galley?

Que le jour est lent de mourir par ces soirs démesurés de l'été!
Marcel Proust
La Fugitive

How slowly the day dies in these endless summer evenings.

Quel vicaire de village ne voudrait pas être Pape?
Voltaire
Lettres Philosophiques

What parish priest would not wish to be Pope?

Quelle affaire!
Marshall Blücher
meeting Wellington at Waterloo

What a business!

Quelle vanité que la peinture, qui attire l'admiration par la ressemblances des choses dont on n'admire point les originaux.
Blaise Pascal
Pensées

How vain painting is, exciting admiration by its resemblance to things of which we do not admire the originals.

Quelques crimes toujours précèdent les grands crimes.
Jean Racine
Phèdre

Some crimes always precede great crimes.

Qui cherche dans la liberté autre chose qu'elle-même est fait pour servir.
Alexis de Tocqueville
L'Ancien régime

He who desires from liberty anything other than itself is born to be a slave.

Qui n'a fait qu'obéir saura mal commader.
Pierre Corneille
Pulchérie

He who has only ever obeyed will make a bad leader.

Qui n'a pas vécu dans les années voisines de 1789 ne sait pas ce qu'est le plaisir de vivre.
Talleyrand

He who did not live in the years around 1789 does not know what living is.

Qui pardonne aisément invite à l'offenser.
Pierre Corneille
Cinna

He who forgives easily invites insult.

Qui rêve, dîne. **Proverb**	*He who dreams, dines.*
Qui s'excuse, s'accuse. **Proverb**	*He who excuses himself, accuses himself.*
Qui se fait brebis, le loup le mange. **Proverb**	*Mugs always get fleeced. (Lit. he who makes a lamb of himself will be eaten by the wolf.)*
Qui se marie pour amour a de bonnes nuits et de mauvais jours. **Meurier** *Trésor des Sentences*	*He who marries for love has good nights and bad days.*
Qui se vainc une fois peut se vaincre toujours. **Pierre Corneille** *Titus et Bérénice*	*He who controls himself once can always control himself.*
Qui vit sans folie n'est pas si sage qu'il croit. **La Rochefoucauld** *Réflexions*	*He who lives without folly is not as wise as he thinks.*
Quiconque a beaucoup vu Peut avoir beaucoup retenu. **La Fontaine** *L'Hirondelle et les Petits Oiseaux*	*He who has seen much can recall much.*
Quoi que vous fassiez, écrasez l'infâme, et aimez qui vous aime. **Voltaire**	*Whatever you do, suppress what is disgraceful and love those who love you.*
Race ennemie, trop perfide Albion! **Song** composed during the Napoleonic War	*Enemy race, most perfidious Albion!*
Rappelez-vous bien qu'il n'est aucun de vous qui n'ait dans sa giberne le bâton de Maréchal du duc de Reggio; c'est à vous à l'en faire sortir. **Louis XVIII** to the cadets of Saint-Cyr	*Keep in mind that every one of you has in his knapsack the Marshal's baton of the Duke of Reggio; it is for you to draw it forth.*
Régime oblige: le pouvoir absolu a des raisons que la République ne connaît pas. **François Mitterand** *Le Coup d'Etat Permanent*	*The order of things requires it; absolute power has reasons which the Republic knows not.*

Renoncer à sa liberté c'est renoncer à sa qualité d'homme, aux droits de l'humanité, même à ses devoirs.
Jean-Jacques Rousseau
Du Contrat Social

To renounce our liberty is to renounce the nature of man, the rights and duties of mankind.

Revenons à ces moutons.
Maistre Pierre Pathelin

Let us get back to those sheep (i.e. to the subject).

Rien n'est plus affreux que le rire pour la jalousie.
Françoise Sagan
La Chamade

To jealousy, nothing is more frightful than laughter.

Rien n'est plus contraire à l'organisation de l'esprit, de la mémoire et de l'imagination... Le nouveau système de poids et mesures sera un sujet d'embarras et de difficultés pour plusieurs générations.
Napoléon I
on the introduction of the metric system, in *Mémoires...écrits à Ste-Hélène*

Nothing is more contrary to the organisation of the mind, of the memory, and of the imagination... The new system of weights and measures will hinder and perplex several generations.

Rien n'est si dangereux qu'un ignorant ami; Mieux vaudrait un sage ennemi.
La Fontaine
L'Ours et l'Amateur de Jardins

Nothing is as dangerous as an ignorant friend; a wise enemy would be better.

Rien ne me serait trop cher pour l'éternité.
Blaise Pascal
Pensées

No price would be too high for eternity

Rien ne nous plaît que le combat, mais non pas la victoire.
Blaise Pascal
Pensées

Nothing pleases us but the struggle, certainly not the victory.

Roland est preux et Olivier est sage.
La Chanson de Roland

Roland is gallant and Oliver is wise.

Saluez-moi, car je suis tout simplement en train de devenir un génie.
Honoré de Balzac
writing to his sister

Salute me, for I am quite simply in the process of becoming a genius.

Savoir dissimuler est le savoir des rois.
Richelieu
Mirame

It is the business of kings to know how to dissimulate.

Se marier, c'est apprendre à être seul.
Proverb

Marriage teaches you to be alone.

Seul le silence est grand, tout le reste est faiblesse.
Alfred de Vigny
La Mort du Loup

Only silence is great, all the rest is weakness.

Si Dieu n'existait pas, il faudrait l'inventer.
Voltaire
Epîtres

If God did not exist, it would be necessary to invent him.

Si j'étais Dieu, j'aurais pitié du coeur des hommes.
Maeterlinck
Pélléas et Mélisande

If I were God I would pity men from my heart.

Si jeunesse savoit; si vieillesse pouvoit.
Henri Estienne
Epigrams

If the young only knew, if the old only could.

Si l'on veut abolir la peine de mort en ce cas, que MM. les assassins commencent.
Alphone Karr
Les Guêpes

If the death penalty is to be abolished, let those gentlemen, the murderers, do it first.

Si la charité est un lait, la dévotion est la crème.
St François de Sales

If charity is milk, devotion is the cream.

Si les triangles faisoient un Dieu, ils lui donneroient trois côtés.
Montesquieu
Lettres Persones no.59

If triangles invented a god, they would give him three sides.

Si nous n'avions point de défauts, nous ne prendrions pas tant de plaisir à en remarquer dans les autres.
La Rochefoucauld
Réflexions

If we had no failings, we would not be so pleased to notice them in others.

Si tous les hommes savaient ce qu'ils disent les uns des autres, il n'y aurait pas quatre amis dans le monde.

If people always knew what they said about each other, there would not be four friends left in the world.

Blaise Pascal
Pensées

Si vous adoptez cette fragrance, vos problèmes d'amour n'existent pas!

If you choose this perfume, your love problems will vanish.

Fragonard
to a nobleman who was having trouble with his mistress

Soldats, songez que, du haut de ces pyramides, quarante siècles vous contemplent.

Think of it, soldiers; from the summit of these pyramids, forty centuries look down upon you.

Napoléon I
speech to the Army of Egypt on 21 July 1798, before the Battle of the Pyramids

Soldats, je suis content de vous!

Soldiers, I am pleased with you.

Napoléon I
Proclamation after the Battle of Austerlitz, 1805

Surtout, Messieurs, point de zèle.

Above all, gentlemen, no zeal.

Talleyrand

Surtout n'ayez pas peur du peuple, il est plus conservateur que vous!

Above all, do not fear the people, they are more conservative than you.

Napoléon III
Mélanges

Ta gloire est dégagée, et ton devoir est quitte.

Your glory is earned, your duty discharged.

Pierre Corneille
Le Cid

Soldats de la légion,
De la Légion Etrangère,
N'ayant pas de nation,
La France est votre Mère.

Soldiers of the legion, the Foreign Legion, with no country of your own, France is your Mother.

War-Song of the Legion

Taisez-vous! Méfiez-vous! Les oreilles enemies vous écoutent.

Be silent! Be suspicious! Enemy ears are listening.

World War I poster

Tes yeux sont la citerne où boivent mes ennuis.

Charles Baudelaire
Sed Non Satiata

Your eyes are the well from which my troubles drink.

Tête de l'armée.

Napoléon I
last words

Head of the army.

Toujours au plus grand nombre on doit s'accommoder.

Molière
L'Ecole des Maris

One should always conform with the majority.

Toujours présent, rarement présenté, et jamais présentable.

Della Cerda
The Happy Summer Days (of family friends)

Always present, rarely presented and never presentable.

Tous hommes se haïssent naturellement l'un l'autre.

Blaise Pascal
Pensées

It is natural for all men to hate each other.

Tous les genres sont bons, hors le genre ennuyeux.

Voltaire
L'Enfant Prodigue

All types of people are fine – except bores.

Tous les jours, à tous points de vue, je vais de mieux en mieux.

Emile Coué

Every day, in every way, I am getting better and better.

Tous pour un, un pour tous.

Alexandre Dumas
Les Trois Mousquetaires

All for one and one for all.

Tout arrive par les idées; elles produisent les faits, qui ne leur servent que d'enveloppe.

Chateaubriand
Analyse Raisonnée de l'Histoire de France

Everything happens through ideas; they produce deeds, which serve them as a covering.

Tout au monde existe pour aboutir à un livre.

Stéphane Mallarmé
Le Livre, Instrument Spirituel

Everything is the world exists to end up in a book.

Tout bonheur que la main n'atteint pas
n'est qu'un rêve.

Soulary
Rêves Ambitieux

*The good fortune that we do not achieve is only
a dream.*

Tout commence en mystique et finit en
politique.

Charles Péguy
Notre Jeunesse

*Everything begins in mysticism and ends in
politics.*

Tout comprendre c'est tout pardonner.
Proverb

*To understand everything is to forgive
everything.*

Tout est bien, tout va bien, tout va le
mieux qu'il soit possible.

Voltaire
Candide

*Everything is fine, everything is going well,
everything is going on as well as it possibly
can.*

Tout homme est capable de faire du bien à
un homme; mais c'est ressembler aux
dieux que de contribuer au bonheur d'une
société entière.

Montesquieu
Lettres

*Any man is capable of doing some good to
another; but to contribute to the welfare of
society as a whole is to resemble the gods.*

Tout influe sur tout.
Proverb

Everything influences everything.

Tout le malheur de l'homme vient d'une
seule chose, qui est de ne savoir pas
demeurer en repos dans une chambre.

Blaise Pascal
Pensées

*All man's unhappiness derives from just one
thing, not being able to stay quietly in a room.*

Tout le plaisir de l'amour est dans le
changement.

Molière
Don Juan

All the pleasure of love lies in variety.

Tout par raison.

Richelieu

Everything in accordance with reason.

Tout Paris.

Molière
L'Impromptu de Versailles

All Paris.

Tout Paris les condamne, et tout Paris les court.

Voltaire
Lettres Philosophiques (of actors)

All Paris condemns them and all Paris courts them.

Tout passe, tout lasse, tout casse.

Proverb

Everything passes, everything wearies, everything breaks.

Toute institution qui ne suppose pas le peuple bon, et le magistrat corruptible, est vicieuse

Robespierre
Déclaration des droits de l'homme

Any institution which does not suppose the people good, and the magistrate corruptible, is evil.

Toute ma vie, je me suis fait une certaine idée de la France.

Charles de Gaulle
the first sentence of his *Mémoires de Guerre*

All my life I have held a certain concept of France.

Toute nation a le gouvernement qu'elle mérite.

Joseph de Maistre
Lettres et Oposcules Inédits

Every country has the government it deserves.

Toute puissance vient de Dieu, je l'avoue; mais toute maladie en vient aussi.

Jean-Jacques Rousseau
Du Contrat Social

All power derives from God, I agree; but so does all illness.

Toutes actions hors les bonnes ordinaires sont sujettes à sinistre interprétation.

Montaigne
De l'Ivrognerie

All unusual actions are open to sinister interpretation.

Toutes choses sont dites déja, mais comme personne n'écoute, il faut toujours recommencer.

André Gide

Everything has been said before, but since no one listens, one must always start again.

Toutes les balles ne tuent pas.

Alphonse Daudet
Tartarin sur les Alpes

Not all bullets kill.

Triste comme la gloire.

Napoléon I

As sad as glory.

Trop de jeunesse et trop de vieillesse empêchent l'esprit, comme trop et trop peu d'instruction.

Blaise Pascal
Pensées

Extreme youth and age impede the mind, like too much or too little education.

Un Anglais, comme homme libre, va au Ciel par le chemin qui lui plaît.

Voltaire
Lettres Philosophiques

An Englishman, being a free man, takes whatever road to heaven pleases him.

Un beau crime m'empoigne comme un beau mâle.

Célestine
Le Journal d'une Femme de Chambre

A fine crime thrills me like a handsome man.

Un beau visage est le plus beau de tous les spectacles; et l'harmonie la plus douce est le son de voix de celle que l'on aime.

La Bruyère
Les Caractères, Des Femmes

A beautiful face is the most pleasing of sights; and the sweetest harmony is to hear the voice of her whom one loves.

Un enfant, c'est un insurgé.

Simone de Beauvoir
Le Deuxième Sexe

A child is a rebel.

Un gentilhomme qui vit mal est un monstre dans la nature.

Molière
Don Juan

A gentleman who lives a wicked life is one of nature's monsters.

Un homme qui a fait une fois un bond dans le Paradis, comment pourrait-il s'accommoder ensuite de la vie de tout le monde?

Alain-Fournier
Le Grand Meaulnes

How can a man who has once made a leap into Paradise accommodate himself again to everyday life?

Un homme sage ne se fait point d'affaires avec les grands.

Beaumarchais
Le Mariage de Figaro

A wise man has no dealings with the great.

Un homme sérieux a peu d'idées. Un homme à idées n'est jamais sérieux.

Paul Valéry
Mauvaises Pensées

A serious-minded person has few ideas. People with ideas are never serious.

Un jour, la France me remerciera d'avoir aidé à sauver son honneur.

Zola
La Vérité en Marche

One day France will thank me for having helped to save her honour.

Un livre n'est après tout qu'un extrait du monologue de son auteur.

Paul Valéry
Choses Tues

A book, after all, is just an extract from its author's monologue.

Un malheureux cherche l'autre.

Marguerite de Navarre
Heptaméron

Unhappy people are attracted to each other.

Un matin, l'un de nous manquant de noir, se servit de bleu; l'impressionisme était né.

Pierre Auguste Renoir

One morning one of us, having no black, used blue instead, and Impressionism was born.

Un premier mouvement ne fut jamais un crime.

Pierre Corneille
Horace

An impulse was never a crime.

Un sou quand il est assuré
Vaut mieux que cinq en espérance.

La Fontaine
Le Berger et la Mer

A coin you have is worth more than five hoped for.

Un vrai chrétien n'examine point ce qu'on lui ordonne de croire.

Nicholas-Sébastien Chamfort
Caractères et Anecdotes

A true Christian never questions what he has been told to believe.

Une armée marche à plat ventre.

Napoléon I
attributed. c. 1819, while in exile on St Helena

An army marches on its stomach.

Une de ces dépêches dont M. de Guermantes avait spirituellement fixé le modèle: "Impossible venir, mensonge suit".

Marcel Proust
Le Temps retrouvé

One of those telegrams of which M. de Guermantes had wittily defined the formula: "Cannot come, lie follows".

Une idée c'est un nain géant qu'il faut sur-
veiller nuit et jour; car l'idée qui rampait
hier à vos pieds demain dominera votre
tête.

Alexandre Dumas
La Dame de Monsoreau

An idea is a young giant that needs to be
watched day and night, for the idea which
yesterday crawled at your feet, tomorrow will
fill your head.

Une maison est une machine-à-habiter.
Le Corbusier
Vers une architecture

A house is a machine for living in.

Victor Hugo – hélas!
André Gide
when asked who was the greatest French
poet

Victor Hugo – alas!

Vienne la nuit, sonne l'heure,
Les jours s'en vont, je demeure.
Guillaume Apollinaire
Le Pont Mirabeau

The night may come, the hour may strike, the
days pass, I remain.

Vieux époux,
Vieux jaloux,
Tirez tous
Les verrous.

Song

Old husband, jealous old man, be sure to shoot
all the bolts.

Vivez joyeux.
Rabelais
motto on the title page of *Gargantua*

Live joyfully.

Vive le Québec Libre!
Charles de Gaulle
speaking in Montreal

Long Live Free Quebec!

Vivre? Les serviteurs feront cela pour
nous.
Philippe-Auguste Villiers de L'Isle-Adam
Axël

Living? The servants will do that for us.

Vogue la galère!
Rabelais

Let things go! (Lit: the ship's under way!)

Voilà un homme!
Napoléon I
on first meeting Goethe, 1808

What a man!

Voir le jour se lever est plus utile que
d'entendre la Symphonie Pastorale.
Claude Debussy
Monsieur Croche Antidilettante

*Seeing the day dawn is more useful than
hearing the Pastoral Symphony.*

Votre coeur est à moi, j'y règne; c'est assez.
Pierre Corneille
Titus et Bérénice

Your heart is mine, I rule there; it is enough.

Vous avez un médecin – que vous fait-il?
Sire, nous causons ensemble; il m'ordonne
des remèdes, je ne les fais point, et je
guéris.
Molière
reply to Louis XIV

*You have a doctor, what does he do for you?
Sire, we chat; he writes a prescription for me, I
ignore it, and I get better.*

Vous aviez mon coeur,
Moi, j'avais le vôtre;
Un coeur pour un coeur,
Bonheur pour bonheur!
Desbordes-Valmore

*You had my heart and I had yours; a heart for
a heart, happiness for happiness.*

Vous êtes une femme pour qui on pourrait
avoir une grande passion!
Benito Mussolini
on first meeting Clare Sheridan

*You are a woman for whom I could feel a great
passion.*

Vous l'avez voulu, Georges Dandin, vous
l'avez voulu.
Molière
Georges Dandin

*It's what you wanted, George Dandin, it's
what you wanted.*

Vous ne connaissez point ni l'amour ni ses
traits;
On peut lui résister quand il commence
à naître,
Mais non pas le bannir quand il s'est
rendu maître.
Pierre Corneille
Horace

*You do not at all understand either love or its
characteristics; you can resist it when it first
begins to grow, but not banish it once it has
mastered you.*

Waterloo! Waterloo! Waterloo! morne
plaine!
Victor Hugo

*Waterloo! Waterloo! Waterloo! melancholy
plain!*

FRENCH INDEX

GERMAN

Voila un homme!

Napoléon after meeting Goethe

There is a man!

Aber hier, wie überhaupt, kommt es
anders, als man glaubt.

Wilhelm Busch
Plisch und Plum

*But in this situation, as usual, it will turn out
differently from what one expects.*

Aber ich, wär ich sehen Sie, ich könnte das
Leiden nicht ertragen - ich würde retten,
retten!

Georg Büchner
Woyzeck

*But if I were omnipotent, you see, I would not
be able to bear the suffering – I would save,
save!*

Ach, daß die Einfalt, daß die Unschuld nie
Sich selbst und ihren heil'gen Wert erkennt!

Goethe
Faust

*Oh, that simplicity and innocence never
recognise themselves and their sacred value!*

Ach, es geschehen keine Wunder mehr!

Schiller
Die Jungfrau von Orleans

Alas, miracles no longer happen!

Ach, ich bin des Treibens müde!

Goethe
Wandrers Nachtlied

O, I am tired of the struggle.

Ach, sie haben einen guten Mann begraben.

Matthias Claudius
Bei dem Grabe meines Vaters

O, they have buried a good man.

Ach, wie gut, daß niemand weiß, daß ich
Rumpelstilzchen heiß!

The Brothers Grimm
Rumpelstilzchen Märchen

*It is just as well that no one knows that my
name is Rumpelstiltskin.*

Ach, wie ist's möglich dann, daß ich dich
lassen kann.

Helmina de Chézy
Revision of a folk song from the
Thüringer Wald

How is it possible that I could leave you?

Acht Bände hat er geschrieben. Er hätte
gewiß besser getan, er hätte acht Bäume
gepflanzt oder acht Kinder erzeugt.

Georg Christoph Lichtenberg
of himself
Aphorismen

*He has written eight volumes. He would surely
have done better to plant eight trees, or produce
eight children.*

Ade, nun, Ihr Lieben! Geschieden muß sein.
Justinus Kerner
Wanderlied

So goodbye, my loved ones! We must part.

Allah braucht nicht mehr zu schaffen,
Wir erschaffen seine Welt.
Goethe
Wiederfinden

Allah need no longer create: we are creating his world.

Alle Kreatur braucht Hilf von allen.
Bertolt Brecht
Von der Kindermörderin, Marie Farrar

All creatures need the help of everyone.

Alle Macht kommt vom Volke.
Proverb

All power comes from the people.

Alle Menschen werden Brüder.
Schiller
An die Freude

All men will become brothers.

Alle rennen nach dem Glück
Das Glück rennt hinterher.
Bertolt Brecht
*Das Lied von der Ünzulänglichkeit
menschlichen Strebens*

Everyone chases after happiness, but happiness is running after them.

Alle streben doch nach dem Gesetz.
Franz Kafka
Der Prozeß

Everyone strives for the law.

Allen zu glauben ist zu viel, keinem
glauben zu wenig.
Proverb

To believe everyone is too much, believing no one is too little.

Alles
Ist nicht es selbst.
Rainer Maria Rilke
Duineser Elegien

Everything is not itself.

Alles Erworbene bedroht die Maschine.
Rainer Maria Rilke
Die Sonette an Orpheus

Machines threaten everything that has ever been achieved.

Alles Getrennte findet sich wieder.
Friedrich Hölderlin
Hyperion

All that is divided will find itself again.

Alles in der Welt läßt sich ertragen, nur nicht eine Reihe von schönen Tagen.

Goethe
Gedichtsammlung, 1815

Everything in the world is bearable, except a series of lovely days.

Alles oder nichts!

Expression

All or nothing!

Alles was geschieht, vom Größten bis zum Kleinsten, geschieht nothwendig.

Artur Schopenhauer

Everything that happens, from the greatest to the least, happens inevitably.

Alles, was über das Leben auf diesem Planeten zu sagen ist, könnte man in einem einzigen Satz von mittlerer Länge sagen.

Bertolt Brecht
Baal

Everything there is to say about life on this planet could be said in a single sentence of moderate length.

Alles, was überhaupt gedacht werden kann, kann klar gedacht werden.

Ludwig Wittgenstein
Tractatus logico-philosophicus

Everything that can be thought at all can be thought clearly.

Alles Wissen hat etwas Puritanisches; es gibt den Worten ein Moral.

Elias Canetti
Aufzeichnungen

All knowledge is somehow puritanical – it gives words a moral.

Als ihr Mund verstummte, wurde ihre Stimme gehört.

Bertolt Brecht
Die heilige Johanna der Schlachthöfe

As her mouth grew silent, one could hear her voice.

Als Gregor Samsa eines Morgens aus unruhigen Träumen erwachte, fand er sich in seinem Bett zu einem ungeheuren Ungeziefer verwandelt.

Franz Kafka
Die Verwandlung

When Gregor Samsa woke one morning from restless dreams, he found himself transformed in his bed into a gigantic insect.

Als wär's ein Stück von mir.

Johann Ludwig Uhland
Ich hatt' einen Kameraden

As if it were part of me.

Also sprach Zarathustra.
Friedrich Nietzsche
Also sprach Zarathustra

Thus spoke Zarathustra.

Am Abend des dritten Tages, als wir bei
Sonnenuntergang gerade durch eine Herde
Nilpferde hindurchfuhren, stand urplötzlich,
von mir nicht geahnt und nicht gesucht, das
Wort "Ehrfurcht vor dem Leben" vor mir.
Albert Schweitzer
Aus meinem Leben und Denken

*Late on the third day, at the very moment
when, at sunset, we were making our way
through a herd of hippopotami, there flashed
upon my mind, unexpected and unsought, the
phrase, "Reverence for Life".*

Am Ende hängen wir doch ab
Von Kreaturen, die wir machten.
Goethe
Faust

*In the end we remain dependent on creatures of
our own making.*

Am Jüngsten Tag, wenn die Posaunen
schallen,
Und alles aus ist mit dem Erdeleben,
Sind wir verpflichtet Rechenschaft zu geben
Von jedem Wort, das unnütz uns entfallen.
Goethe
Warnung

*On the Day of Judgement, when the trumpets
sound and earthly life is finished, we shall have
to account for every idle word that has fallen
from our lips.*

An den langen Tischen der Zeit
Zechen die Krüge Gottes.
Paul Celan
Die Krüge

*The tankards of God make merry at the long
table of time.*

An diesem Tage hatte die Weltgeschichte
ihren Sinn verloren.
Walter Rathenau
on the outbreak of World War I

*On this day the history of the world seems to
have lost its mind.*

Andrea: Unglücklich das Land, das keine
Helden hat!
Galilei: Nein. Unglücklich das Land, das
Helden nötig hat.
Bertolt Brecht
Leben des Galilei

Andrea: *Unhappy the land that has no heroes!*
Galileo: *No. Unhappy the land that needs
heroes.*

Anklagen ist mein Amt und meine
Sendung.
Schiller
Wallenstein

Accusation is my duty and my mission.

Arbeit ist das halbe Leben,
Und die andre Hälfte auch.

Erich Kästner
Bürger, schont eure Anlagen

Architektur ist überhaupt die erstarrte
Musik.

Friedrich von Schelling

Arbeit macht frei.
Inscription over the gates of Dachau (and
subsequently those of Auschwitz), 1933

Auch das Schöne muß sterben!

Schiller
Nänie

Auf der Welt ist kein Bestand,
Wir müssen alle sterben,
Das ist uns wohlbekannt!

Folk song

Auf dem Grunde aller dieser vornehmen
Rassen ist das Raubtier, die prachtvolle
nach Beute und Sieg lüstern schweifende
blonde Bestie nich zu verkennen.

Friedrich Nietzsche
Zur Genealogie der Moral

Auferstanden aus Ruinen.

Johannes R. Becher
National anthem of the DDR

Auf Flügeln des Gesanges.

Heinrich Heine
title of a song

Aus der Kriegsschule des Lebens – was
mich nicht umbringt, macht mich stärker.

Friedrich Nietzsche
*Götzen-Dämmerung oder Wie man mit dem
Hammer philosophiert*

Work is half of life – and the other half, too.

Architecture is frozen music.

Work liberates.

Even beauty must die!

*There is no permanence in the world; we must
all die – we are well aware of that!*

*At the base of all these aristocratic races the
predator is not to be mistaken, the splendrous
blond beast, avidly rampant for plunder and
victory.*

Risen from the ruins.

On wings of song.

*From the war-school of life – whatever does not
kill me makes me stronger.*

Aus so krummem Holze, als woraus der
Mensch gemacht ist, kann nichts ganz
Gerades gezimmert werden.

Immanuel Kant
*Idee zu einer allgemeinen Geschichte in
weltbürgerlicher Absicht*

*From the crooked timber of humanity nothing
straight can ever be made.*

Beim wunderbaren Gott! Das Weib ist
schön.

Schiller

By the wonderful God! Women are beautiful.

Beitet unz iuwer jugent zergê:
Swaz ir in tuot, daz rechent iuwer jungen.

Walther von der Vogelweide
Die Veter habent ir Kint erzogen

*Wait until your youth is gone! Your children
will reckon with you for what you did to them.*

Beruf ist mirs, zu rühmen Höhers.

Hölderlin
Die Prinzessin Auguste von Homburg

My profession is to praise higher things.

Besiegen könnt ihr uns, aber täuschen
nicht mehr.

Ludwig Börne
Briefe aus Paris

*You may be able to conquer us, but you can no
longer deceive us.*

Bestechlichkeit ist unsre einzige Aussicht.
Solangs die gibt, gibts milde Urteilssprüche,
und sogar der Unschuldige kann
durchkommen vor Gericht.

Bertolt Brecht
Mutter Courage und ihre Kinder

*Corruption is our only hope. As long as we
have that there will be lenient sentences and
even the innocent will survive a trial.*

Bettler sind Könige.

Schiller
Die Räuber

Beggars are kings.

Bezähme jeder die gerechte Wut
Und spare für das Ganze seine Rache:
Denn Raub begeht am allgemeinenen Gut,
Wer selbst sich hilft in seiner eignen Sache.

Goethe
Werke

*Everyone should control his righteous anger
and save his revenge for the whole. For whoever
helps himself robs the common good.*

Blut ist ein ganz besondrer Saft.

Goethe
Faust

Blood is a very special juice.

Brennt Paris?
Adolf Hitler

Is Paris burning?

Courage ist gut, aber Ausdauer ist besser.
Theodor Fontane

Courage is good, but endurance is better.

Da rast der See und will sein Opfer haben.
Schiller
Wilhelm Tell

The sea is raging and demands its sacrifice.

Da wo wir lieben,
Ist Vaterland;
Wo wir genießen
Ist Hof und Haus.
Goethe
Felsweihegesang an Psyche

The place that we love is the fatherland; the places in which we enjoy ourselves are the garden and home.

Das strebende Stemmen,
Grau aus vergehender Stadt oder aus
fremder, des Doms.
Rainer Maria Rilke
Duineser Elegien

The striving grey mass of the cathedral rising from a strange or dying town.

Das allgemeine Verhältnis erkennet nur
Gott.
Proverb

Only God understands the overall relationship of things.

Das alte romantische Land.
Wieland

The old land of romance.

Das alte stürzt, es ändert sich die Zeit.
Schiller
Wilhelm Tell

The old order is crumbling; times are changing.

Das älteste Sprichwort ist wohl: Allzuviel
ist ungesund.
Georg Christoph Lichtenberg
Aphorismen

The old proverb is right: excess is unhealthy.

Das Bild ist ein Modell der Wirklichkeit.
Ludwig Wittgenstein
Tractatus logico-philosophicus

A picture is a model of reality.

Das Buch ist ein Spiegel; wenn ein Affe hineinguckt, so kann freilich kein Apostel heraussehen.

Georg Christoph Lichtenberg
Aphorismen

A book is a mirror; if an ape looks into it, an apostle cannot look out of it.

Das Edle schwindet von der weiten Erde,
Das Hohe sieht vom Niedern sich
                                verdrängt,
Und Freiheit wird sich nennen die
                                Gemeinheit,
Als Gleichheit brüsten sich der dunkle Neid.

Franz Grillparzer
Libussa

Nobility is fading from the wide world, the lofty sees itself being driven out by the lowly. Vulgarity will call itself freedom, and dark envy will boast of itself as equality.

Das Ewig-Weibliche
Zieht uns hinan.

Goethe
Faust

The eternal feminine draws us upwards.

Das freie Meer befreit den Geist.

Proverb

The free ocean releases the spirit.

Das Ganze macht, nicht das Einzelne.

Proverb

It is the whole, not the detail, which counts.

Das gesamte Leben läßt sich in drei Thesen zusammenfassen: der Kampf ist der Vater aller Dinge, die Tugend ist eine Angelegenheit des Bluts, Führertum ist primär entscheidend.

Adolf Hitler
Letter to Heinrich Brüning

The whole of life can be summed up in three propositions: struggle is the father of all things; virtue lies in the blood; leadership is primarily decisiveness.

Das Gesetz hat noch keinen großen Mann gebildet, aber die Freiheit brütet Kolosse und Extremitäten aus.

Schiller
Die Räuber

Laws have never yet produced a great man, but freedom incubates both giants and extremists.

Das Glück ist eine leichte Dirne,
Sie weilt nicht gern am selben Ort;
Sie streicht das Haar dir aus der Stirne
Und küßt dich rasch und flattert fort.

Heinrich Heine
Romanzero

Good fortune is a loose woman who does not like to tarry in the same place for long; she strokes the hair back from your forehead, kisses you quickly and flutters off.

Das Haß ist parteiisch, aber die Liebe ist es noch mehr.

Goethe

Hate is unfair, but love even more so.

Das Leben der Reichen ist ein langer Sonntag.

Georg Büchner

The life of rich people is one long Sunday.

Das Leben ist eine Tortur ...
Andererseits kommen wir
Gerade in den Angstzuständen
Zu uns selbst.

Thomas Bernhard
Die Jagdgesellschaft

Life is torture... On the other hand, we get to know ourselves only when we are in a state of panic.

Das leiseste Zucken des Schmerzes, und rege es sich nur in einem Atom, macht einen Riß in der Schöpfung von oben bis unten.

Georg Büchner
Dantons Tod

The faintest twinge of pain, even if only in an atom, creates a fissure in creation from top to bottom.

Das Schicksal benutzt meistens doch unsere schwachen Punkte, um uns auf das uns Dienliche aufmerksam zu machen.

Wilhelm Raabe
Stopfkuchen

Fate generally uses our weak points to teach us something useful.

Das Sorgenschränkchen, das Allerheiligste der innersten Seelenökonomie, das nur des Nachts geöffnet wird.

Georg Christoph Lichtenberg
Aphorismen

The little cupboard of worries, the inner sanctum of the soul's innermost economy, which is opened only at night.

Das Weib war der zweite Fehlgriff Gottes.
Friedrich Nietzsche
Der Antichrist

Woman was God's second blunder.

Das Wort baut Brücken in unerforschte Gebiete.

Adolf Hitler

Words build bridges in unexplored areas.

Das Wunderreich der Nacht.
Richard Wagner
Tristan und Isolde

The wonder-realm of Night.

Daz si dâ heizent minne, de ist niwan
senede leit.

Walther von der Vogelweide
Daz si dâ heizent Minne

*That which they call love is nothing but
yearning sorrow.*

Dem Herzen folg' ich, denn ich darf ihm
trauen.

Schiller
Wallensteins Tod

I follow my heart, for I can trust it.

Dem Wandersmann gehört die Welt
In allen ihren Weiten.

F. Rückert

To the wanderer belongs the whole wide world.

Den Himmel überlassen wir den Engeln
und den Spatzen.

Heinrich Heine
Deutschland. Ein Wintermärchen

*We will leave heaven to the angels and the
sparrows.*

Denken ist danken.

Proverb

To think is to thank.

Denn ein Haifisch ist kein Haifisch,
Wenn man's nicht beweisen kann.

Bertolt Brecht
Die Dreigroschenoper

*For a shark is not a shark if it cannot be
proved.*

Den für dieses Leben
Ist der Mensch nicht schlau genug.

Bertolt Brecht
*Das Lied von der Unzulänglichkeit
menschlichen Strebens*

Man is not crafty enough for this life.

Denn, Ihr Deutschen, auch Ihr seid
Tatenarm und gedankenvoll.

Friedrich Hölderlin
An die Deutschen

*For you Germans are also poor in deeds and
full of thought.*

Denn nur vom Nutzen wird die Welt regiert.

Schiller
Wallensteins Tod

The world is ruled only according to profit.

Denn schwer ist zu tragen
Das Unglück, aber schwerer das Glück.

Friedrich Hölderlin
Der Rhein

*Although misfortune is hard to bear, good
fortune is even harder.*

Der alte Jude, das ist der Mann.
Otto von Bismarck
about Disraeli at the Congress of Berlin

The old Jew, that's the man.

Der Aberglaube ist die Poesie des Lebens.
Goethe

Superstition is the poetry of life.

Der brave Mann denkt an sich selbst zuletzt.
Schiller
Wilhelm Tell

The good man thinks of himself last.

Der die dunkle Zukunft sieht, der muß auch
sehen den Tod und allein ihn fürchten.
Friedrich Hölderlin
Der Mensch

*He who sees the dark future must also see
death, and fear it alone.*

Der Druck der Geschäfte ist schön der
Seele; wenn sie entladen ist, spielt sie
freier und genießt des Lebens.
Goethe
Tagebuch

*Business pressures are good for the soul; when
it has unburdened itself of them, it plays all the
more freely and enjoys life.*

Der du die weite Welt umschweiffst, ge-
schäftiger Geist, wie nah fühl ich mich dir.
Goethe
Faust

*You who wander the wide world, busy spirit,
how close I feel to you.*

Der eine fragt: Was kommt danach?
Der andere fragt nur: Ist es recht?
Und so unterscheidet sich
Der Freie von dem Knecht.
Theodor Storm
Der eine fragt: Was kommt danach?

*One person asks "What happens next?" The
other asks only "Is it right?" And the free man
is thus distinguished from the serf.*

Der Erfolgreiche hört nur noch
Händeklatschen. Sonst ist er taub.
Elias Canetti
Aufzeichnungen

*The successful person hears only applause – he
is deaf to all else.*

Der ewige Friede ist ein Traum und nicht
einmal ein schöner.
Helmuth von Moltke
letter to Johann Kaspar Bluntschli, 11
December 1880

*Eternal peace is a dream, and not even a nice
one.*

Der früh Geliebte,
Nicht mehr Getrübte,
Er kommt zurück!

Goethe
Faust

The beloved of long ago, no more befogged, is
coming back!

Der ganzen modernen Weltanschauung
liegt die Täuschung zugrunde, daß die
sogennanten Naturgesetze die
Erklärungen der Naturerscheinungen
seien.

Ludwig Wittgenstein
Tractatus logico-philosophicus

The entire modern world view supports an
illusion that the so-called laws of nature are the
explanation of natural phenomena.

Der Gedanke ist der sinnvolle Satz.

Ludwig Wittgenstein
Tractatus logico-philosophicus

A thought is a meaningful proposition.

Der Glaube an einen Gott ist Instinkt, er ist
dem Menschen natürlich, so wie das
Gehen auf zwei Beinen.

Georg Christoph Lichtenberg
Aphorismen

Belief in a god is instinctive; it is as natural to
mankind as walking on two legs.

Der Glaube ist schwerer zu erschüttern als
das Wissen.

Adolf Hitler
Mein Kampf

Belief is harder to shake than knowledge.

Der Glaube ist wie die Liebe: er läßt sich
nicht erzwingen.

Goethe

Faith is like love: neither can be forced.

Der größte Lump im ganzen Land, das ist
und bleibt der Denunziant.

**August Heinrich Hoffmann von
Fallersleben**
Politische Gedichte aus der Vorzeit Deutschlands

The greatest rogue in the whole land is, and
will remain, the informer.

Der Haß ist so gut erlaubt als die Liebe,
und ich hege ihn im vollsten Maße gegen
die, welche ihn verachten.

Georg Büchner
letter to his family, February 1824

Hatred is just as allowable as love, and I
harbour it in the fullest measure against
those who scorn it.

Der Kaiser ist Alles, Wien ist nichts!

Prince Metternich

The Emperor is everything, Vienna is nothing!

Der Kampf hat den Menschen groß gemacht.

Adolf Hitler
letter to Heinrich Brüning

Struggle has made mankind great.

Der kann sich manchen Wunsch gewähren,
Der kalt sich selbst und seinem Willen lebt;
Allein wer andre wohl zu leiten strebt,
Muß fähig sein, viel zu entbehren.

Goethe
Ilmenau

He who lives coldly and according to his will can grant his own wishes; but he who strives to lead others must be capable of many sacrifices.

Der König hat eine Bataille verloren. Jetzt ist die Ruhe die erste Bürgerpflicht.

F. W. von der Schulenburg-Kehnert
7 October 1806, after the battle of Jena and Auerstedt

The king has lost a battle. Calm is now the primary duty of all citizens.

Der Kopf steht mir wie eine Wetterfahne, wenn ein Gewitter heraufzieht und die Windstöße veränderlich sind.

Goethe
letter to J.D. Salzmann, 1771

My head feels like a weathervane when a thunderstorm is approaching and the gusts of wind are changeable.

Der Krieg findet immer einen Ausweg.

Bertolt Brecht
Mutter Courage und ihre Kinder

War always finds a way.

Der Krieg ist nichts als eine Fortsetzung des politischen Verkehrs mit Einmischung anderer Mittel.

Karl von Clausewitz

War is nothing else but a continuation of politics with an admixture of other means.

Der Leichnam ist nicht das ganze Tier.

Goethe
letter to Herr Hetzler, 1770

The body is not the entire animal.

Der Mensch denkt, Gott lenkt.

Proverb

Man proposes, God disposes. (Lit. Man thinks, God directs.)

Der Mensch für andere.

Dietrich Bonhoeffer
about Jesus

The man for others.

Der Mensch ist, was er ißt.
Ludwig Feuerbach

Man is what he eats.

Der Mensch hat die Weisheit all seiner
Vorfahren zusammengenommen, und seht,
welch ein Dummkopf er ist!
Elias Canetti
Aufzeichnungen

*Man has assimilated the collective wisdom of
all his ancestors, and see, what a fool he is!*

Der Mensch ist doch wie ein Nachtgänger;
er steigt die gefährlichsten Kanten im
Schlafe.
Goethe
letter to Charlotte von Stein, 1780

*Man is like a sleepwalker; he climbs dangerous
ledges in his sleep.*

Ich lehre euch den Übermenschen. Der
Mensch ist etwas, das überwunden wer-
den soll.
Friedrich Nietzsche
Also sprach Zarathustra

*I teach you the superman. Man is something
that has to be overcome.*

Der Mensch spielt nur, wo er in voller
Bedeutung des Worts Mensch ist, und er
ist nur da ganz Mensch, wo er spielt.
Schiller
*Über die ästhetische Erziehung des Menschen
in einer Reihe von Briefen*

*Man plays only where he is, in the full sense of
the word, human, and he is an entire man only
there where he plays.*

Der schwerster Schlag den die Menschheit
je erlebte, war die Einführung des
Christentum.
Adolf Hitler

*The heaviest blow that mankind has ever
experienced was the introduction of
Christianity.*

Der Soldat allein ist der freie Mann.
Schiller
Wallensteins Lager

The soldier is the only free man.

Der Staat wird nicht "abgeschafft", er
stirbt ab.
Friedrich Engels

The State is not "abolished", it withers away.

Der Tag.
Kaiser Wilhelm II
referring to the anticipated outbreak of war

*The Day. (A pre-World War I toast. See
"Herrliche Tage.")*

Der Tod ist kein Ereignis des Lebens. Den Tod erlebt man nicht.

Ludwig Wittgenstein
Tractatus logico-philosophicus

Death is not an event of life; one does not experience death.

Der Tod ist ein Meister aus Deutschland.

Paul Celan
Todesfuge

Death is a master from Germany.

Der Umgang mit Frauen ist das Element guter Sitten.

Goethe

The company of women is the school of good manners.

Der Wahn ist kurz, die Reu ist lang.

Schiller

The illusion [of love] *is brief, the repentance long.*

Der wahre Bettler ist
Doch einzig und allein der wahre König!

Gotthold Ephraim Lessing
Nathan der Weise

The true beggar is the only true king.

Der Weg der neueren Bildung geht
Von Humanität
Durch Nationalität
Zur Bestialität.

Franz Grillparzer
epigram of 1849

The path of the new education leads from humanity to nationality to bestiality.

Der Weisheit erster Schritt ist: alles
                anzuklagen.
Der letzte ist: sich mit allem zu vertragen.

Georg Christoph Lichtenberg
Aphorismen

The first step of wisdom is to accuse everything. The last is to come to terms with everything.

Der Wind, das einzige Freie in der Zivilisation.

Elias Canetti
Aufzeichnungen

The wind is the only free thing in civilization.

Der Zufall wohl pathetische, niemals aber tragische Situationen hervorbringen dürfe; das Schicksal hingegen muße immer fürchterlich sein.

Goethe
Wilhelm Meisters Lehrjahre

Chance may create pathetic, but never tragic, situations; fate, on the other hand, must always be awesome.

Der Zweck des Lebens ist das Leben selbst. **Goethe**	*The purpose of life is life itself.*
Der Zweifel zeugt den Zweifel an sich selbst. **Franz Grillparzer** *Ein Bruderzwist in Habsburg*	*Doubt generates doubt of itself.*
Des Menschen Leben ist ein ähnliches Gedicht: Es hat wohl einen Anfang, hat ein Ende, Allein ein Ganzes ist es nicht. **Goethe** *Faust*	*Human life resembles a poem: it certainly has a beginning and an end; but it is not complete.*
Deutschland, Deutschland über alles. **August Heinrich Hoffmann von Fallersleben** *Das Lied der Deutschen*	*Germany, Germany, above everything else.*
Deutschland, ein geographischer Begriff. **Metternich** about the country's disunity; he had previously said the same about Italy	*Germany is a geographical expression.*
Die barbarische Genauigkeit; winselnde Demut. **Georg Christoph Lichtenberg** *Aphorismen*	*Barbaric precision; whimpering humility!*
Die breite Masse eines Volkes fällt einer großen Lüge leichter zum Opfer als einer kleinen. **Adolf Hitler**	*The broad mass of the people will fall victim more easily to a big lie than a small one.*
Die deutsche Revolution hat im Saale stattgefunden. **Kurt Tucholsky** *Schnipsel, 'Wir Negativen'*	*The German revolution took place in a room.*
Die Doggen der Wortnacht. **Paul Celan** *Abend der Worte*	*The mastiffs of the night of words.*
Die edle Einfalt und stille Größe der griechischen Statuen ist zugleich das	*The noble simplicity and calm greatness of the Greek statues are also hallmarks of Greek*

wahre Kennzeichen der griechischen
Schriften aus den besten Zeiten.
Johann Joachim Winckelmann
Werke

writing in the best periods.

Die ewigen Götter sind
Voll Lebens allzeit; bis in den Tod
Kann aber ein Mensch auch
Im Gedächtnis doch das Beste behalten,
Und dann erlebt er das Höchste.
Friedrich Hölderlin
Der Rhein

The eternal gods are always full of life; but a man too can keep the best in his memory until his death. Then he will experience the highest things.

Die finstern Wolken lagern
Schwer auf dem greisen Land,
Die welken Blätter rascheln,
Was glänzt, ist Herbstes-Tand.
Otto Erich Hartleben
Trutzlied

The dark clouds lie heavily over the ancient land; the wilted leaves rustle, and what gleams are the trinkets of autumn.

Die ganze Natur ist ein gewaltiges Ringen
zwischen Kraft und Schwäche.
Adolf Hitler
to Heinrich Brüning

The whole of nature is a mighty struggle between strength and weakness.

Die Gelehrsamkeit kann auch ins Laub
treiben, ohne Früchte zu tragen.
Georg Christoph Lichtenberg
Aphorismen

Erudition can also sprout leaves without bearing fruit.

Die gesamte Wirklichkeit ist die Welt.
Ludwig Wittgenstein
Tractatus logico-philosophicus

The sum of reality is the world.

Die Gesamtheit der wahren Gedanken
istein Bild der Welt.
Ludwig Wittgenstein
Tractatus logico-philosophicus

The totality of true thought is a picture of the world.

Die Geschichte aller bisherigen Gesellschaft
ist die Geschichte von Klassenkämpfen.
Karl Marx and **Friedrich Engels**
Manifest der Kommunistischen Partei

The history of all previous society is the history of class war.

Die Geschichte der Welt ist sich selbst gleich wie die Gesetze der Natur und einfach wie die Seele des Menschen. Dieselben Bedingungen bringen dieselben Erscheinungen zurück.

Schiller
lecture, 1789

The history of the world itself resembles the laws of nature and is simple, like the human soul. The same conditions bring back the same phenomena.

Die Geschichte kennt kein letztes Wort.
Willy Brandt
Erinnerungen

History does not recognise a last word.

Die Gesetze der Welt sind Würfelspiele worden.

Schiller
Die Räuber

The laws of the world have become games of dice.

Die gleiche weiße Decke aller Straßen,
Hüllt und bedeckt die Mühsal auf der Erde.
Es stirbt ein Jahr, lautlos, entsühnt, gelassen,
Gibt dem Geschicke heim, was dauert
werde.
Erwin Guido Kolbenheyer
Wintersonnenwende

The same white blanket on all the streets shrouds and covers earthly tribulations. A year is dying, silently, expiated and calm, returning to fate that which will endure.

Die Grenzen meiner Sprache bedeuten die Grenzen meiner Welt.
Ludwig Wittgenstein
Tractatus logico-philosophicus

The limits of my language mean the limits of my world.

Die großen Tage stehn, bedeckt vom Staube,
Verweilend, breit und still im ebnen Land.
In ihren heißen Händen reift die Traube,
Vergilbt das Feld, verbrennt das Gartenland.
Fritz Diettrich
Heißer Sommer

The long days linger, covered in dust, standing wide and still in the flat land. Their hot hands ripen the grape, gild the field and scorch the gardens.

Die großen Worte aus den Zeiten, da Geschehen noch sichtbar war, sind nicht für uns. Wer spricht von Siegen? Überstehn ist alles.

Rainer Maria Rilke
Requiem für Wolf, Graf von Kalckreuth

Those great words from the times when we could see what was going to happen are not for us. Who speaks of victories? Survival is everything.

Die Gründe kenne ich nicht, aber ich muß sie mißbilligen.

Julius Kell
February 1849, to the state parliament of Saxony

I do not know the reasons, but I have to disapprove of them.

Die Guillotine ist der beste Arzt!

Georg Büchner
Dantons Tod

The guillotine is the best doctor!

Die Idee des Kampfes ist so alt wie das Leben selbst.

Adolf Hitler

The idea of struggle is as old as life itself.

Die Krähen schrein
Und ziehen schwirren Flugs zur Stadt:
Bald wird es schnein. -
Wohl dem, der jetzt noch Heimat hat!

Friedrich Nietzsche
Vereinsamt

The crows shriek and move towards the town in whirling flight. Soon it will snow. Happy is he who still has a home.

Die Kunst geht nach Brod.

Martin Luther

Art comes after bread.

Die Kunst hat die Tendenz, wieder die Natur zu sein.

Arno Holz
Die Kunst, ihr Wesen und ihre Gesetze

Art has a tendency to revert to nature.

Die Kunst ist eine verführerische, verbotene Frucht.

Wilhelm Heinrich Wackenroder
'Ein Brief Joseph Berglingers' in *Phantasien über die Kunst, für Freunde der Kunst*

Art is a seductive, forbidden fruit.

Die Logik erfüllt die Welt; die Grenzen der Welt sind auch ihre Grenzen.

Ludwig Wittgenstein
Tractatus logico-philosophicus

Logic fills the world; the limits of the world are its limits too.

Die Luft ging durch die Felder,
Die Ähren wogten sacht,
Es rauschten leis die Wälder,
So sternklar war die Nacht.

Joseph von Eichendorff
Mondnacht

The breeze blew through the fields, the ears of corn undulated gently, the woods rustled quietly, so starry clear was the night.

147

Die meisten Menschen sind so subjektiv,
daß im Grunde nichts Interesse für sie hat,
als ganz allein sie selbst.
Artur Schopenhauer

*Most men are so subjective that fundamentally
nothing interests them except themselves.*

Die meisten Philosophen haben eine zu
geringe Vorstellung von der Variabilität
menschlicher Sitten und Möglichkeiten.
Elias Canetti
Aufzeichnungen

*Most philosophers have too narrow a
conception of the variability of human customs
and potential.*

Die Menschen sind im ganzen Leben blind.
Goethe
Faust

Men are blind throughout their entire lives.

Die Nachahmung ist uns angeboren, das
Nachzuahmende wird nicht leicht erkannt.
Goethe
Wilhelm Meisters Lehrjahre

*Imitation is natural to us, but it is not easy to
recognise what should be imitated.*

Die Nacht der langen Messer.
Adolf Hitler
quoting a Nazi marching song, applied to
the killing of Roehm and his colleagues

The night of the long knives.

Die Nachwelt ist mir gleichgültig - ich
schreibe für heute.
Kurt Weill

*I don't care about posterity – I am writing for
today.*

Die Natur gab die Schönheit des Baues,
die Seele gibt die Schönheit des Spiels.
Schiller
Über Anmut und Würde

*Nature gave constructive work its beauty; the
soul gives beauty to playfulness.*

Die Philosophen haben die Welt nur
verschieden interpretiert; es kommt aber
darauf an, sie zu verändern.
Karl Marx
Thesen über Feuerbach

*The philosophers have merely interpreted the
world in different ways. Changing it is what
matters, however.*

Die Philosophie ist ein Kampf gegen die
Verhexung unseres Verstandes durch die
Mittel unserer Sprache.
Ludwig Wittgenstein
Philosophische Untersuchungen

*Philosophy is a battle against the bewitchment
of our intelligence by means of language.*

Die Philosophie ist keine Lehre, sondern eine Tätigkeit.

Ludwig Wittgenstein
Tractatus logico-philosophicus

Philosophy is not a doctrine, but an occupation.

Die Politik ist die Lehre vom Möglichen.
Otto von Bismarck

Politics is the art of the possible.

Die Politik ist keine Wissenschaft, wie viele der Herren Professoren sich einbilden, sondern eine Kunst.
Otto von Bismarck

Politics are not a science, as many professors declare, but an art.

Die Presse ist die Artillerie der Freiheit.
Hans-Dietrich Genscher

The press is the artillery of freedom.

Die Proletarier haben nichts zu verlieren als ihre Ketten.
Karl Marx and **Friedrich Engels**
Manifest der Kommunistischen Partei

The proletariat have nothing to lose except their chains.

Die Religion...ist das Opium des Volkes.
Karl Marx
*Zur Kritik der Hegelschen Rechtsphilosophie
Einleitung*

Religion...is the opium of the people.

Die Revolution ist wie Saturn, sie frißt ihre eignen Kinder.

Georg Büchner
Dantons Tod

The [French] Revolution is like Saturn – it devours its own children.

Die schöne Seele hat kein anderes Verdienst, als daß sie ist.

Schiller
Über Anmut und Würde

A beautiful soul has no other merit than its existence.

Die Schönheit gibt schlechterdings kein einzelnes Resultat weder für den Verstand noch für den Willen, sie führt keinen einzelnen, weder intellektuellen noch moralischen Zweck aus, sie findet keine einzige Wahrheit, hilft uns keine einzige Pflicht erfüllen und ist, mit einem Worte, gleich ungeschickt, den

Beauty has absolutely no result, either for the intellect or for the will; it pursues no purpose, neither intellectual nor moral; it uncovers no truth, does not help us fulfil any duty and is, in a word, unsuited to form the character or to enlighten the mind.

Charakter zu gründen und den Kopf
aufzuklären.

Schiller
Werke

Die sieht den Menschen in des Lebens
                          Drang
Und wälzt die größre Hälfte seiner Schuld
Den unglückseligen Gestirnen zu.

Schiller
Wallenstein

*Art sees men amid life's struggle, and shifts
the greater part of their guilt on to the hapless
stars.*

Die Statue der Freiheit ist noch nicht
gegossen, der Ofen glüht, wir alle
können uns noch die Finger dabei
verbrennen.

Georg Büchner
Dantons Tod

*The Statue of Liberty has not yet been cast.
The oven is glowing and we could still burn
our fingers on it.*

Die Sternbilder waren als Ratschläge
gedacht, doch niemand hat sie ver-
standen.

Elias Canetti
Aufzeichnungen

*The constellations were considered as a source
of advice, but no one could understand them.*

Die Sünde ist im Gedanken. Ob der
Gedanke Tat wird, ob ihn der Körper
nachspielt, das ist Zufall.

Georg Büchner
Dantons Tod

*Sin is in the thought. It is a matter of chance if
the thought becomes a deed, if the body acts it
out.*

Die Treue, sie ist doch kein leere Wahn.

Schiller
Die Bürgschaft

Loyalty is, however, no empty illusion.

Die unbegrenzte Welt, voll Leiden überall,
in unendlicher Vergangenheit, in
unendlicher Zukunft.

Artur Schopenhauer
Die Welt als Wille und Vorstellung

*The limitless world, everywhere full of
suffering, in an unending past, in an unending
future.*

Die Unruhe und Ungewissenheit sind
unser Theil.

Goethe
letter to Sophie von La Roche, 1774

Unrest and uncertainty are our lot.

Die Wahlverwandtschaften.
Goethe
title of a book

Elective affinities.

Die Wahrheit finden wollen ist Verdienst,
wenn man auch auf dem Wege irrt.
Georg Christoph Lichtenberg
Aphorismen

*There is merit in wanting to discover the truth,
even if one makes mistakes along the way.*

Die Wahrheit ist das Ganze.
Georg Hegel

Truth is the whole.

Die Welt des Glücklichen ist eine andere
als die des Unglücklichen.
Ludwig Wittgenstein
Tractatus logico-philosophicus

*The world of fortunate people is different from
that of the unfortunate.*

Die Welt ist die Gesamtheit der Tatsachen,
nicht der Dinge.
Ludwig Wittgenstein
Tractatus logico-philosophicus

The world is the totality of facts, not of things.

Die Welt ist unabhängig von meinem
Willen.
Ludwig Wittgenstein
Tractatus logico-philosophicus

The world is independent of my will.

Die Weltgeschichte ist das Weltgericht.
Schiller
Resignation

*The history of the world is the judgement seat
of the world.*

Die Zeit hat ungeheuren Schwung
Paar Jahre bist du stark und jung
Dann sackst du langsam auf den Grund
Der Weltgeschichte.
Wolf Biermann
Bilanzballade im dreißigsten Jahr

*Time has a tremendous momentum; you are
strong and young for a few years, and then
you sag slowly on to the ground of the world's
history.*

Die Zeit wird Herr.
Goethe
Faust

Time will become master.

Dieses war der erste Streich,
Doch der zweite folgt sogleich.
Wilhelm Busch
Max und Moritz

*This was the first prank, but the second will
follow immediately.*

Diu werlt ist ûzen schoene, wîz grüene
                                                    unde rôt,
Und innân swarzer varwe, vinster sam
                                                    der tôt.
Walther von der Vogelweide
Elegy (or Palinode)

*The world is beautiful on the outside: white,
green and red; but it inside it is black and dark
as death.*

Doch alles, was dazu mich trieb
Gott, war so gut! ach, war so lieb!
Goethe
Faust

*But everything that drove me to it, God, was
so good, so lovely!*

Doch uns ist gegeben,
Auf keiner Stätte zu ruhn.
Friedrich Hölderlin
Hyperions Schicksalslied

*We are fated, however, not to find a resting
place.*

Dort erblick' ich schöne Hügel
Ewig jung und ewig grün!
Hätt' ich Schwingen, hätt ich Flügel,
Nach den Hügeln zög' ich hin!
Schiller
Sehnsucht

*I saw there beautiful hills that were eternally
young and eternally green. If I had wings I
would fly to them.*

Dort, wo man Bücher verbrennt, verbrennt
man am Ende auch Menschen.
Heinrich Heine
Almansor

*Whenever books are burned, in the end men
too are burned.*

Du bist der Lenz, nach dem ich verlangte.
Richard Wagner
Die Walküre

You are the spring for which I longed.

Du bleibst doch immer, was du bist.
Goethe
Faust

You will always remain what you are.

Du danke Gott, wenn er dich preßt,
Und dank' ihm, wenn er dich wieder entläßt.
Goethe
Gesprächte mit JP Eckermann

*You should thank God when he oppresses you,
and thank him when he releases you again.*

Du gehst zu Frauen? Vergiß die Peitsche
nicht!
Friedrich Nietzsche
Also Sprach Zarathustra

*You are going to a woman? Do not forget the
whip!*

Du mußt dein Leben ändern!
Rainer Maria Rilke
Archaischer Torso Apollos

You must change your life!

Du mußt herrschen und gewinnen,
Oder dienen und verlieren,
Leiden oder triumphieren
Amboß oder Hammer sein.
Goethe
Der Groß-Cophta

One must be master and win or serve and lose,
grieve or triumph, be the anvil or the hammer.

Du sprichst ein großes Wort gelassen aus.
Goethe

Calmly you speak a momentous word.

Du wohnst bei mir Urquell der Natur,
Leben und Freude der Creatur.
Goethe
Des Künstlers Erdewallen

You live within me, primal fountain of nature,
life and joy of creation.

Durch zweier Zeugen Mund
Wird allerwegs die Wahrheit kund.
Goethe
Faust

Truth is established everywhere from the
mouths of two witnesses.

Ehrlicher Makler.
Otto von Bismarck

An honest broker.

Eigentlich weiß man nur, wenn man wenig
weiß; mit dem Wissen wächst der Zweifel.
Goethe
Maximen und Relexionen

One is knowledgeable only when one knows
little; doubt grows with knowledge.

Ein Abgrund von Landesverrat.
Konrad Adenauer
November 1962, to the Bundestag

A bottomless pit of treason.

Ein Blick von dir, ein Wort, mehr unterhält
Als alle Weisheit dieser Welt.
Goethe
Faust

One of your glances, one word, says more than
all the wisdom in this world.

Ein Diadem erkämpfen ist groß. Es weg-
werfen ist göttlich.
Schiller
Fiesko

To win a crown is greatness. To throw it away
is godlike.

Ein echter deutscher Mann mag keinen Franzen leiden, Doch ihre Weine trinkt er gern.

Goethe
Faust

A true German cannot bear the French, but he enjoys drinking their wine.

Ein einz'ger Augenblick kann alles umgestalten.

Christoph Martin Wieland
Oberon

Everything can change in the blink of an eye.

Ein feste Burg ist unser Gott.

Martin Luther

A strong citadel is our God.

Ein freies Leben ist ein paar knechtischer Stunden wert.

Schiller
Fiesko

A life of freedom is worth a few hours of servitude.

Ein Fuchs riecht den andern.

Proverb

One fox smells another.

Ein Gespenst geht um in Europa - das Gespenst des Kommunismus.

Karl Marx and **Friedrich Engels**
Manifest der Kommunistischen Partei

A spectre is haunting Europe – the spectre of communism.

Ein gewissermaßen oberflächliche Schicht des Unbewußten ist zweifellos persönlich. Wir nennen sie das *persönliche Unbewußte*. Dieses ruht aber auf einer tieferen Schicht, welche nicht mehr persönlicher Erfahrung und Erwerbung enstammt, sondern angeboren ist. Diese tiefere Schicht ist das sogenannte *kollektive Unbewußte*.

Carl Jung

A certain superficial level of the unconscience is without doubt personal. I call it the personal unconscious. *But this personal unconscious rests upon a deeper level, which does not derive from personal experience and is not a personal acquisition but is inborn. This deeper level I call the* collective unconscious.

Ein Grab ist doch immer die beste Befestigung wider Stürme des Schicksals.
Georg Christoph Lichtenberg
Aphorismen

The grave, however, remains the best fortress against the storms of fate.

Ein jeder wird besteuert nach Vermögen.
Schiller
Wilhelm Tell

Everyone will be taxed according to his means.

Ein Kuß von rosiger Lippe,
Und ich fürchte nicht Sturm nicht Klippe!
Folk song

A kiss from rosy lips, and I fear neither storm nor cliff!

Ein Mensch, der kein Gefühl für Geschichte hat, ist wie einer ohne Augen und Ohren.
Adolf Hitler

A person who has no feeling for history is like a man who has no eyes and ears.

Ein Onkel, der Gutes mitbringt, ist besser als eine Tante, die bloß Klavier spielt.
Wilhelm Busch
Aphorismen und Reime

An uncle who brings nice things with him is better than an aunt who only plays the piano.

Ein rechter Schütze hilft sich selbst.
Schiller
Wilhelm Tell

A true marksman helps himself.

Ein Reich, ein Volk, ein Führer.
Nazi Party slogan

One realm, one people, one leader.

Eine notwendige Operation des Dichters ist Idealisierung seines Gegenstandes, ohne welche er aufhört seinen Namen zu verdienen.
Schiller
Review of GA Bürger's Gedichte

A necessary process of what poets do is to idealise their subject – without which they no longer deserve the name.

Eine seltsamere Ware als Bücher gibt es wohl schwerlich in der Welt. Von Leuten gedruckt, die sie nicht verstehen; von Leuten verkauft, die sie nicht verstehen; gebunden, rezensiert und gelesen von Leuten, die sie nicht verstehen; und nun gar geschrieben von Leuten, die sie nicht verstehen.
Georg Christoph Lichtenberg
Aphorismen

It would be difficult to find any products in the world that are as strange as books. Printed by people who don't understand them; sold by people who don't understand them; bound, reviewed and read by people who don't understand them; and now, even written by people who don't understand them.

Eine Weltkatastrophe kann zu manchem dienen. Auch dazu, ein Alibi finden vor Gott. Wo warst du, Adam? Ich war im Weltkrieg.
Heinrich Böll
Wo warst du, Adam?
quoting Haechel

A world catastrophe can be useful for some things, including finding an alibi before God. Where were you, Adam? I was in the world war.

Einen Menschen recht zu verstehen, müßte
man zuweilen der nämliche Mensch sein,
den man verstehen will.

Georg Christoph Lichtenberg
Aphorismen

*To understand a man properly, one would need
sometimes to be the person one wants to
understand.*

Eines kann ich den Fleischessern
prophezeien: Die Gesellschaft der Zukunft
wird vegetarisch leben.

Adolf Hitler

*There is one thing that I can predict to the
flesh-eaters: the society of the future will be
vegetarian.*

Einmal werd ich die Wahrheit sagen - das
meint man, aber die Lüge ist ein Egel, sie
hat die Wahrheit ausgesaugt.

Max Frisch
Andorra

*One day I shall tell the truth – that is what
one thinks, but the lie is a leech and has sucked
the truth dry.*

Einsam steigt er dahin, in die Berge des
Urleids,
Und nicht einmal sein Schritt klingt aus
dem tonlosen Los.
Rainer Maria Rilke
Duineser Elegien

*Lonely he climbs the mountains of primeval
sorrow, and not even his footsteps ring out
from the tonelessness of destiny.*

Em jeder Engel ist schrecklich.
Rainer Maria Rilke
Duineser Elegien

Every angel is frightening.

Endlich giebt es einen Imperativ, der, ohne
irgend eine andere durch ein gewisses
Verhalten zu erreichende Absicht als
Bedingung zum Grunde zu legen, dieses
Verhalten unmittelbar begeitet, Dieser
Imperativ ist categorisch ... Dieser
Imperativ mag der Sittlichkeit heißen.
Immanuel Kant
Grundlegung zur Metaphisik der Sitten

*Finally, there is an imperative which requires a
certain conduct immediately, without having
as its condition any other purpose to be
attained by it. This imperative is categorical...
This imperative may be called that of Morality.*

Englands Beherrscher brauchen nichts zu
scheuen, als ihr Gewissen und ihr
Parlament.

Schiller
Maria Stuart

*England's rulers need fear nothing except their
conscience and their parliament.*

Entbehren sollst Du! Sollst entbehren! Das ist der ewige Gesang.

Goethe
Faust

Deny yourself! You must deny yourself! That is the eternal song.

Er ging auf wie ein Meteor und schwindet wie eine sinkende Sonne.

Schiller
review of a production of *Die Räuber*

He rose like a meteor and faded away like the setting sun.

Er nennt's Vernunft und braucht's allein,
Nur tierischer als jedes Tier zu sein.

Goethe
Faust

He calls it reason but only uses it to be more bestial than any beast.

Er sagt, was das Herz seiner Zuhörer zu hören wünscht.

Otto Strasser
of Hitler, 1930

He says what the heart of his audience wants to hear.

Er ward geboren,
Er lebte, nahm ein Weib und starb.

Christian Fürchtegott Gellert
Der Greis

He was born, he lived, took a wife, and died.

Erloschen sind die heitern Sonnen,
Die meiner Jugend Pfad erhellt.

Schiller
Die Ideale

The cheerful sunshine that brightened my young path has been extinguished.

Ersatz für's Unersätzliche.

Expression

A replacement for the irreplaceable.

Erst kommt das Fressen, dann kommt die Moral.

Bertolt Brecht
Die Dreigroschenoper

Food comes first, then morals.

Erst wenn du dich selbst erkannt,
verurteile deinen Nächsten.

Proverb

Only when you have understood yourself can you judge your neighbours.

Erst wägen und dann wagen.
von Moltke's maxim

Look before you leap. (Lit. First weigh it up, then act.)

Es bildet ein Talent sich in der Stille,
Sich ein Charakter in dem Strom der Welt.
Goethe
Torquato Tasso

Talent is shaped in tranquility, character in the stream of life.

Es ehret der Knecht nur den Gewaltsamen.
Friedrich Hölderlin
Menschenbeifall

Servants honour only the powerful.

Es geht alles vorüber,
Es geht alles vorbei,
Auf jeden Dezember
Folgt wieder ein Mai.

Kurt Feltz
Es geht alles vorüber

Everything passes, everything ends, a May always follows every December.

Es gibt Leute, die ihre Nase in gar alle
Angelegenheiten hineinstecken müssen.
Wenn man solchen Leuten den kleinen
Finger reicht, nehmen sie gleich die ganze
Hand.
Bertolt Brecht
Mann ist Mann

There are people who have to stick their noses into absolutely everything. If you reach out your little finger to such people, they will take your whole hand.

Es gibt nur ein Recht in der Welt, und
dieses Recht liegt in der eigenen Stärke.
Adolf Hitler
Munich, 22 September 1928

There is only one sort of justice in the world, and that lies in individual strength.

Es irrt der Mensch, so lang er strebt.
Goethe
Faust

Man will err as long as he strives.

Es ist der Gang Gottes in der Welt, daß der
Staat ist: sein Grund ist die Gewalt der sich
als Wille verwirklichenden Vernunft.
Georg Hegel
Grundlinien der Philosophie des Rechts

It is God's way with the world that the State exists, based on the power of reason which realises itself as will.

Es ist die letzte territoriale Forderung, die
ich Europa zu stellen habe, aber es ist die
Forderung, von der ich nicht abgehe, und
die ich, so Gott will, erfüllen werde.

Adolf Hitler
about the Sudetenland

*It is the last territorial claim which I have in
Europe, but it is the claim from which I will
not retreat, and which, God willing, I shall
achieve.*

Es ist nicht das Bewußtsein der Menschen,
das ihr Sein, sondern umgekehrt ihr
gesellschaftliches Sein, das ihr Bewußtsein
bestimmt.

Karl Marx
Vorwort: Zur Kritik der politischen Ökonomie

*It is not the consciousness of men that
determines their existence; it is the other way
round: their collective existence determines
their consciousness.*

Es ist nicht leicht, Mensch zu sein.

Expression

Being human is not easy.

Es ist nicht wahr, daß die kürzeste Linie
immer die gerade ist.

Gotthold Ephraim Lessing
Die Erziehung des Menschengeschlechts

*It is not true that the shortest line is always
the straightest.*

Es is oft besser, in Ketten als frei zu sein.

Franz Kafka
Der Prozeß

It is often better to be in chains than to be free.

Es muß etwas geschehen!

Heinrich Böll
*Doktor Murkes gesammeltes Schweigen und
andere Satiren*

Something must happen!

Es war getan, fast eh' gedacht.

Goethe
Willkommen und Abschied

*It was done almost as soon as it was conceived
of.*

Es weiß vielleicht ein Gott, wohin wir
                                    ziehn.
Wir wissen nicht das Ziel und nicht
                                    zurück.

Fritz Usinger
Große Elegie

*Perhaps a god knows where we are going. We
do not know our goal, or the way back.*

Ethik und Ästhetik sind Eins.

Ludwig Wittgenstein
Tractatus logico-philosophicus

Ethics and aesthetics are one.

Falsche Begriffe und schlechtes Wissen kön- | False ideas and scanty knowledge can be
nen durch Belehrung beseitigt werden. | eliminated by instruction.

Adolf Hitler

Feig, wirklich feig ist nur, wer sich vor | The only person who is truly cowardly is he
seinen Erinnerungen fürchtet. | who is afraid of his own memories.

Elias Canetti
Aufzeichnungen

Folgte Begierde dem Blick, folgte Genuß | Desire followed a glance, and pleasure followed
der Begier. | desire.

Goethe
Römische Elegien

Freiheit ist immer nur Freiheit des anders | Freedom is always and only the freedom to
Denkenden. | think differently.

Rosa Luxemburg

Freude heißt die starker Feder | Joy is the powerful spring of eternal nature;
In der ewigen Natur, | joy, joy drives the wheels of the great world
Freude, Freude, treibt die Räder | clock.
In der großen Weltenuhr.

Schiller
An die Freude

Friede den Hütten! Krieg den Palästen! | Peace to the shacks! War on the palaces!

Georg Büchner
Der Hessische Landbote

Füllest wieder Busch und Tal | You quietly fill thickets once more and valleys
Still mit Nebelglanz, | with the gleam of fog, and also finally and
Lösest endlich auch einmal | completely release my soul.
Meine Seele ganz.

Goethe
An den Mond

Für einen Kammerdiener giebt es keinen | No man is a hero to his valet.
Held.

Georg Hegel

Gäbe es das Wort 'Tod' in unserem Sprach- | If the word "death" did not exist in our
schatz nicht, wären die großen Werke der | vocabulary, the great works of literature
Literatur nie geschrieben worden. | would never have been written.

Arthur Koestler
Mensch

Galgenhumor gibt es nicht. Wer ihn zu
haben glaubt, hängt schon.
Wolfdietrich Schnurre
Der Schattenfotograf

*Gallows humour does not exist; whoever
believes that he possesses it will soon hang.*

Geburt und Grab, ein ewiges Meer.
Goethe
Faust

Birth and the grave, an eternal sea.

Gefährlich ist's, den Leu zu wecken,
Verderblich ist des Tigers Zahn,
Jedoch der schrecklichste der Schrecken,
Das ist der Mensch in seinem Wahn.
Schiller
Das Lied von der Glocke

*It is dangerous to awaken a lion, and the
tiger's tooth is sharp, but the most terrible of
all terrors is the mania of man.*

Gefühl ist alles:
Name ist Schall und Rauch,
Umnebelnd Himmelsglut.
Goethe
Faust

*Feeling is everything: a name is but the sound
and smoke that cloud the heavenly fire.*

Gegen Demokraten helfen nur Soldaten.
Wilhelm von Merckel
Die fünfte Zunft

*Soldiers are the only protection against
democrats.*

Gehorsam ist des Christen Schmuck.
Schiller
Der Kampf mit dem Drachen

Obedience is the ornament of the Christian.

Gelebte ich noch die lieben zît
Daz ich daz lant solt aber schouwen,
Dar inne al min fröude lît
Nu lange an einer schoenen frouwen.
Friedrich von Hausen
Heimweh

*If only I still lived in that blessed time when I
could see my own country and when all my
pleasure lay in a beautiful woman.*

Geschichte schreiben ist eine Art, sich das
Vergangene vom Halse zu schaffen.
Goethe
Maximen und Reflexionen

*Writing history is a way of getting rid of the
past which hangs around one's neck.*

Getauft geimpft gefirmt geschult.
Gespielt hab ich mit Bombensplittern

*Baptised, vaccinated, confirmed, educated, I
played with fragments of bombs and grew up*

Und aufgewachsen bin ich zwischen
Dem Heiligen Geist und Hitlers Bild.

between the Holy Spirit and Hitler's portrait.

Günter Grass
Kleckerburg

Gib meine Jugend mir zurück!

Give me back my youth!

Goethe
Faust

Glaube und Zweifel verhalten sich zueinan-
der wie Regierung und Opposition in
einem parlamentarischen Gemeinwesen.

*Belief and doubt relate to each other in the
same way as government and opposition in a
parliamentary body.*

Hans Egon Holthusen
Verstehen

Glauben ist Vertrauen, nicht Wissenwollen.

Belief is trust, not knowledge.

Hermann Hesse
Lektüre für Minuten

Glaubt es mir! - das Geheimnis, um die
größte Fruchtbarkeit und den größten
Genuß vom Dasein einzuernten, heißt:
gefährlich leben!

*Believe me! The secret of reaping the most
fruitful harvest and the greatest enjoyment
from life is to live dangerously!*

Friedrich Nietzsche
Die fröhliche Wissenschaft

Gott hat den Menschen einfach gemacht,
aber wie er gewickelt und sich verwickelt
ist schwer zu sagen.

*God made man simple. How he evolved and
became complicated is hard to say.*

Goethe
letter to Charlotte von Stein, 11 Dec. 1778

Gott hielt dein und mein Leben
Wie Blumen in seiner Hand.

*God held my life and your life like flowers in
his hand.*

Agnes Miegel
Blumen

Gott ist tot! Gott bleibt tot! Und wir haben
ihn getötet!

*God is dead! God will remain dead! And we
have killed him!*

Friedrich Nietzsche
Die fröhliche Wissenschaft

Gott schafft die Tiere, der Mensch schafft
sich selber.

God creates the animals, man creates himself.

Georg Christoph Lichtenberg
Aphorismen

Gott schuf den Menschen nach seinem
Bilde, das heißt vermutlich, der Mensch
schuf Gott nach dem seinigen.
Georg Christoph Lichtenberg
Aphorismen

*God created man in his own image; this
presumably means that man created God in
his own image.*

Gott straffe England!
Alfred Funke

God punish England!

Gottes Mühlen mahlen langsam, mahlen
aber trefflich klein.
Friedrich von Logau

*The mills of God grind slowly, yet they grind
exceeding small.*

Gottseidank geht alles schnell vorüber
Auch die Liebe und der Kummer sogar.
Bertolt Brecht
Nannas Lied

*Everything passes quickly, thank God – even
love and sorrow.*

Grau, teurer Freund, ist alle Theorie,
Und grün des Lebens goldner Baum.
Goethe
Faust

*Grey, my dearest friend, is the colour of all
theory, and green is the colour of the golden
tree of life.*

Greif nicht in ein Wespennest;
Doch wenn du greifst, so stehe fest.
Matthias Claudius
Ein gülden ABC

*Do not reach into a wasps' nest; but if you do,
stand firm.*

Groß kann man sich im Glück, erhaben
nur im Unglück zeigen.
Schiller
Vom Erhabenen

*One can show oneself to be great in times of
good fortune, but merely noble in times of
misfortune.*

Guten Kaufs macht den Beutel leer.
Proverb

Good purchases make empty purses.

Hab Sonne im Herzen
ob's stürmt oder schneit,
ob der Himmel voll Wolken,
die Erde voll Streit!
Cäsar Flaischlen
Aus den Lehr- und Wanderjahren des Lebens

*Carry the sun in your heart even if it is stormy
or snowing, if the sky is cloudy or the earth
resounds with strife.*

Haben die Tiere weniger Angst, weil sie ohne Worte leben?

Elias Canetti
Aufzeichnungen

Are animals less afraid because they live without words?

Halte fest: du hast vom Leben doch am Ende nur dich selber.

Theodor Storm
Für meine Söhne

Hold fast: in the end all you will have from life is yourself.

Handle so, daß du die Menschheit, so wohl in deiner Person, als in der Person eines jeden andern, jederzeit zugleich als Zweck, niemals bloß als Mittel brauchest.

Immanuel Kant
Grundlegung `ur Mataphisik der Sitten

So act as to treat humanity, whether in thine own person or in that of another, always as an end, never as a means only.

Hätte Gott mich anders gewollt, so hätt' er mich anders gemacht.

Goethe

If God had wanted me to be different, he would have created me differently.

Hätte ich nicht die Welt durch Anticipation bereits in mir getragen, ich wäre mit sehenden Augen blind geblieben.

Goethe
letter to J.P. Eckermann, 26 February 1824

If I had not already borne the world within me through anticipation, despite my seeing eyes I would have remained blind.

Heftige Ehrgeiz und Mißtrauen habe ich noch allemal beisammen gesehen.

Georg Christoph Lichtenberg
Aphorismen

I have always seen burning ambition accompanies by distrust.

Heiajoho! Grane! Grüß deinen Herren! Siegfried! Siegfried! Sieh'! Selig grüßt dich dein Weib!

Richard Wagner
Die Walküre
Brünnhilde's last words as she rides her horse, Grane, into Siegfried's funeral pyre

Heiajoho! Grane! Greet your master! Siegfried! Siegfried! See! Joyfully you wife greets you!

Heilige Gefäße sind die Dichter.

Friedrich Hölderlin
Buonaparte

Poets are sacred vessels.

Heilige Gluten!
Wen sie umschweben,
Fühlt sich im Leben
Selig mit Gutem.

Goethe
Faust

Sacred fires! He around whom they hover feels his life blessed with goodness.

Herr: Es ist Zeit. Der Sommer war sehr
groß.
Leg deinen Schatten auf die Sonnenuhren,
Und auf den Fluren laß die Winde los.

Rainer Maria Rilke
Herbsttag

Lord, it is time! It was a great summer. Lay your shadows across the sundials, and unleash the winds across the open fields.

Herr, ich bin ein arm und kaum noch
glühend
Döchtlein am Altare deiner Gnade.

Annette von Droste-Hülshoff
Das geistliche Jahr

Lord, at the altar of your mercy I am but the poor, small wick of a candle which scarcely still glows.

Herr, ich kann nicht mehr beten!
Ich bin müde vom Elend des Menschen,
Vom Leiden der Kreatur.
Deine Schöpfung ist herrlich,
Aber erbarmungslos.

Christina Busta
Salzgärten

Lord, I can pray no longer. I am tired of the misery of mankind, and of the suffering of creation. Your creation is marvellous, but merciless.

Herren-Moral and Sklaven-Moral.

Friedrich Nietzsche
Jenseits von Gut und Böse

Master-morality and slave-morality.

Herrlichen Tagen führe ich euch entgegen.

Kaiser Wilhelm II
February 1892, to the provincial state
parliament of Brandenburg

I am leading you towards wonderful times.

Heut dies und morgen das.

Proverb

Today this and tomorrow that.

Hier gilt's der Kunst.

Richard Wagner
Die Meistersinger von Nürnberg

Art reigns here.

Hier stehe ich, ich kann nicht anders. Gott helfe mir. Amen

Martin Luther
1521 in Worms

Here I stand – I can do nought else. God help me. Amen.

Höchstes Glück der Erdenkinder
Sei nur die Persönlichkeit.

Goethe
West-östliche Divan

The highest fortune of earth's children is seen in personality alone.

Höflichkeit ist Klugheit; folglich ist Unhöflichkeit Dummheit.

Artur Schopenhauer

Politeness is wisdom, therefore impoliteness is folly.

Hört ihr das Glockchen klingeln? Kniet nieder - Man bringt die Sakramente einem sterbenden Gotte.

Heinrich Heine

Do you hear the little bell tinkling? Kneel down. The sacrament is being brought to a dying god.

Hütet Euch vor Weibertücken!

Wolfgang Amadeus Mozart
libretto of *Die Zauberflöte*

Beware women's waywardness.

Ich aber soll zum Meißel mich erniedern,
Wo ich der Künstler könnte sein?

Schiller
Werke

Why should I lower myself to the level of a chisel, when I could be the artist?

Ich bin ein Berliner.

John F Kennedy
26 June 1963, in Berlin

I am a citizen of Berlin. (But "Berliner" also means a kind of doughnut.)

Ich bin es müde, über Sklaven zu herrschen.

Frederick the Great
c. 1786, to his cabinet

I am tired of ruling slaves.

Ich bin der Geist, der stets verneint.

Goethe
Faust
the reply of Mephistopheles when asked
his name

I am the spirit that always says no.

Ich bin mein Himmel und meine Hölle.

Schiller
Die Räuber

I am my heaven and my hell.

Ich bin nun wie ich bin;
So nimm mich nur hin!

Goethe
Liebhaber in allen Gestalten

I am what I am, so accept me as such!

Ich bin wie immer bald leidlich bald
unleidlich.

Goethe
letter to Johanna Fahlmer, 31 Oct. 1773

*As always, I am reasonable one moment,
unreasonable the next.*

Ich bin ze lange arm gewesen âne mînen
danc.

Walther von der Vogelweide
Ich hân mîn Lêhen

I have been poor for too long against my will.

Ich brauche Thau und Nachtluft wie die
Blumen.

Georg Büchner
Leonce und Lena

Like flowers, I need dew and night air.

Ich dien.
 motto of the Prince of Wales, assumed after
Crecy by the Black Prince, from the banner of
 the King of Bohemia, who had been killed

I serve.

Ich glaube, daß die Quelle des meisten
menschlichen Elends in Indolenz und
Weichlichkeit liegt. Die Nation, die die
meiste Spannkraft hatte, war auch allezeit
die freiste und glücklichste.

Georg Christoph Lichtenberg
Aphorismen

*I believe that the source of most human misery
lies in indolence and weakness. The nation that
had the most vigour was always the freest and
the happiest too.*

Ich hab' mich so an Künstliches verloren,
Daß ich die Sonne sah aus toten Augen
Und nicht mehr hörte als durch tote. Ohren.

Hugo von Hofmannsthal
Der Tor und der Tod

*I had so abandoned myself to artificiality that I
saw the sun with dead eyes, and could no
longer hear except with deaf ears.*

Ich habe geliebt manch schönes Kind
Und manchen guten Gesellen.
Wo sind sie hin? Es pfeift der Wind,
Es schäumen und wandern die Wellen.

Heinrich Heine
Träumen

*I have loved many a pretty child, and some
good fellows. Where have they gone? The wind
whistles, and the waves foam and move on.*

Ich habe gerochen alle Gerüche
In dieser holden Erdenküche;
Was man genießen kann in der Welt,
Das hab' ich genoßen wie je ein Held!
Heinrich Heine
Rückschau

I have smelled all the aromas there are in this sweet earthly kitchen; everything that one can enjoy in the world, I have enjoyed like a hero!

Ich habe jetzt keine Zeit, müde zu sein.
Kaiser Wilhelm I

I've no time to be tired.

Ich habe meine Lehrzeit
Hinter mir.
Erich Fried
Fast Alles

My apprenticeship is behind me.

Ich hatt einen Kamaraden,
Einen bessern find'st du nicht.
Die Trommel schlug zum Streite,
er ging an meiner Seite
In gleichem Schritt und Tritt.
Johann Ludwig Uhland

I had a comrade, a better one you'd never find. When the drum called us to war, he marched beside me step by step.

Ich kenne die Leute wohl, die ihr meint; sie
sind bloß Geist und Theorie und können
sich keinen Knopf annähen.
Georg Christoph Lichtenberg
Aphorismen

I know the people well whom you mean: they are just intellect and theory and could not sew on a button for themselves.

Ich kenne keine Parteien mehr, ich kenne
nur Deutsche.
Kaiser Wilhelm II
4 August 1914, to the Reichstag in Berlin

I no longer recognise political parties; I recognise only Germans.

Ich leb und weiß nit wie lang,
Ich stirb und weiß nit wann,
Ich fahr und weiß nit wohin,
Mich wundert, daß ich fröhlich bin.
Martinus von Biberach
Ich leb und weiß nit wie lang

I am alive, but don't know for how long; I will die, but don't know when; I am travelling, but don't know whither; I am surprised that I am still happy.

Ich liebe eine gesinnungsvolle Opposition.
Friedrich Wilhelm IV

I love an opponent with convictions.

Ich seh sie dort, ich seh sie hier
Und weiß nicht auf der Welt,
Und wie und wo und wann sie mir
Warum sie mir gefällt.

Goethe
Auf Christiane R

I see her here, I see her there, and do not know why in the world, how, where, and when, she appeals to me.

Ich studierte die Geschichte der Revolution. Ich fühlte mich wie zernichtet unter dem gräßlichen Fatalismus der Geschichte.

Georg Büchner
letter to Minna Jaegle, 10 March 1834

I studied the history of the revolution. I felt as if I had been destroyed by the abominable fatalism of history.

Ich weiß nicht, was in mir das andere
belügt.

Georg Büchner
Dantons Tod

I do not know what it is inside me that lies to the other part.

Ich weiß nicht, was soll es bedeuten,
Daß ich so traurig bin;
Ein Märchen aus alten Zeiten,
Das kommt mir nicht aus dem Sinn.

Heinrich Heine
"Die Lorelei", Buch der Lieder

I don't know what it portends that I should feel so sad. A fairy story from olden times keeps running through my mind.

Ich will in mein Küchel gehn,
Will mein Süpplein kochen,
Steht ein bucklicht Männlein da,
Hat mein Töpflein brochen.

Folk tale

I want to go into my little kitchen to make my little soup; a little bent man is standing there who has broken my little saucepan.

Ihr Racker, wollt ihr ewig leben?

Frederick the Great
to his hesitant troops

Rascals, would you live forever?

Im echten Manne ist ein Kind versteckt:
das will spielen. Auf, ihr Frauen, so entdeckt mir doch das Kind im Manne!

Friedrich Nietzsche
Also sprach Zarathustra

A child is hidden in the real man, and it wants to play. Come on, you women, discover the child in the man!

Im Haufen steht die Tierwelt gar zu nah.

Franz Grillparzer
Ein Bruderzwist in Habsburg

In crowds of people the animal kingdom seems far too close.

Im Kleinen liegt das Große.
Proverb

Greatness lies in small things.

Im Lieben und im Haßen
Wie einig waren wir!
Wenn alle dich verlassen,
Kehrst du zurück zu mir!
Max Herrmann-Neisse
Verlassen

How united we were in love and in hate! When everyone deserts you, you will return to me!

Immer zierlicher die Uhren, immer
gefährlicher die Zeit.
Elias Canetti
Aufzeichnungen

The more delicate the clocks, the more dangerous is time.

In Bezug auf das sudetendeutsche Problem
ist meine Gedul jetzt zu Ende!
Adolf Hitler

With regard to the problem of the Sudeten Germans my patience is now at an end.

In den Asphaltstädten bin ich daheim.
Bertolt Brecht
Vom armen B.B.

I am at home in the asphalt cities.

In der Ewigkeit ist alles am Anfang, duf-
tender Morgen.
Elias Canetti
Aufzeichnungen

In eternity everything is just beginning, a sweet-scented fragrant morning.

In der Kunst ist das Beste gut genug.
Goethe

In art the best is good enough.

In der Logik ist nichts zufällig.
Ludwig Wittgenstein
Tractatus logico-philosophicus

Nothing in logic is coincidental.

In der Natur ist alles einzeln.
Proverb

In nature everything is individual.

In Erstaunen setzen, ist das nicht die
Natur des Poeten?
Ernst Penzoldt
Der Delphin

Is it not the nature of poets to astonish?

In Gefahr und großer Not bringt der
Mittelweg Tod.
Friedrich von Logau

In times of danger and great distress, compromise will bring death.

In jedes Menschen Gesichte
Steht seine Geschichte,
Sein Hassen und Lieben
Deutlich geschrieben.
Friedrich von Bodenstedt
Liedern des Mirza-Schaffy

One can see their life history in the face of all men: their loves and hates are clearly written there.

In seiner Fülle ruhet der Herbsttag nun.
Friedrich Hölderlin
Mein Eigentum

Now the autumn day rests amid its rich plenty.

Ist dir ein Heiligtum ganz unbekannt,
Das, in dem Lager, Vaterland sich nennt?
Heinrich von Kleist
Prinz Friedrich von Homburg

Is that holy place quite unknown to you which, within our camp, is called Fatherland?

Ist es dem Land nicht egal, wer auf dem Apfelschimmel sitzt, der es staubig stampft?
Bertolt Brecht
Die heilige Johanna der Schlachthöfe

Does the land really care who sits on the dapple-grey horse which paws dustily at it?

Ja, ja, Prozeße müßen sein.
Christian Fürchtegott Gellert
Der Prozeß

Yes, yes, there must be trials.

Ja süß, himmlisch süß ists, eingewiegt zu werden in den Schlaf des Todes von dem Gesang des Geliebten.
Schiller
Die Räuber

Yes, it is sweet, heavenly sweet, to be rocked into the sleep of death by the songs of one's beloved.

Jâ leider desn mac niht gesîn,
Daz guot und weltlich êre
Und gotes hulde mêre
Zesamene in ein herze komen.
Walther von der Vogelweide
Ich saz ûf eime Steine

Unfortunately it is not possible for wealth and worldly honour and God's grace all to come together in one heart.

Je mehr du fühlst, ein Mensch zu sein,
Desto ähnlicher bist du den Göttern!
Goethe
Zahme Xenien

The more you feel yourself to be human, the more you resemble the gods!

Je mehr er hat, je mehr er will,
Nie schweigen seine Klagen still.

Johann Martin Miller
Zufriedenheit

The more he has the more he wants; his
complaints never cease.

Jede Sprache hat ihr eigenes Schweigen.

Elias Canetti
Aufzeichnungen

Every language has its own silence.

Jeder Affekt hat seine spezifiken Äußer-
ungen und, so zu sagen, seinen eigentüm-
lichen Dialekt, an dem man ihn kennt.

Schiller
Werke

Every emotion has its specific expression and,
so to speak, its characteristic dialect, by which
one recognises it.

Jeder glaubt,
Es sei auch schicklich, was ihm nützlich ist.

Goethe
Torquato Tasso

Everyone believes that what is useful to him is
also proper.

Jeder ist Kaiser in seiner Lage.

Proverb

Everyone is king in his own camp.

Jeder ist werth, daß man ihn aufmerksam
betrachte; wenn auch nicht Jeder, daß man
mit ihm redet.

Artur Schopenhauer

Every man is worth careful study; but not
every man is worth talking to.

Jeder Krieg enthält alle früheren.

Elias Canetti
Aufzeichnungen (1951)

Every war contains all earlier wars within it.

Jeder liebt sich selber nur am meisten.

Gotthold Ephraim Lessing
Nathan der Weise

Everyone loves himself the most.

Jeder Mensch glaubt, weil er spricht, über
die Sprache sprechen zu dürfen.

Proverb

Everyone believes that because he can speak, he
may talk about language.

Jeder Mensch hat auch seine moralische
'Backside', die er nicht ohne Not zeigt, und
die er solange als möglich mit der Hosen
des guten Anstandes zudeckt.

Georg Christoph Lichtenberg
Aphorismen

Every person also has his moral "backside",
which he does not expose needlessly, and which
he covers for as long as possible with the
trousers of politeness.

Jeder Mensch ist ein Abgrund; es
schwindelt einem, wenn man hinabsieht.
Georg Büchner
Woyzeck

*Every man is a chasm into which it makes one
dizzy to look down.*

Jeder Mensch ist ein Adam; denn jeder
wird einmal aus dem Paradiese der war-
men Gefühle vertrieben.
Goethe
letter to J.C. Lobe, July 1820

*Every man is an Adam, for everybody is one
day driven out of the paradise of warm feelings.*

Jeder muß nach seiner Fasson selig werden.
Frederick the Great

Everyone must find his own salvation.

Jedes vollkommene Gedicht ist Ahnung
und Gegenwart, Sehnsucht und Erfüllung
zugleich. Gespräch über Gedichte.
Hugo von Hofmannsthal

*Every perfect poem is simultaneously a
premonition and the present, longing and
fulfilment. A conversation more than a poem.*

Jemand mußte Josef K. verleumdet haben,
denn ohne daß er etwas Böses getan hätte,
wurde er eines Morgens verhaftet.
Franz Kafka
Der Prozeß

*Someone must have slandered Joseph K., for
without having done anything bad, he was
arrested one morning.*

Jetzt ergeht es ihm wie jedem Schwärmer,
der von seiner herrschenden Idee über-
wältigt wird. Er kennt keine Grenzen mehr.
Schiller
Werke

*Now he is becoming like every zealot who is
overwhelmed by his ruling idea. He no longer
recognises any limits.*

Jetzt wächst zusammen, was zusammen-
gehört.
Willy Brandt
10 Nov. 1989, on the fall of the Berlin Wall

*Now that which belongs together is growing
together.*

Jugend ist Trunkenheit ohne Wein.
Goethe
Westöstliche Diwan, 'Schenkenbuch'

Youth is drunkenness without wine.

Kein Feuer, keine Kohle
Kann brennen so heiß
Als heimliche Liebe,
Von der niemand nichts weiß.
Folk song

*No fire nor coals could burn as hotly as the
secret love which no one knows.*

Kein lebendiges ist ein Eins,
Immer ist's ein Vieles.

Goethe
Epirrhema

No living creature is a single thing, it is always a multiple.

Kein Talent, doch ein Charakter.

Heine

No talent, but a character.

Kennst Du das Land, wo die Zitronen
blühn?
Im dunkelm Laub die Gold-Orangen glühn,
Ein sanfter Wind vom blauen Himmel weht,
Die Myrte still und hoch der Lorbeer steht –
Kennst du es wohl?
Dahin! Dahin
Möcht' ich mit dir, o mein Geliebter, ziehn!

Goethe
Wilhelm Meisters Lehjahre

Do you know the country where the lemons bloom? Among the dark leaves the golden oranges glow, a soft wind wafts from the blue sky, the myrtle is still and the laurel stands high – do you know it well? There, there, would I go, oh my beloved, with thee.

Kinder, Kirche, Küche.

Traditional
the proper concerns for a German woman

Children, church, kitchen.

Kleiner Mann hat auch sein Stolz.

Proverb

The little man also has his pride.

Komme, Tod, und raub mich, Tod, im
Kuße!

Thomas Mann
Der Kamerad

Come, death, carry me off in your kiss!

Könnten Sie nicht ein wenig vergessen,
berühmt zu sein?

Robert Walser
to Hugo von Hofmannsthal

Couldn't you forget your fame just a little?

Kraft durch Freude.

Robert Ley
German Labour Front slogan from 1933

Strength through joy.

Kraft ist oberstes Gesetz.

Adolf Hitler

Power is the highest law.

Kulturkampf.
historical name for the struggle with the
Clerical Party

Culture struggle.

Lerne leiden, ohne zu klagen, das ist das einzige, was ich dich lehren kann.

Kaiser Friedrich III
advice to his son

Learn to suffer without complaint; this is the only thing I can teach you.

Lieb Vaterland, magst ruhig sein
Fest steht und treu die Wacht am Rhein.

Max Schnekkenburger
Die Wacht am Rhein

Dear Fatherland, you can be calm, for the watch stands firm and faithful on the Rhine.

Liebe ist nichts als Angst des sterblichen Menschen vor dem Alleinsein.

Theodor Storm
Im Schloß

Love is nothing but the human fear of being alone.

Lieber ein Ende mit Schrecken als ein Schrecken ohne Ende.

Ferdinand von Schill
to his troops in 1809

Better a terrifying end than terror without end.

Lieber ein kleiner Herr als ein großer Knecht.

Proverb

It is better to be a minor lord than an important servant.

Mâc hilfet wol, friunt verre baz.

Walther von der Vogelweide
Man hôchgemâc

Kinsmen may help, but friends are better.

Mache mich bitter.
Zähle mich zu den Mandeln.

Paul Celan
Zähle die Mandeln

Make me bitter. Include me among the almonds.

Macht geht vor Recht.
attributed by his opponents to Bismarck, who repudiated it

Might before right.

Macht mir den rechten Flügel stark!

Alfred von Schlieffen
1913, on his death bed

Make the right wing strong for me!

Mags schnell geschehn, was muß geschehn!

Goethe
Faust

Let that which must happen happen quickly!

Man darf Heldentaten nicht in der Nähe betrachten.

Theodor Fontane
Ein Sommer in London

One should not examine heroic deeds closely.

Man hat's, oder man hat's nicht.

Theodor Fontane
Man hat es oder man hat es nicht

One either has it, or one doesn't.

Man kann doch Menschen nicht für ein leeres Wort sterben lassen!

Wolfgang Borchert
Draußen vor der Tür

But we cannot let people die for the sake of an empty word!

Man löst sich nicht allmählich von dem Leben!

Schiller
Werke

One cannot gradually release oneself from life.

Mehr Licht!

Goethe
dying

More light!

Mein armer Kopf
Ist mir verrückt,
Mein armer Sinn
Ist mir zerstückt.

Goethe
Faust

My poor head is in disarray, my poor mind is breaking up.

Mein Geist dürstet nach Taten, mein Atem nach Freiheit.

Schiller
Die Räuber

My spirit yearns for action, my breath for freedom.

Mein Handwerk ist Wiedervergeltung - Rache ist mein Gewerbe.

Schiller
Die Räuber

My trade is retaliation; revenge is my profession.

Mein Herz ich will dich fragen:
Was ist denn lieber? Sag'!
"Zwei Seelen und ein Gedanke,
Zwei Herzen und ein Schlag!"

Friedrich Halm

What love is, if thou wouldst be taught,
Thy heart must teach alone.
Two souls with but a single thought,
Two hearts that beat as one.

Mein Kind, ich hab' es klug gemacht:
Ich habe nie über des Denken gedacht.

> **Goethe**
> *Zahme Xenien*

My child, I have behaved very cleverly – I have never thought about thinking.

Meine Ruh' ist hin,
Mein Herz ist schwer.

> **Goethe**
> *Faust*

My peace is gone, my heart is heavy.

Mensch werden ist eine Kunst.

> **Novalis** (Friedrich von Hardenberg)
> *Fragmente*

Becoming a human is an art.

Minister fallen wie Butterbrote: gewöhn-
lich auf die gute Seite.

> **Ludwig Börne**
> *Aphorismen*

Ministers fall like buttered bread: usually on their good side.

Mir fällt zu Hitler nichts ein... Ich fühle
mich wie vor den Kopf geschlagen.

> **Karl Kraus**
> *Die Fackel, July 1934*

I can't think of anything to say about Hitler... I feel as though I have been hit over the head.

Mit der Dummheit kämpfen Götter selbst
vergebens.

> **Schiller**
> *Die Jungfrau von Orleans*

Against stupidity even the gods struggle in vain.

Mit der Wahrheit hat die Kunst doch
nichts zu tun!

> **Wolfgang Borchert**
> *Draußen vor der Tür*

Art has got nothing to do with truth!

Mit der Wahrheit ist das wie mit einer
stadtbekannten Hure. Jeder kennt sie, aber
es ist peinlich, wenn man ihr auf der
Straße begegnet.

> **Wolfgang Borchert**
> *Draußen vor der Tür*

Truth is similar to a well-known town whore. Everyone knows her, but it is embarrassing when one meets her in the street.

Mit einem Worte: wir wollen niemand in
den Schatten stellen, aber wir verlangen
auch unseren Platz an der Sonne.

> **Prince Bernhard von Bülow**
> to the Reichstag, 6 December 1897

In a word, we desire to throw no one into the shade [in East Asia], but we also demand our own place in the sun.

Mit gewaltsamer Hand
Löset der Mord auch das heiligste Band.

Schiller
Die Braut von Messina

Murder dissolves even the most sacred bond with its violent hands.

Möhte ich verslâfen des winters zît!

Walther von der Vogelweide
Uns hât der Winter geschât über al

If only I could sleep through the winter time!

Mönchlein, Mönchlein, du gehst einen schweren Gang.

Martin Luther
on the eve of his departure for Worms

Little monk, little monk, you are following a difficult path.

Musik, das Hohlmaß des Menschen.

Elias Canetti
Aufzeichnungen, 1956

Music is the measure of humanity.

Muß es sein? Es muß sein.

Ludwig von Beethoven

Must it be? It must be.

Nach innen geht der geheimnisvolle Weg. In uns oder nirgends ist die Ewigkeit mit ihren Welten, die Vergangenheit und Zukunft.

Novalis
(Friedrich von Hardenberg)
Heinrich von Ofterdingen

The secret path leads inwards. In us and nowhere else lies eternity, with its past and future worlds.

Nach Canossa gehen wir nicht.

Otto von Bismarck
during the Kulturkampf, meaning that he would not submit to the Vatican

We are not going to Canossa.

Naiv muß jedes wahre Genie sein.

Schiller
Über naïve und sentimentalische Dichtung

Every true genius must be naïve.

Neugier nur beflügelt jeden Schritt.

Goethe
Faust

Curiosity alone inspires every step.

Nicht bloß wissen, sondern auch für die Nachwelt tun, was die Vorwelt für uns getan hat, heißt ein Mensch sein.

Georg Christoph Lichtenberg
Aphorismen

Being a man means not just knowing, but also doing for posterity, that which our predecessors did for us.

Niemand ist mehr Sklave, als der sich für frei hält, ohne es zu sein.

Goethe

No one is more truly a slave than he who thinks himself free without being so.

Niemand kann sagen, ob die kommende Generation eine Generation von Giganten sein wird.

Adolf Hitler

No one can say whether the coming generation will be a generation of giants.

Noch ein Endlichstes zu wissen! Welt ist Traum und Traum wird Welt.

Georg Berneck
Letzte Sehnsucht

There is still a final thing to know! The world is a dream, and the dream will become the world.

Nur das Unerwartete macht glücklich, aber es muß auf viel Erwartetes stoßen, das es zerstreut.

Elias Canetti
Aufzeichnungen

Only the unexpected brings happiness, but it must push against much that is expected and scatter it.

Nur die Toten kommen nicht wieder.

Georg Büchner
Dantons Tod

Only the dead never return.

Nur rastlos betätigt sich der Mann.

Goethe
Faust

Man acts only through restlessness.

O Minnetrug! O Lieberzung! Der Welt holdester Wahn!

Richard Wagner
Tristan und Isolde

O deception of love! O passion's force! Most beautiful of the world's illusions!

O sink hernieder
Nacht der Liebe,
Gibt vergessen
Daß ich lebe.

Richard Wagner
Tristan und Isolde

Oh descend here, night of love, and let me forget that I am alive.

O Tannenbaum, O Tannenbaum, Wie grün sind deine Blätter!

Louis Schnieder
Der Kurmärker und die Picarde

O pinetree, o pinetree, How green are thy leaves.

O über mich Narren, der ich wähnete, die Welt duch Greuel zu verschönen und die Gesetze durch Gesetzlosigkeit aufrecht zu halten. Ich nannte es Rache und Recht.

Schiller
Die Räuber

Oh how foolish I was to dream that I could make the world more beautiful by means of atrocity and that I could uphold the law by means of lawlessness. I called it revenge and justice.

Ob er heilig, ob er böse,
Jammert sie den Unglücksmann.

Goethe
Faust

Whether he's holy or evil, this unlucky man is pitied.

Oft fühl ich jetzt... [und] je tiefer ich einsehe, daß Schicksal und Gemüt Namen *eines Begriffes* sind.

Novalis (Friedrich von Hardenberg)
Heinrich von Ofterdinger

I often feel, and ever more deeply I realize, that fate and character are the same *conception.*

Oh, wär' ich nie geboren!

Goethe
Faust

Oh, if only I had never been born!

Ohne Beweis ist der Mensch überhaupt kein Mensch, sondern ein Orang.

Bertolt Brecht
Elephantenkalb

Without proof man is actually no man, but an ape.

Ohne Butter werden wir fertig, ohne nicht beispielsweise ohne Kanonen. Wenn wir einmal überfallen werden, dann können wir uns nicht mit Butter, sondern nur mit Kanonen verteidigen.

Joseph Goebbels

We can manage without butter, but not, for example, without guns. If we are attacked we cannot defend ourselves with butter, only with guns.

Ohne Hast, aber ohne Rast.

Goethe
Zahme Xenien

Without haste but without pause.

Ohne mich.

slogan of disillusioned post-war German voters

Without me.

Ordnung führt zu allen Tugenden! Aber was führt zur Ordnung?

Georg Christoph Lichtenberg
Aphorismen

Order leads to all virtues. But what leads to order?

Ouwê war sint verswunden alliu mîniu jâr?
Walther von der Vogelweide
Elegy (or *Palinode*)

Where have they disappeared, all my years?

Pack schlägt sich, Pack verträgt sich.
Proverb

The rabble is at each other's throats one minute, and friends again the next.

Poesie und Wissenschaft erscheinen als die größten Widersacher.
Goethe
Zur Morphologie

Poetry and science appear the greatest adversaries.

Proletarier aller Länder, vereinigt euch!
Karl Marx and **Friedrich Engels**
Manifest der Kommunistischen Partei

Workers of the world, unite!

Prosit!
German toast

Good luck.

Recht ist nur der ausgeschmückte Name
Für alles Unrechte, das die Erde hegt.
Franz Grillparzer
Libussa

Justice is only the decorative name for all the injustice that the world harbours.

Reue und Verzweiflung über ein begangenes Verbrechen zeigen uns die Macht des Sittengesetzes nur später, nicht schwächer.
Schiller
Werke

Remorse and despair about having committed a crime reveal the power of the moral law belatedly, but no less forcefully.

Ruhe, ruhe, du Gott!
Richard Wagner
Götterdämerung
Brünnhilde to Wotan

Rest, rest, thou God!

Sagen Sie mir nicht, daß Friede ausgebrochen ist, wo ich eben neue Vorräte eingekauft hab.
Bertolt Brecht
Mutter Courage und ihre Kinder

Don't tell me peace has broken out just when I have bought new supplies.

Schön ist die Jugend, sie kommt nicht mehr.
Folk song

Youth is beautiful and will not return.

Sein Geld hebt er in seinem Herzen auf,
die Schläge zählen es.

Elias Canetti
Aufzeichnungen

He captures his money in his heart, and his heartbeats count it.

Sein Schicksal schafft sich selbst der Mann.
Gottfried Kinkel
Otto der Schütz

Man creates his own destiny.

Selig wer sich vor der Welt
Ohne Haß verschließt.

Goethe
Der Mondlied

Blessed is he who can shut himself off from the world without hating it.

Selten wird das Treffliche gefunden, selt-
ner geschätzt.

Goethe
Wilhelm Meisters Lehrjahre

Excellence is rarely found; even more rarely is it valued.

Setzen wir Deutschland, sozusagen, in den
Sattel! Reiten wird es schon können.
Otto von Bismarck
11 March 1867, in a speech to the North
German Reichstag

Let us put Germany in the saddle, so to speak; it already knows how to ride.

Sie konnen einwenden, daß es ja überhaupt kein Verfahren ist. Sie haben sehr
recht, denn es ist ja nur ein Verfahren,
wenn ich es als solches anerkenne.
Franz Kafka
Der Prozeß

You may object that this is really not a trial. You are right. It is only a trial when I recognise it as such.

*Sie macht sich nur durch Blut und Eisen.
Otto von Bismarck
speaking to the Prussian House of Deputies,
1886

It can be done only through blood and iron.

Sieh nach den Sternen! Gib acht auf die
Gassen!

Wilhelm Raabe
Die Leute aus dem Walde

Look to the stars! Keep an eye on the alleyways!

So geschieht es denn nicht selten, das [der
Idealist] über dem unbegrenzten Ideale

It often happens that [the idealist], filled with limitless idealism, overlooks the practical limits

* Compare p.194

den begrenzten Fall der Anwendung über-
siehet und, von einem Maximum erfüllt,
das Minimum verabsäumt, aus dem noch
alles Große in der Wirklichkeit erwächst.

Schiller
Über naïve und sentimentalische Dichtung

of application, and, inspired by the maximum, neglects the minimum, from which, after all, grows everything that is great in the real world.

So ist jede schöne Gabe
Flüchtig wie des Blitzes Schein,
Schnell in ihrem düstern Grabe
Schließt die Nacht sie wieder ein.

Schiller
Die Gunst des Augenblicks

Thus every beautiful talent is as fleeting as a flash of lightning, and is quickly enclosed again in night's gloomy grave.

So kann es Leute geben, die zuletzt
mechanisch
Gutes oder Böses tun.

Schiller
Werke

Therefore there are people who, in the end, do good or evil quite mechanically.

So lang man lebt, sei man lebendig!

Goethe
Maskenzug

As long as we live, let us be alive!

So leben wir und nehmen immer
Abschied.

Rainer Maria Rilke
Duineser Elegien

So we live, forever saying goodbye.

So stürben wir um ungetrennt, ewig einig
ohne End', ohn' Erwachen, ohn' Erbange,
namelos in Lieb' umfangen, ganz uns selbst
gegeben, der lieb nur zu leben!

Richard Wagner
Tristan und Isolde

So might we die together, eternally, one without end, without awakening, without fearing, nameless in love's embrace, giving ourselves wholly, to live only for love.

So tauml' ich von Begierde zu Genuß,
Und im Genuß verschmacht' ich nach
Begierde.

Goethe
Faust

I stagger thus from desire to enjoyment, and in enjoyment I languish for desire.

So weit im Leben, ist zu nah am Tod!

Friedrich Hebbel
Sommerbild

To be advanced in life is to be too close to death!

So wie die Welt nicht von Kriegen lebt, so leben die Völker nicht von Revolutionen.

Adolf Hitler
Mein Kampf

Just as the world does not live by wars, neither do people live by revolutions.

Soldaten sehn sich alle gleich
Lebendig und als Leich.

Wolf Biermann
Soldat, Soldat

Soldiers always resemble each other: whether they are alive or whether they are corpses.

Sphären in einander lenkt die Liebe,
Weltsysteme dauern nur durch sie.

Schiller
Phantasie an Laura

Love guides the spheres together, and world-systems endure only through love.

Sprich mir von allen Schrecken des Gewissens, von meinem Vater sprich mir nicht.

Schiller
Don Karlos

Tell me about all the terrors of the conscious mind, but do not speak of my father.

Staub soll er fressen, und mit Lust.

Goethe
Faust

He shall gobble dust and enjoy it.

Sterben, ach! sterben
Soll ich allein!

Folk song

Oh, I must die alone!

Stirb und werde!

Goethe
Selige Sehnsucht

Die and become!

Sturm und Drang.

Christoph Kaufmann

Storm and stress.

Swer guotes wîbes minne hât,
Der schamt sich aller missetât.

Walther von der Vogelweide
Einniuwer Sumer

Whoever has the love of a good woman will be ashamed of every misdeed.

Swes brot ich ezz', des liet ich sing'.

Minstrels' motto

I will sing the song of him whose bread I eat.

Tiefe Nacht ist drauß und drinnen,
Tiefe Nacht in euren Sinnen,
Tiefe Nacht allumgetan.

Albrecht Schaeffer
Die lange Nacht

*Deep night is outside and inside, deep night is
in your consciousness, deep night is complete.*

Todesangst ist ärger als Sterben.

Schiller
Die Räuber

The fear of death is worse than dying.

Tu nur das Rechte in deinen Sachen; das
andre wird sich von selber machen.

Goethe
Gedichtsammlung, 1815

*Make sure that you only do the right thing in
life; everything else will take care of itself.*

Über allen Gipfeln ist Ruh'.

Goethe
Wanderers Nachtlied

Over all the mountain tops is peace.

Überhaupt beobachtet man, daß die
Bösartigkeit der Seele gar oft in kranken
Körpern wohnt.

Schiller

*One can generally observe that maliciousness
of the soul often dwells in sick bodies.*

Überhaupt ist es für den Froscher ein guter
Morgensport, täglich vor dem Frühstück
eine Lieblingshypothese einzustampfen -
das erhält jung.

Konrad Lorenz

*It is generally a good morning exercise for a
scientist to discard some pet theory every day
before breakfast – it keeps him young.*

Überlegung ist eine Kranckheit der Seele,
und hat nur krancke Taten getan.

Goethe
Götz von Berlichingen (first version)

*Reflection is a disease of the soul, and has
performed only sick deeds.*

Und der Haifisch, der hat Zähne
Und er tragt sie im Gesicht
Und Macheath, der hat ein Messer
Doch das Messer sicht man nicht.

Bertholt Brecht
Die Dreigroschenoper

*Oh, the shark has pretty teeth, dear,
And he shows them pearly white.
Just a jacknife has Macheath, dear,
And he keeps it out of sight.*

Und die Größe ist gefährlich
Und der Ruhm ein leeres Spiel.

Franz Grillparzer
Der Traum ein Leben

*Greatness is dangerous, and glory is an empty
game.*

Und doch, welch Glück, geliebt zu werden!
Und lieben, Götter, welch ein Glück!
Goethe
Willkommen und Abschied

And even so, what happiness to be loved! And,
oh you gods, what happiness it is to love!

Und was der ganzen Menschheit zugeteilt
ist,
Will ich in meinem innern Selbst genießen.
Goethe
Urfaust

I want to savour in my inner self that which is
granted to the whole of mankind.

Und weil der Mensch ein Mensch ist,
drum will er was zu essen, bitte sehr!
Bertolt Brecht
Einheitsfrontlied, Svendborger Gedichte

And because man is a man, he would like
something to eat, please!

Und wir müssen wandern, wandern,
Keiner weiß vom andern.
August Heinrich Hoffmann von
Fallersleben
Niemals wieder

And we must wander, wander, no one being
aware of the other's existence.

Unsre Taten sind nur Würfe
In des Zufalls blinder Nacht.
Franz Grillparzer
Die Ahnfrau

Our deeds are only throws of the dice in the
blind night of chance.

Vater werden ist nicht schwer,
Vater sein dagegen sehr.
Wilhelm Busch
Julchen

Becoming a father is not difficult; being a
father, on the other hand, is very hard.

Vereint sind Liebe und Lenz!
Richard Wagner
Die Walküre

Spring and love are made one!

Verstücke den Donner in seine einfache
Silben, und du wirst Kinder damit in der
Schlummer singen; schmelze sie zusam-
men in einen plötzlichen Schall, und der
monarchische Laut wird den ewigen
Himmel bewegen.
Schiller
Fiesko

Divide the thunder into its simple syllables,
and you will be able to sing children to sleep
with them; but, melt them together into one
sudden roar, and the royal sound will move
the eternal heavens.

Viele Unternehmungen mißlingen bloß, weil man die Früchte davon noch gerne erleben wollte.

Georg Christoph Lichtenberg
Aphorismen

Many enterprises fail simply through eagerness to experience their fruits.

Von der Gewalt, die alle Wesen bindet Befreit der Mensch sich, der sich überwindet.

Goethe
Die Geheimnisse

He who masters himself is freed from the force which binds all creatures.

Von diesen Städten wird bleiben: der durch sie hindurchging, der Wind!

Bertolt Brecht
Vom armen B.B.

All that remains of these cities will be the wind that blew through them.

Von hier und heute geht eine neue Epoche der Weltgeschichte aus, und ihr könnt sagen, ihr seid dabeigewesen.

Goethe
19 September 1792, on the eve of the barrage of Valmy

Here and today begins a new era in world history, and you can say that you were there.

Vor der Kunst wie vor dem Gesetz sind alle Menschen gleich.

Gerhart Hauptmann
Die Ratten

All men are equal before art, as before the law.

Vor diesem einschlicßlich der Sowjetunion riesigen Territorium würde sich sofort ein eiserner Vorhang heruntersenken.

Joseph Goebbels
in 1945, on the consequences if Germany were to surrender

An iron curtain would at once descend on this territory which, including the Soviet Union, would be of gigantic size.

Vorsprung durch Technik.
Advertisement for Audi motors

Progress through technology.

Vorwärts.
the motto and the nickname of
Gebbard Blücher

Forward!

Wanderjahre.
German expression for the travels of a journeyman after his *Lehrjahre*, the year of apprenticeship

The years of wandering.

Was den politischen Enthusiasten bewegt, ist nicht was er siehet, sondern was er denkt.

Schiller
Werke

What moves the political enthusiast is not what he sees, but what he thinks.

Was einem angehört, wird man nicht los, und wenn man es wegwürfe.

Goethe
Maximen und Reflexionen

One cannot get rid of that which belongs to one, even if one throws it away.

Was für Plündern!

Gebbard Blücher

What a city to plunder!
(A misquotation. He actually said "Was für Plunder!" What a lot of rubbish.)

Was glänzt, ist für den Augenblick geboren.

Goethe

A thing that glitters is made only for the moment.

Was Hände bauten, können Hände stürzen.

Schiller
Wilhelm Tell

What hands have built, hands can cause to fall.

Was ist dein Ziel in der Philosophie? Der Fliege den Ausweg aus dem Fliegenglas zeigen.

Ludwig Wittgenstein
Philosophische Untersuchungen

What is your aim in philosophy? To show the fly the way out of the fly-bottle.

Was man aufgibt, hat man nie verloren.

Proverb

What one sacrifices is never lost.

Was man scheint, hat jedermann zum Richter, was man ist, hat keinen.

Schiller
Maria Stuart

Everyone judges you by how you appear, no one judges by what you are.

Was soll all der Schmerz und Lust?
Süßer Friede,
Komm, ach komm in meine Brust!

Goethe
Wanderers Nachtlied

Why all the pain and pleasure? Sweet peace, enter, oh enter, my breast!

Was unsterblich im Gesang soll leben,
Muß im Leben untergehn.

Schiller
Die Götter Griechenlands

What is immortalised in song must be destroyed in life.

Waz hât diu werlt ze gebenne
Liebers dan ein wîp,
Daz sende herze baz gefreuwen müge?
             Walther von der Vogelweide
                Waz hât diu Werlt?

What dearer thing has the world to offer than a woman who can gladden a yearning heart?

Wehret den Anfängen.
             Proverb

Beware of beginnings.

Weil ich ihm nicht trau, wir sind befreundet.
             Bertolt Brecht
       Mutter Courage und ihre Kinder

Because I don't trust him, we are friends.

Weisheit kommt nicht gratis mit dem
Alter.
             Proverb

Wisdom does not come free with age.

Welch Haupt steht fort, wenn dieses
heil'ge fiel!
             Schiller
           Maria Stuart

Whose head will remain upright if this blessed one were to fall?

Wenige wissen
Das Geheimnis der Liebe,
Fühlen Unersättlichkeit
Und ewigen Durst.
    Novalis (Friedrich von Hardenberg)
             Hymne

Few know the secret of love; they feel insatiability and perpetual thirst.

Wenn deine Schrift dem Kenner nicht
             gefällt
So ist es schon ein böses Zeichen:
Doch wenn sie gar des Narren Lob erhalt
So ist es Zeit, sie auszustreichen.
            Salomon Gessner

When your writings fail to please knowledgeable critics, that is certainly a bad sign: but when they are praised by fools, it is time to expunge them.

Wenn es in den alten Apfelbäumen
            rauscht, ist es anders.
Und wenn es in Tannenwipfeln rauscht, ist
            es anders.
Wenn es über Felder braust, ist es anders.
Wenn es im Weidenbusche rauscht, ist es
            anders.
            Peter Altenberg
            Geräusche

[Of the wind.] It's different when it rustles through the old apple trees; and it's different when it rustles across the tops of the pine trees. It's different when it roars across the fields; and it's different when it rustles through the willow bushes.

Wenn Frauen Fehler machen wollen,
Dann soll man ihnen nicht in Wege stehen.

Erich Kästner
*Bei Durchsicht meiner Bücher 'Hotelsolo für
eine Männerstimme'*

*If women want to make mistakes, one should
not stand in their way.*

Wenn ich Kultur höre entsichere ich meine
Browning.

Hans Johst
but usually attributed to Goering

*When I hear the word "culture", I slip the
safety-catch of my Browning.*

Wenn ich nicht sinnen oder dichten soll,
So ist das Leben mir keinen Leben mehr.

Goethe
Torquato Tasso

*If I may not ponder or write, then life is no
longer any sort of life for me.*

Wenn ich nicht morgen nachmittag Sieger
bin, bin ich ein toter Mann!

Adolf Hitler
Munich, 8 November 1923

*If I am not the victor by tomorrow afternoon, I
shall be a dead man.*

Wer den kleinsten Theil eines
Geheimnisses hingibt, hat den andern
nicht mehr in der Gewalt.

Jean Paul Richter

*When one reveals the smallest part of a secret
one can no longer be said to possess the rest of
it.*

Wer den Zweck will, will (so fern die
Vernunft auf seine Handlungen entschei-
denden Einfluß hat), auch das dazu unent-
behrlich nothwendige Mittel, das in seiner
Gewalt ist.

Immanuel Kant
Grundlegung zur Metaphisik der Sitten

*Whoever wills the end, wills also (so far as
reason decides his conduct) the means in his
power which are indispensably necessary
thereto.*

Wer dunkel ist, bleibe dunkel, wer
Unrein ist, unrein. Lobet
Mangel, lobet Mißhandlung, lobet
Die Finsternis.

Bertolt Brecht
Leben Eduards des Zweiten von England

*Whoever is gloomy, stay gloomy, whoever is
unclean, remain unclean. Praise shortcomings,
praise ill treatment, praise the darkness.*

Wer gar zuviel bedenkt, wird wenig
leisten.

Schiller
Wilhelm Tell

He who reflects too much will achieve little.

Wer immer strebend sich bemüht
Den können wir erlösen.

Goethe
Faust

We can rescue him who constantly strives.

Wer lange lebt, hat viel erfahren,
Nichts Neues kann für ihn auf dieser Welt
geschehn.

Goethe
Faust

He who has lived for a long time has experienced much. For him, nothing new can happen in this world.

Wer möchte ohne den Trost der Bäume
leben?

Günter Eich
Ende eines Sommers

Who would want to live without the consolation of the trees?

Wer nicht die Kraft hat, dem nutzt das
"Recht an sich" gar nichts.

Adolf Hitler

Having "right on one's side" is absolutely useless if one has no power.

Wer nie sein Brot mit Tränen aß,
Wer nie die kummervollen Nächte
Auf seinem Bette weinend saß,
Der Kennt euch nicht, ihr himmlischen
Mächte.

Goethe
Wilhelm Meisters Lehjahre

Who never ate his bread with tears nor spent a mournful night upon his bed knows you not, you heavenly powers.

Wer saß nicht bang vor seine Herzens
Vorhang?

Rainer Maria Rilke
Duineser Elegien

Who has not sat in uneasy anticipation before the stage curtain of his heart?

Wer Schnaps hat, ist gerettet!

Wolfgang Borchert
Draußen vor der Tür

Whoever has schnaps is saved!

Wer sich stets viel geschont hat, der
kränkelt zuletzt an seiner vielen Schonung.
Gelobt sei, was hart macht.

Friedrich Nietzsche
Also sprach Zarathustra

He who has always cushioned himself will in the end become sick of his great indulgence. That which makes things hard should be praised.

Wie anstrengend es ist, böse zu sein!

Bertolt Brecht
Die Maske des Bösen

How demanding it is to be wicked!

Wie ein Kind am Tischtuch zerrt, aber
nichts gewinnt, sondern nur die ganze
Pracht hinunterwirft und sie sich für
immer unerreichbar macht.

Franz Kafka
Das Schloß

*Like a child who tugs at the tablecloth but gains
nothing, only throwing its entire splendour
to the ground, thus making it permanently
unattainable.*

Wie in verwehte Jugendtage blickst du
zurück,
Und irgendeiner sagt dir weise: 'Es ist
dein Glück!'
Da denkt man, daß es vielleicht so ist,
Wundert sich still, daß man doch nicht
froh ist!

Peter Altenberg
Sehnsucht

*As one looks back on the long-gone days of
youth, and somebody wisely tells you: "You
are fortunate!", you think that perhaps it is
true, and are quietly surprised that you are
still not happy!*

Wie klein denken doch kleine Menschen!

Adolf Hitler

*What little thoughts are thought by little
people!*

Will vom Krieg leben
Wird ihm wohl müssen auch etwas geben.

Bertolt Brecht
Mutter Courage und ihre Kinder

*He who would live off war must eventually
give something to it.*

Willst du dich selber erkennen, so sieh, wie
die Andern es treiben; Willst du die Andern
verstehn, blick'in dein eigenes Herz.

Schiller

*If you want to know yourself, see how others
behave; if you want to understand others, look
in your own heart!*

Wir führen einen Kampf auf Leben und
Tod und können zur Zeit keine Geschenke
machen.

Adolf Hitler
letter to Franco, 1940

*We are waging a life and death struggle and
can make no concessions to time.*

Wie selig lebt ein Mann, der seine
Pflichten kennt!

Christian Fürchtegott Gellert
Der Menschenfreund

How blessed is the man who knows his duty!

Wir Deutsche fürchten Gott, aber sonst nichts
in der Welt. Und die Gottesfurcht ist es schon,
die uns den Frieden lieben und pflegen läßt.

Otto von Bismarck
February 1888, to the Reichstag

*We Germans fear God but nothing else in the
world, and it is the fear of God which allows us
to love and cherish peace.*

Wir haben der Schmerzen nicht zu viel,
wir haben ihrer zu wenig, denn durch den
Schmerz gehen wir zu Gott ein!

Georg Büchner
on his death bed

We do not have too much pain, but too little,
for it is through pain that we attain God.

Wir stehen selbst enttäuscht und sehn
betroffen
Den Vorhang zu und alle Fragen offen.
...Verehrtes Publikum, los, such dir selbst
den Schluß!
Es muß ein guter da sein, muß, muß, muß!

Bertolt Brecht
Der gute Mensch von Sezuan

We stand there in disappointment and look in
consternation at the closed stage curtain that
leaves all questions open... Honoured audience,
go, find your own conclusion! There must be a
good one, there must, there must, there must!

Wir wollen mehr Demokratie wagen.

Willy Brandt
28 October 1969

We want to risk more democracy.

Wo Hunger herrscht, kann Friede nicht
Bestand haben.

Willy Brandt
Erinnerungen

Peace cannot endure where hunger rules.

Wo ist er nun, der große Traum der Erde,
Der Traum von Vogelflug und Pflanzensein?
Die Dinge bleiben doch, ihr altes Werde,
Ihr alter Tod und ach, ihr altes Nein.

Günter Eich
Märztag

Where is it now, the great dream of the earth,
the dream of the flight of birds and the existence
of plants? Things remain, with their ancient
development, their ancient death, and oh, their
ancient denial.

Wo Mäßigung ein Fehler ist, da ist
Gleichgültigkeit ein Verbrechen.

Georg Christoph Lichtenberg
Aphorismen.

If restraint is weakness, indifference is a crime.

Wo steht das geschrieben?

Martin Luther
*Kleinen Katechismus and Lehrstück von Amt
der Schlüssel*

Where is it written?

Wo wird einst des Wandermüden
Letzte Ruhestätte sein?

Heinrich Heine
Wo

Where will the final resting place be for him
who is tired of wandering?

Wohin wir nur sehen, so sehen wir bloß uns.

Georg Christoph Lichtenberg
Aphorismen

Wherever we look, we can only see ourselves.

Wovon man nicht sprechen kann, darüber muß man schweigen.

Ludwig Wittgenstein
Tractatus logico-philosophicus

We should keep quiet about that of which we cannot speak.

Wüchsen die Kinder in der Art fort, wie sie sich andeuten, so hätten wir lauter Genies.

Goethe
Dichtung und Wahrheit

If children continued to develop according to their early indications, we would have nothing but genius.

Wunder ist des Glaubens liebstes Kind.

Goethe
Faust

Wonder is belief's favourite child.

Wunderlich nah ist der Held doch den jugendlich Toten.

Rainer Maria Rilke
Duineser Elegien

The hero is strangely close to those who died young.

Zeit ist teuer.

Proverb

Time is expensive.

Zufriedenheit geht über Reichtum.

Proverb

Contentment is worth more than riches.

Zum erstenmal einen Silberstreifen an dem sonst düsteren Horizont.

Gustav Stresemann
1924, after the second London conference on war reparations

For the first time we can see a silver streak on the otherwise murky horizon.

*Zwar der Tapfere nennt sich Herr der Länder
Durch sein Eisen, durch sein Blut.

Ernst Arndt
reputedly the source of Bismarck's phrase

The brave man calls himself lord of the land through his iron, through his blood.

*Compare p.182

Zwein Dinge erfüllen das Gemüt mit immer neuer und zunehmender Bewunderung und Ehrfurcht, je öfter und anhaltender sich das Nachdenken damit beschäftigt: der bestirnte Himmel über mir, und das moralische Gesetz in mir.

Immanuel Kant
Kritik der praktischen Vernunft

Two things fill the mind with ever new and increasing wonder and awe, the more often and the more seriously reflection concentrates upon them: the starry heaven above me and the moral law within me.

Zwei Seelen wohnen, ach! in meiner Brust!
Goethe
Faust

Alas! Two souls live within my breast!

GERMAN INDEX

197

ITALIAN

Dante, who loved well because he hated,
Hated wickedness that hinders loving.

Browning

A pensare male si fa peccato, ma spesso si indovina.

Giulio Andreotti

To think badly [of someone] is a sin, but often it turns out to be true.

A re malvagio, consiglier peggior.

Torquato Tasso
Gerusalemme liberata

To an evil king, worse counsellor.

A una a una le foglie d'acacia si tolsero senza vento, col leggero fremito d'anima che passi.

Giovanni Pascoli
Prose

One by one, the acacia leaves dropped, without a hint of wind, with the slight quiver of a passing soul.

'A vita è tosta e nisciuno ti aiuta, o meglio ce sta chi t'aiuta ma una vota sola, pe' puté di': "t'aggio aiutato..."

Eduardo de Filippo
Questi fantasmi

Life is tough and no-one helps you, or rather there are those who help once, so that they can say, "I did help you..."

Abbiamo tutti dentro un mondo di cose; ciascuno un suo mondo di cose! E come possiamo intenderci, signore, se nelle parole ch'io dico metto il senso e il valore delle cose come sono dentro di me; mentre chi le ascolta, inevitabilmente le assume col senso e col valore che hanno per sé, del mondo com'egli l'ha dentro? Crediamo d'intenderci; non c'intendiamo mai!

Luigi Pirandello
Six Characters in Search of an Author

Each one of us has a whole world of things inside him; and each one of us has his own particular world. How can we understand each other if I put into my words the sense and the value of things as I understand them within myself... While at the same time whoever is listening to them inevitably assumes them to have the sense and value that they have for him... The sense and value that they have in the world that he has within him? We think we understand one another... But we never really do understand!

Ad un governo ingiusto nuoce più il martire che non il ribelle.

Massimo d'Azeglio
I miei ricordi

To an unjust government a martyr is more harmful than a rebel.

Addio, monti sorgenti dall'acque, ed elevati al cielo; cime inuguali, note a chi è cresciuto tra voi, e impresse nella sua mente, non meno che lo sia l'aspetto de' suoi più familiari.

Alessandro Manzoni
I Promessi sposi

Farewell, mountains springing from the waters and rising to the sky; rugged peaks, familiar to any man who has grown up in your midst, you are impressed upon his mind as clearly as the features of his nearest and dearest.

Ai mali estremi, estremi rimedi.

Proverb

For severe ills, severe remedies.

Al giovanile
Bollor tutto par lieve.

Vittorio Alfieri

To the fire of youth all tasks seem light.

Alla domanda: "Che cos'è l'arte?" si
potrebbe rispondere celiando (ma non
sarebbe una celia sciocca): che l'arte è ciò
che tutti sanno che cosa sia.

Benedetto Croce
Breviario di estetica

To the question "What is art?" one could
jokingly reply (although it would not be so
outlandish a joke) that art is that which everyone recognises as such.

Amici vicini e lontani, buona sera.

Ruggero Orlando
the opening greeting of RAI-TV's (Italian
state television) former New York news
correspondent

Good evening, friends near and far.

Amor, ch'al cor gentil ratto s'apprende.

Dante
Divina Commedia, Inferno

Love, whose lesson a gentle heart doth quickly
learn.

Amor mi mosse, che mi fa parlare.

Dante
Divina Commedia, Inferno

Love moved me, as it moves me now to speak.

Amore e 'l cor gentil sono una cosa.

Dante
Vita Nuova

Love and the gentle heart are but one thing.

Arcano è tutto, fuor che il nostro dolor.

Giacomo Leopardi
Ultimo canto di Saffo

All is dark, except our pain.

Arte piú misera, arte piú rotta
Non c'è del medico che va in condotta.

Arnaldo Fusinato
Il medico condotto

There's no more thankless nor tiring a job than
that of a country doctor. (Also translated as:
Of all the arts unhappy, arts accurst, that
of the general practitioner's the worst.)

Aspettare è ancora un'occupazione. È non
aspettar niente che è terribile.

Cesare Pavese
Il mestiere di vivere, September 15, 1946

Waiting is still an occupation. It's not
having anything to wait for that is terrible.

Assai acquista chi perdendo impara.
Michelangelo Buonarroti
Rime

Much is gained by those who learn from their losses.

Avrei voluto sentirmi scabro ed essenziale siccome i ciottoli che tu volvi, mangiati dalla salsedine.
Eugenio Montale
Mediterraneo

I should like to have felt myself rough and fundamental, like the pebbles you are turning over, eaten by the salt tides.

Bacco, tabacco e Venere
Riducon l'uomo in cenere.
Proverb

Wine, the weed and women will finish a man off. (Lit: Bacchus, tobacco and Venus reduce a man to ashes.)

Balaustrata di brezza
per appoggiare stasera
la mia malincolia.
Giuseppe Ungaretti
L'Allegria

Balustrade of breeze where leans my melancholy this evening.

Bella Italia, amate sponde
Pur vi torno a riveder!
Trema in petto e si confonde
L'alma oppressa dal piacer.
Vincenzo Monti
Bella Italia

*Beautiful Italy, beloved shores,
again at last I behold you!
My heart throbs in my breast,
and my soul is overwhelmed with joy.*

Berna è grande il doppio del cimitero di Vienna, ma ci si diverte solo la metà.
Luciano De Crescenzo

Berne is twice the size of the Vienna cemetery, but one enjoys Berne only half as much.

Biondo era e bello e di gentile aspetto.
Dante
Divina Commedia, Purgatorio

He was fair-haired and handsome and his aspect was noble.

C'è un' Ape che si posa
su un bottone di rosa:
lo succhia e se ne va...
Tutto sommato, la felicità
è una piccola cosa.
Trilussa (Carlo Alberto Salustro)
La felicità

*A bee on a rosebud comes to light,
Drinks the nectar and then takes flight:
All things considered, how slight
Are the things which bring us most delight.*

C'è un tale bisogno d'amore nel mondo, che certe donne amano persino il proprio marito.
Pitigrilli (Dino Segre)

There is such a need for love in the world that some women even love their own husbands.

Carneade! Chi era costui?
           Alessandro Manzoni
              I promessi sposi

Carneades! Now who was he?

Caro m'è il sonno e piú l'esser di sasso,
Mentre che 'l danno e la vergogna la dura.
Non veder, non sentir m'è gran ventura;
Però non mi destar, deh! parla basso.
       Michelangelo Buonarroti
           Rime, Epigramma

Slumber is sweet, but it were sweeter still
To turn to stone while shame and sorrow last,
Nor see, nor hear, and so be freed from ill;
Ah, wake me not! Whisper as you go past!

Casta Diva che inargenti queste sacre piante.
           Felice Romani
          Bellini's *Norma*

Chaste goddess, who silvers these ancient
sacred trees.

Celeste Aida, forma divina.
         Antonio Ghislanzoni
           Verdi's *Aida*

Heavenly Aida, divine form.

Certo, certissimo, anzi probabile.
           Ennio Flaiano
          Diario notturno

Of course, most certainly. Or rather, probably.

Cessate d'uccidere i morti,
Non gridate piú, non gridate
Se li volete ancora udire,
Se sperate di non perire.
Hanno l'impercettibile sussurro,
Non fanno piú rumore
Del crescere dell'erba,
Lieta dove non passa l'uomo.
           Giuseppe Ungaretti
    Sentimento del tempo, Non gridate piú

Stop killing the dead,
Cry out no more, do not cry out
If you would hear them still,
If you would hope not to die.
Their whisper is slight,
They are no louder
Than the growing of grass,
Happy where man does not pass.

Che deve far'altro un Re, che cercar sempre
Di far maggior lo stato, di acquistarsi
Maggior potenza?
      Cinthio Giambattista Giraldi
            Euphimia

What else should a king do, but always try to
increase his state and acquire greater power for
himself?

Che fai tu, luna, in ciel? dimmi, che fai,
Silenziosa luna?
Sorgi la sera, e vai,
Contemplando i deserti; indi ti posi.
           Giacomo Leopardi
 Canto notturno di un pastore errante dell'Asia

What are you doing, moon, there in the sky?
Tell me, what are you doing, silent moon?
You rise at evening, then go,
Gazing upon the deserts, and then set.

Che gelida manina! Se la lasci riscaldar.
   Giuseppe Giacosa and **Luigi Illica**
     Puccini's *La Bohème*

Your tiny hand is frozen. Let me warm it into life.

Che giova nelle fata dar di cozzo?
      Dante
   Divina Commedia, Inferno

What do you gain by locking horns with fate?

Che la pace mal finge nel volto
Chi sente la guerra nel cor.
    Pietro Metastasio

It is difficult for a man who has war in his heart to wear a look of peace upon his brow.

Chi la pace non vuol, la guerra s'abbia.
    Torquato Tasso
   Gerusalemme liberata

He who doesn't want peace shall have war.

Che molte volte al fatto il dir vien meno
      Dante
   Divina Commedia, Inferno

I often have to tell less than I saw.

Che paese l'Italia: mi sono distratto un
attimo e non è successo niente.
  Tullio Pericoli and **Emanuele Pirella**

What a country Italy is: I was distracted for a second and nothing at all happened.

Chè sovente addivien che 'l saggio e 'l forte
Fabbro a sè stesso è di beata sorte.
    Torquato Tasso
   Gerusalemme liberata

The wise and bold man often creates his own good fortune.

Che ti fa ciò che quivi si pispiglia? Vien
dietro a me, e lascia dir le genti: sta come
torre ferma, che non crolla già mai la cima
per soffiar di venti.
      Dante
   Divina Commedia, Purgatorio

Why should you care about what's whispered here? Come follow me, and let these people talk: stand like a sturdy tower that does not shake its summit though the winds may blast.

Che'l nome di Dio e di guadagno.
    Francesco Datini
  motto on the accounting books of
  Francesco Datini, the Merchant of Prato

In the name of God and of profit.

Chi ama l'Italia mi segua!
    Giuseppe Garibaldi

He who loves Italy, follow me!

Chi fa presto fa bene, e chi fa subito fa meglio.

Carlo Goldoni
Il Talismano

It is good to act swiftly, and even better to act suddenly.

Chi ha denti, non ha pane; e chi ha pane, non ha denti.

Proverb

He who has teeth, has no bread; and he who has bread, has no teeth.

Chi non fa, non falla.

Proverb

He who does nothing makes no mistakes.

Chi non punisce il male comanda lo si faccia.

Leonardo da Vinci
Scritti letterari

He who does not punish evil commands it to be done.

Chi non risica non rosica.

Proverb

He who risks not, nibbles not.

Chi non trova un biografo deve inventare la propria vita da solo.

Giovanni Guareschi

He who doesn't find a biographer must invent his own life.

Chi sa fare la musica la fa, chi la sa fare meno la insegna, chi la sa fare ancora meno la organizza, chi la sa fare cosí cosí la critica.

Luciano Pavarotti

Those who know how to make music do so; those who know a little less, teach it; those who know less still, arrange it; and those who do it only so-so, criticize.

Chi si leva a tempo, fa buona giornata e si può riposare all'albergo.

Niccolò Dell'Ammannato

The early riser makes a good profit and can rest at night in an inn.

Chi trova l'amico, trova il tesoro, e se in bilancia metti l'oro e l'argento, piú l'amico pesa.

Carlo Gozzi

He who has found a friend has found a treasure, and if you add gold and silver to the equation, the friendship is worth still more.

Chi va piano va sano, e chi va sano va lontano.

Proverb
(used by Carlo Goldoni in *I Volponi*, with the wording: "Chi va piano va sano e va lontano.")

He who goes slowly goes wisely, and he who goes wisely goes far.

Chi vuol essere ricco in un dí, è impiccato
in un anno.
Leonardo da Vinci
Scritti letterari

He who seeks wealth in a day will hang in a
year.

Chiamavi 'l cielo 'ntorno vi si gira,
mostrandovi le sue bellezze etterne,
e l'occhio vostro pur a terra mira.
Dante
Divina Commedia, Purgatorio

Heaven would call you and encircle you;
would show you its eternal beauties; yet your
eyes would only see the ground.

Chiare fresche e dolci acque ove le belle
membra pose colei che sola a me par
donna.
Francesco Petrarch
Chiare fresche e dolci acque

Clear, fresh and sweet waters where she who
alone seems woman to me rested her lovely
limbs.

Chiodo schiaccia chiodo, ma quattro
chiodi di seguito formano una croce.
Cesare Pavese

One pain drives out another, but four in a row
will crucify you.

Co' nemici la clemenza è bella piú assai
che la vendetta.
Vincenzo Monti
Galcotto Manfredi

Clemency towards the enemy is better than
starting a vendetta.

Cogli la rosa, o ninfa, or ch'è il bel tempo.
Lorenzo Medici
Corinto

Gather the rose, o nymph, while the weather is
fair.

Cogliam' la rosa in sul mattino adorno
Di questo di che tosto il seren perde.
Torquato Tasso
Gerusalemme liberata

Gather the rose while time thou hast.
Short is the day once it has begun.

Col mare
mi sono fatto
una bara
di freschezza
Giuseppe Ungaretti
L'Allegria

Of the sea I have made me a coffin of coolness.

Colui che non intende ed ode.
Dante
Divina Commedia, Paradise

He who hears and does not understand.

Come dell'oro il fuoco
Scopre le masse impure,
Scoprono le sventure
De' falsi amici il cor.

Pietro Metastasio
Olimpiade

As fire is the test of pure gold, adversity is the test of true friendship.

Come esistono oratori balbuzienti, umoristi tristi, parrucchieri calvi, potrebbero esistere benissimo anche dei politici onesti.

Dario Fo

Just as there are stuttering orators, sad comics, bald hairdressers, so too there could be honest politicians.

Considerate se questo è un uomo
Che lavora nel fango
Che non conosce la pace
Che lotta per mezzo pane
Che muore per un sì o per un no.
Considerate se questa è una donna,
Senza capelli e senza nome
Senza piú forza di ricordare
Vuoti gli occhi e freddo il grembo
Come una rana d'inverno.

Primo Levi
introductory poem to *Se questo è un uomo*

Reflect whether this is a man
Who toils in the mud
Who knows not peace
Who squabbles for a crust of bread
Who perishes because of a "yes" or "no".
Reflect whether this is a woman
Who has had her hair shorn and is nameless,
Without the strength to remember,
Vacant eyes and frozen loins
Like a frog stranded in the winter.

Coraggio, il meglio è passato.

Ennio Flaiano

Courage, the best has passed.

Cosí è se vi pare.

Luigi Pirandello
title of a play

So it is, if you think so.

Cosí fan tutte.

Lorenzo Da Ponte
title of Mozart's opera

That's what all women do.

Curioso fatto, che il vivere arrabbiato piaccia tanto! Vi si pone una specie d'eroismo. Se l'oggetto contro cui ieri si fremeva è morto, se ne cerca subito un altro. "Di chi mi lamenterò oggi? Chi odierò? Sarebbe mai quello il mostro?... Oh gioia! L'ho trovato."

Silvio Pellico
Le mie prigioni

What a strange thing it is, that living with anger is all the rage! It becomes a type of heroism. If the object of yesterday's vexation drops dead, one goes right out in search of another. "About whom will I complain about today? Whom can I hate? Might it just be that monster over there?... Oh great! I've found him!"

Dal dire al fare c'è di mezzo il mare.

Proverb

Between saying and doing lies a divide as great as the sea.

Datemi una nota della lavandaia e la metterò in musica.

Gioacchino Rossini
attrib.

Give me a laundry bill and I will put it to music.

Della verità e del bene non si ride. Ecco perché Cristo non rideva. Il riso è fomite di dubbio.

Umberto Eco
The Name of the Rose

One does not laugh about truth or goodness. That is why Christ never laughed. Laughter is a cause of doubt.

Dolce e chiara è la notte e senza vento, e queta sovra i tetti e in mezzo agli orti Posa la luna, e di lontan rivela serena ogni montagna.

Giacomo Leopardi
La sera del dì di festa

The night is soft and clear, and no wind blows, the quiet moon stands over roofs and orchards, revealing from afar each peaceful mountain.

Dove forza non val giunga l'inganno.

Pietro Metastasio
Didone abbandonata

Where force cannot prevail, cunning steps in.

E avanti a lui tremava tutta Roma.

Giuseppe Giacosa and **Luigi Illica**
Puccini's *Tosca*
Tosca, standing over Scarpia's body

Before him all Rome trembled.

E caddi, come corpo morto cade.

Dante
Divina Commedia, Inferno

Then swooning, to the ground like a corpse he fell.

E del mio vaneggiar vergogna è 'l frutto e'l pentersi e'l conoscer chiaramente che quanto piace al mondo è breve sogno.

Francesco Petrarch
Voi ch'ascoltate in rime sparse il suono

And the fruit of my vanity is shame, and repentance, and the clear knowledge that whatever the world finds pleasing is but a brief dream.

'E denare teneno 'e piede, 'e denare teneno 'e rote.

Eduardo De Filippo
Il sindaco del rione Sanità

Money has feet, money has wheels.

E dietro la venia sí lunga tratta
di gente, ch'io non avei mai creduto,
che morte tanta n'avesse disfatta.

Dante
Divina Commedia, Inferno
about the Trimmers

*And behind came so long a train of people that
I should never have believed death had undone
so many.*

È figlie so' figlie.

Eduardo De Filippo
Filumena Marturana

A child is a child.

È l'alba: si chiudono i petali
un poco gualciti; si cova,
dentro l'urna molle e segreta,
non so che felicità nuova.

Giovanni Pascoli
The Jasmine at Night

*It is dawn: the petals close, slightly crumpled;
some new happiness nests in the soft and secret
urn, I cannot say what.*

E l'armonia
vince di mille secoli il silenzio.

Ugo Foscolo
Dei sepolcri

*Harmony overcomes the silence of a thousand
centuries.*

È la fede degli amanti
come l'Araba fenice:
che vi sia ciascun lo dice,
dove sia, nessun lo sa.

Pietro Metastasio
Demetrio

*The faithfulness of lovers is like the Arabian
phoenix: everyone says that it does exist, but
exactly where, nobody knows.*

E la nave va.

Federico Fellini
title of a film

And the ship departs.

E li uomini hanno meno respetto a offend-
ere uno che si facci amare che uno che
facci temere; perché l'amore è tenuto da un
vinculo di obligo, il quale, per essere li
uomini tristi, da ogni occasione di propria
utilità è rotto; ma il timore è tenuto da una
paura di pena che non ti abbandona mai.

Niccolò Machiavelli
The Prince

*Men hesitate less to offend one who makes
himself loved than one who makes himself
feared; for love is held by a chain of obligation,
which, men being selfish, is broken whenever
it serves their purpose; but fear is maintained
by a dread of punishment, which never fails.*

È meglio aver oggi un uovo, che domani
una gallina.

Proverb

*It is better to have an egg today than a hen
tomorrow.*

È meno male non aver leggi, che violarle
ogni giorno.

Ugo Foscolo
Opere

It is better not to have laws than to break them
every day.

È minestra senza sale
Nobilità senza il poter.

Carlo Goldoni
Il re alla caccia

Nobility without power is like soup without
salt.

È natural' degli uomini, d'essere benigni,
e mansueti estimatori delle azioni pro-
prie, ma severissimi censori delle azioni
d'altri.

Francesco Guicciardini

It is in the nature of men to look benignly and
gently upon their own acts, but to judge the
actions of others most severely.

E nelle azioni di tutti gli uomini, e mas-
sime de' principi, dove non è iudizio a chi
reclamare, si guarda al fine. Facci dunque
uno principe di vincere a mantenere lo
stato: e mezzi saranno sempre iudicati
onorevoli e da ciascuno laudate.

Niccolò Machiavelli
The Prince

In the actions of men, and especially of princes,
from which there is no appeal, the result is
what matters. Let a prince therefore aim at
conquering and maintaining the state, and the
means will always be judged honourable and
praised by everyone.

E piove su i nostri volti silvani,
Piove su le nostre mani ignude,
Su i nostri vestimenti leggieri,
Su i freschi pensieri che l'anima schiude
                                    novella,
Su la favola bella che ieri
m'illuse, che oggi ti illude,
O Ermione.

Gabriele D'Annunzio
Alcyone: La pioggia nel pineto

And it rains upon our woodwild faces, it rains
on our naked hands, on our light clothes, on
the fresh thoughts which the soul, renewed,
discloses, on the lovely fable that yesterday
beguiled me, that today beguiles you, O
Hermione.

E quindi uscimmo a vivander le stella.
Dante
Divina Commedia, Inferno

Thence we came forth to see the stars again.

È un tipico caso di convergenze parallele.
Aldo Moro
Moro's elliptical way of describing Christian
Democrat and Communist cooperation; in a
speech at Benevento, November 18, 1977

It is a classic case of converging parallels.

E'n la sua volontade è nostra pace.

Dante
Divina Commedia, Paradiso

In his will is our peace.

Eppur si muove!

Galilei Galileo
having recanted before the Pope

Nevertheless it does move.

Eran trecento, eran giovani e forti,
e sono morti!

Luigi Mercantini
La spigolatrice di Sapri

They were three hundred; they were young and strong; and now they are dead!

Essere donna è cosí affascinante. È
un'avventura che richiede un tale coraggio, una sfida che non annoia mai.

Oriana Fallaci
Intervista a un bambino mai nato

To be a woman is so fascinating. It's an adventure that demands such courage, a challenge that is never boring.

Figaro... Figaro...
Son qua, son qua.
Figaro qua, Figaro là,
Figaro su, Figaro giú
Pronto prontissimo
Son come il fulmine:

Cesare Sterbini
Rossini's *Il Barbiere di Siviglia*

Figaro... Figaro...
I'm here, I'm here
Figaro... I'm here, Figaro... I'm there
Figaro here, Figaro there
Figaro up, Figaro down
I'm like a streak of lightning:

Fiorentin mangia fagioli
Lecca piatti e tovaglioli.

Florentine saying

The Florentine who eats beans
licks the plate and tablecloth clean

Forse che sì forse che no.

Gabriele D'Annunzio
title of a book (inspired by a motto incised
on the ceiling of the Ducal Palace at Mantua,
which, in turn, was inspired by an old
Tuscan expression)

Perhaps yes, perhaps no.

Fratelli d'Italia
L'Italia s'è desta;
Dell'elmo di Scipio
S'è cinta la testa.

Goffredo Mameli
Fratelli d'Italia
first lines of the Italian national anthem

Brothers of Italy, Italy has awakened and placed the helmet of Scipio on her head.

Fuoco e fiamme per un anno, cenere per trenta.

Giuseppe Tomasi di Lampedusa

Fire and flames for one year, ashes for thirty.

Genti v'eran con occhi tardi e gravi, di grande autorità ne' lor sembianti; parlavan rado, con voci soavi.

Dante
Divina Commedia, Inferno

There people were whose eyes were calm and grave, whose bearing told of great authority; they spoke seldom and always quietly.

Giusto! l'ha detto! lo scandalo è il concime della democrazia.

Dario Fo
Accidental Death of an Anarchist

Right! You said it! Scandal is the fertilizer of democracy.

Gli italiani guadagnano netto, ma vivono lordo.

Giuseppe Saragat

Italians earn net, but they live gross.

Gli italiani non hanno costumi; essi hanno delle usanze.

Giacomo Leopardi
Zibaldone

The Italians have no customs: they only have habits.

Gli italiani sono sempre pronti a correre in soccorso dei vincitori.

Ennio Flaiano

Italians are always ready to rush to the aid of winners.

Gli uomini nelle cose generali s'ingannano assai, nelle particolari non tanto.

Niccolò Machiavelli
The Prince

Men are apt to deceive themselves over generalities, less so over particulars.

Gli uomini sono buoni coi morti quasi quanto son cattivi coi vivi.

Indro Montanelli
Gli incontri

Men are kindly disposed towards the dead almost as much as they are cruelly disposed towards the living.

Godiamoci il papato poiché Dio ce lo ha dato!

Pope Leo X
attrib.

God has given us the Papacy: now let us enjoy it.

Guarda com'entri e di cui tu ti fide.

Dante
Divina Commedia, Inferno

Take care how you enter and in whom you trust.

Ha da passà 'a nuttata.
Eduardo De Filippo
Napoli milionaria!

We must get through the night.

Hanno un modo d'inginocchiarsi, che è
piúttosto uno stare in piedi con le gambe
piegate: al contrario di tutti gli altri italiani, che anche quando stan ritti sembra
che stiano in ginocchio.
Curzio Malaparte (Kurt Erich Suckert)
Maledetti Toscani

*They have a way of kneeling that is a sort of
standing straight with bent legs, whereas all
other Italians, even when they stand straight,
look as though they are kneeling.*

Ho bisogno di mille morti per sedermi al
tavolo della pace.
Benito Mussolini

*I need one thousand dead to sit down at the
peace table.*

I benefizi debbono scriversi in bronzo e le
ingiurie nell'aria
Galilei Galileo
Opere

*Good things should be cast in bronze and bad
ones cast to the winds.*

I fantasmi non esistono, li abbiamo creati
noi, siamo noi i fantasmi.
Eduardo De Filippo
Questi fantasmi

*There are no such things as ghosts. It is we
who have invented them. We are the ghosts.*

I giovani hanno la memoria corta, e hanno
gli occhi per guardare solo a levante; e a
ponente non ci guardano altro che i vecchi,
quelli che hanno visto tramontare il sole
tante volte.
Giovanni Verga
I Malavoglia

*The young have short memories and gaze only
eastward. Those who look west are the elderly,
who have already seen the sun set many times
before.*

I miracoli si possono fare, ma con il sudore.
Giovanni Agnelli
from an interview in *Corriere della Sera*, 1994

Miracles can be achieved, but only with sweat.

I pensieri stretti e il viso sciolto.
Scipione Alberti

Secret thoughts and open countenance [will
go safely over the whole world].

I privilegi si accantonano ma non si
perdono mai.
Luigi Pintor
Servabo: Il matrimonio

*Privileges may be set aside, but they are never
lost.*

I timidi non hanno, meno amor proprio
che gli arroganti; anzi piú, o vogliamo dire
piú sensitivo; e perció temono.

Giacomo Leopardi
Pensieri

The timid have no less self-esteem than the
arrogant, indeed more, or perhaps a more
sensitive kind; and that is why they are afraid.

Il bel paese
Ch'Appenin parte, e'l mar
circonda e l'Alpe

Francesco Petrarch
Sonetto in vita di M. Laura

The lovely land ridged by the Apennines,
which sea and Alps environ.

Il buon si perde,
Talor cercando il meglio.

Pietro Metastasio
Ipermestra

Sometimes good is lost in trying to achieve
better.

Il diavolo fa le pentole, ma non i coperchi.

Proverb

The devil makes pots, but he doesn't make the
lids (i.e. you can conceal a bad deed but it's
liable to be exposed).

Il diavolo invecchioto, si fece frato.

Proverb

The devil grows old, he becomes a friar.

Il falso amico è come l'ombra che ci segue
fin che dura il sole.

Carlo Dossi
Note azzurre

The false friend is like a shadow that follows
you as long as there is daylight.

Il giovinetto cor s'appaga e gode
Del dolce suon della verace lode.

Torquato Tasso
Gerusalemme liberata

The young one's heart is fulfilled and enjoys
The sweet sound of true praise.

Il Maestro di color che sanno.

Dante
(about Aristotle)
Divina Commedia, Inferno

The Master of them that know.

Il mentitore dovrebbe tener presente che
per essere creduto non bisogna dire che le
menzogne necessarie.

Italo Svevo
La coscienza di Zeno

The liar ought to bear in mind that, in order to
be believed, he should tell only those lies which
are necessary.

Il mio motto è sempre stato: pessimismo dell'intelligenza, ottimismo della volontà.

Antonio Gramsci
Lettere dal carcere

My motto has always been: pessimism of mind and optimism of will.

Il mondo è un bel libro, ma poco serve a chi non lo sa leggere.

Carlo Goldoni

The world is a beautiful book but it is of little use to him who cannot read it.

Il peggio che può capitare a un genio è di essere compreso.

Ennio Flaiano

The worst thing that could happen to a genius is to be understood.

Il Piave mormorava
Calmo e placido al passaggio.

E. A. Mario (Gioviano E. Gaeta)
I canti delle trincee

The Piave [river] murmured quietly and peacefully in passing.

Il pittoresco ci ha fregati per tre secoli.

Benito Mussolini
party speech of 25 October, 1938

The picturesque has duped us for three centuries.

Il piú bel fior ne coglie.

Motto of the Accademia della Crusca
which oversees the "purity of the Italian language"

It collects only the finest flowers.

Il potere logora chi non ce l'ha.

Giulio Andreotti

Power wears down those who don't have it.

Il sogno è vita.

Luigi Pirandello
La vita che ti diedi

Dreams are life.

*Il treno arriva all'orario.

Infanta Eulalia of Spain
quoting the first observable advantage of Mussolini's rule in Italy

The train is on time.

Il vero amore é una quiete accesa.

Giuseppe Ungaretti
Sentimento del tempo, Silenzio in Liguria

True love is an illuminated calm.

* Compare p.241

Immensità s'annega il pensier mio: E il naufragar m'è dolce in questo mare.

Giacomo Leopardi
L'infinito

In this immensity my thought is drowned; and sweet it is to me to be a shipwreck in this sea.

In Italia quando una cosa non è piú proibita diventa obbligatoria.

Pietro Nenni

In Italy, when something is no longer forbidden, it becomes obligatory.

In questa vita per lo piú o si pena, o si spera, e poche volte si gode.

Carlo Goldoni
Arlecchino – Servitore di due padroni

In this life, for the most part, you suffer or you hope, only rarely do you enjoy it.

In Russia sta proprio cambiando tutto. Ho visto dei bambini che mangiavano i comunisti.

Michele Mozzati and Gino Vignali

In Russia, things are really changing. I saw some children eating communists.

Inglese italianizzato, Diavolo incarnato.

Proverb

An Englishman Italianized is the devil incarnate.

Io parlo per ver dire
Non per odio d'altrui nè per disprezzo.

Francesco Petrarch
Canzoni sopra vari argomenti, IV

*I speak to tell the truth
And not in hatred or contempt of others.*

L'amico mio, e non della ventura.

Dante
Divina Commedia, Inferno

My friend, who is no friend of Fortune.

L'amor che move il sole e l'altre stelle.

Dante
Divina Commedia, Paradiso; last line

The love that moves the sun and the other stars.

L'Angelo della famiglia è la Donna. Madre, sposa, sorella, la Donna è la carezza della vita, la soavità dell'affetto diffusa sulle sue fatiche, un riflesso sull'individuo della Provvidenza amorevole che veglia sull'Umanitá.

Giuseppe Mazzini
Opere scelte

The Guardian Angel of the family is the woman. Mother, wife and sister, she is the gentle caress of life, sweet affection diffused throughout her toils, an individual reflection of loving Providence, keeping watch over humanity.

L'aritmetica non è un'opinione.

attrib. **Bernardino Grimaldi**

Arithmetic is not an opinion.

L'arte si regge unicamente sulla fantasia: la sola sua ricchezza sono le immagini. Non classifica gli oggetti, non li pronunzia reali o immaginari, non li qualifica, non li definisce: li sente e rappresenta. Niente di piú.

Benedetto Croce
Problemi di Estetica

Art is controlled purely by the imagination. Images are its only wealth. It does not classify objects, does not pronounce them real or imaginary, does not qualify them, does not define them; it feels and presents them. Nothing more.

L'arte stà nel deformare.

Ettore Petrolini
on acting
Al mio pubblico: I pirati della varietà

The art of distortion.

L'attimo...fuggiva, oh, che altro può fare un attimo?

Carlo Emilio Gadda
Quel pasticciaccio brutto de via Merulana

The moment flashed by. Well, what else could a moment do?

L'educazione è il pane dell'anima.

Giuseppe Mazzini
Dei doveri dell'uomo

Education is the bread of the soul.

L'errore parla con una doppia voce, una delle quali afferma il falso, ma l'altra lo smentisce.

Benedetto Croce
Breviario di estetica

Error speaks with two tongues, one of which utters a falsehood, while the other denies it.

L'esperienza non falla mai, ma sol fallan i nostri giudizi promettendosi di lei cose che non sono in sua potestà.

Leonardo da Vinci
The Notebooks

Experience never errs; it is only our judgement that errs in promising itself things that experience has shown are not possible.

L'essere canzonati un pochino, e qualche volta un po' di piú, è cosa che attrae molto, tanto gli uomini che le donne, piú assai che l'essere trattati con serietà e rispetto.

Aldo Palazzeschi
Le Sorelle Materassi

To be ribbed a little – and sometimes even a bit more – really appeals to men as well as women far more than to be taken seriously and respectfully

L'invidia è come una palla di gomma che più la spingi sotto e più ti torna a galla.

Alberto Moravia
Racconti romani

Envy is like a rubber ball: the more you push it under, the more it bobs to the surface.

L'ispettore delle imposte crede esattamente il doppio di quello che gli si dice.

Ugo Tognazzi

The tax inspector believes exactly double what he is told.

L'Italia si sta tirando fuori il suo dente; che ciascuno degli altri Paesi provi a cavare il suo di dente.

Antonio Di Pietro
speech delivered in Toronto, 1993

Italy is pulling out her own rotten teeth; let all other countries pull out their own.

L'operaio conosce 300 parole, il padrone 1000. Per questo lui è il padrone.

Dario Fo
Grande Pantomima

The worker knows 300 words while the boss knows 1000. That is why he is the boss.

L'umanità...la divido in cinque categorie: gli uomini, i mezz'uomini, gli uominicchi, i pigliainculo e i quaquaraquà.

Leonardo Sciascia

I divide humanity into five categories: men, half-men, arse-crawlers, pigmies and duck-like quackers.

L'umiltà è una virtù stupenda. Ma non quando si esercita nella dichiarazione dei redditi.

Giulio Andreotti

Humility is a splendid virtue. But not when used in declaring income.

L'uomo è nato per soffrire, e ci riesce benissimo.

Roberto Gervaso

Man was born to suffer and succeeds at it very well.

L'uomo ha grande discorso, del quale la più parte è vano e falso; gli animali l'hanno piccolo, ma è utile e vero. È meglio la piccola certezza che la grande bugia.

Leonardo da Vinci
Scritti letterari

Men talk largely and most of it is pointless and incorrect. Animals on the other hand speak but little. What they say is useful and true. Thus a small certainty is better than a big lie.

L'uomo infelice ed arrabbiato è tremenda-mente ingegnoso a calunniare i suoi simili e lo stesso Creatore. L'ira è più immorale, più scellerata che generalmente non si pensa.

Silvio Pellico
Le mie prigioni

The unhappy and angry man is extremely clever at slandering his fellow men and even his Creator. Anger is more immoral, more wicked, than one generally thinks.

L'Uomo qualunque.

Guglielmo Giannini
title of a weekly newspaper

The ordinary man.

La bellissima e famosissima figlia di Roma, Fiorenza.

Dante
Il Convivio

Rome's most beautiful and most famous daughter, Florence.

La botte piena non fa rumore.

Proverb

The full barrel makes no noise.

La buona fortuna degli uomini è spesso il maggior inimico che abbiano.

Francesco Guicciardini
Ricordi politici e civili

Man's good fortune is frequently his worst enemy.

La camera a gas è l'unico punto di carità, nel campo di concentramento.

Elsa Morante
La storia

The gas chamber is the only charitable place in the concentration camp.

La civiltà contadina è una civiltà senza stato, e senza esercito: le sue guerre non possono essere che questi scoppi di rivolta; e sono sempre, per forza, delle disperate sconfitte.

Carlo Levi
Cristo si è fermato a Eboli

The peasant world has neither government nor army; its wars are only sporadic outbursts of revolt, doomed to repression.

La commedia è finita.

Ruggiero Leoncavallo
I Pagliacci; last line

The comedy is ended.

La critica è un fucile molto bello: deve sparare raramente!

Benedetto Croce

Criticism is like a very beautiful gun: it should be fired rarely!

La donna è mobile
qual piuma al vento,
muta d'accento
e di pensiero.
Sempre un amabile
leggiadro viso,
in pianto o in riso,
è menzognero.

Francesco Maria Piave
Verdi's *Rigoletto*

*Woman is fickle,
as a feather in the wind,
she changes her tune
and her thoughts.
A sweet, fair face,
in tears or in laughter,
always deceives us.*

La forza d'un bel viso a che mi prone?
C'altro non è c'al mondo mi diletti:
ascender vivo fra gli spiriti eletti, per
grazia tal, c'ogn'altra par men buona.
Michelangelo Buonarroti

What does the power of a beautiful face spur
me to? Nothing on earth I hold so rich a prize:
To soar, while still alive, to paradise, by way of
such incomparable grace.

La gola e 'l sonno e l'oziose piume hanno
del mondo ogni virtù sbandita; ond'è dal
corso suo quasi smarrita nostra natura,
vinta dal costume.
Francesco Petrarch

Gluttony and dullness and slothful couches
have banished every virtue from the world;
so that our nature, overcome by habit,
has all but lost the way.

La legge della Vita è PROGRESSO.
Giuseppe Mazzini
Dei doveri dell'uomo

The law of life is PROGRESS.

La lingua batte dove il dente duole.
Proverb

The tongue always touches the aching tooth.

La maggior saviezza che sia, è conoscere
se stesso.
Galilei Galileo
Opere

The greatest wisdom there is is to know
oneself.

La nostra individualità è una parvenza
fissata dal nome, cioè da una convenzione.
Benedetto Croce
Etica e politica: Frammenti di etica

One's individuality is seemingly affixed to a
name, in short, to a convention.

La parola d'ordine è vincere. E vinceremo.
Benito Mussolini
on declaring war against France

The password is win. And win we will.

La Pittura è una Poesia muta, e la Poesia è
una Pittura cieca.
Leonardo da Vinci

Painting is a mute poem and poetry a blind
painting.

La ricchezza della vita è fatta di ricordi,
dimenticati.
Cesare Pavese
Il mestiere di vivere

Life's wealth is in its memories, forgotten
memories.

La ricchezza nei molti secoli di esistenza
si era mutata in ornamento, in lusso, in
piaceri; soltanto in questo.
Giuseppe Tomasi di Lampedusa
Il Gattopardo

The wealth of centuries had been reduced to
ornament, luxury, pleasure and nothing more.

La vita vi fu ... data da Dio perché ne usiate a benefizio dell'umanitá ...Dovete educarvi ed educare, perfezionarvi e perfezionare.

Giuseppe Mazzini
Doveri dell'uomo

Life is given by God to be used for the benefit of mankind. You must educate yourselves and teach others. You must better yourselves and better others.

Largo! Sono il poeta!
Io vengo da lontano,
il mondo ò traversato
per venire a trovare
la mia creatura da cantare!

Aldo Palazzeschi
L'incendiario: L'incendiario

Make way! I am the poet!
I've come from afar,
I've travelled the globe
to come and find
my muse of song!

Lasciate ogni speranza, voi ch'entrate.

Dante
Divina Commedia, Inferno

Abandon all hope, ye who enter here.

Lasso! non di diamante, ma d'un vetro
Veggio di man cadermi ogni speranza:
E tutti miei pensier romper nel mezzo.

Francesco Petrarch
Sonnets

Ah, wretched me! Now I can see only too well that each hope, unlike a diamond, is but a fragile mirror shattered into fragments.

Laudato si', mi' Signore, per sor' aqua, la quale è molto utile et humile et pretiosa et casta.

St Francis
Cantico delle creature

Be praised, my Lord, for sister water, who is very useful and humble and chaste.

Laudato si', mi' Signore, per sora luna e le stelle: in celu l'hai create clarite preziose e belle.

Ibid

Be praised, my Lord, for sister moon and the stars in heaven you have made them clear and precious and lovely.

Laudato sie, mi' Signore, cum tucte le tue creature, spetialmente messer lo frate sole, lo qual'è iorno, et allumini noi per lui. Et ellu è bellu e radiante cum grande splendore: de te, Altissimo, porta significatione.

Ibid

Be praised, my Lord, with all your creatures, especially master brother sun, who brings day, and by whom you give us light. He is fair and radiant with a great splendour – he draws his meaning, most High, from you.

Lavorare stanca.

Cesare Pavese
title of a book

Work is tiring.

Le bugie sono per natura cosí feconde, che una ne suole partorir cento.

Carlo Goldoni
Il bugiardo

Lies are, by nature, so fertile that one begets a hundred.

Le cose tutte quante
Han ordine tra loro.

Dante
Divina Commedia, Paradiso

Among all things there reigns an order.

Le iniurie si debbano fare tutte insieme, acciò che, assaporandosi meno, offendino meno: e benefizii si debbano fare a poco a poco, acciò si assaporino meglio.

Niccolò Machiavelli
The Prince

Injuries should be inflicted all together, so that, being less tasted, they will give less offence. Benefits should be granted little by little, so that they may be better enjoyed.

Le lezioni non si danno, si prendono.

Cesare Pavese
Il mestiere di vivere

Lessons are not given. They are taken.

Li uomini dimenticano piú presto la morte del padre che la perdita del patrimonio.

Niccolò Machiavelli

Men forget the death of their fathers more rapidly than the loss of their inheritance.

Libertà va cercando, ch'è sí cara, come sa chi per lei vita rifiuta.

Dante
Divina Commedia, Purgatorio

He goes in search of Liberty, and how dear that is, as he who renounces life for her well knows.

Libro e moschetto, fascista perfetto.

Benito Mussolini
Il Libro Unico
Italian schoolchildren's textbook

A book and a gun make a perfect Fascist.

Lo sanno tutti che razza di egoisti sono i morti.

Curzio Malaparte (Kurt Erich Suckert)
La Pelle

Everyone knows what a bunch of egoists the dead are.

Lo spirito è pronto, ma la carne è debole.

Francesco Petrarch
Rapido fiume, che d'alpestra vena

The spirit is willing but the flesh is weak.

Lo spendere quello d'altri non ti toglie
reputazione, ma te ne aggiunge.

Niccolò Machiavelli
The Prince

You will increase rather than diminish your
reputation by spending the wealth of others.

M'illumino d'immenso

Giuseppe Ungaretti
L'Allegria; Mattina

I fill myself with the light of immensity.

Ma facciam noi ciò che a noi fare conviene;
Darà il Ciel, darà il mondo ai piú forti!

Torquato Tasso

Let us do what suits us; Heaven will provide,
and give the world to the ablest.

Mal comune mezzo gaudio.

Proverb

A sorrow shared is almost a joy.

Me ne frego.

Gabriele D'Annunzio
motto during the seizure of Fiume

I don't give a damn.

Maledetta sei tu, antica lupa, che piú di
altre bestie ha preda per la tua fame sanza
fine cupa!

Dante
Divina Commedia, Purgatorio

May you be damned, o ancient wolf, whose
power can claim more prey than all other
beasts, for your hunger is deep and insatiable.

Meglio un morto in case che un pisano
all'uscio.

Italian insult
though not always about Pisans

It is better to have a corpse in the house than a
Pisan on your doorstep.

Memento Audere Semper. (Ricorda di
osare sempre.)

Gabriele D'Annunzio
motto created by D'Annunzio

Remember always to dare.

Meriggiare pallido e assorto
Presso un rovente muro d'orto.

Eugenio Montale
Meriggiare pallido e assorto

To laze at noon, pale and absorbed,
by a scorching garden wall.

Mi accade spesso di svegliarmi di notte e
cominciare a pensare a una serie di gravi
problemi e decidere di parlarne col Papa.
Poi mi sveglio completamente e mi ricordo
che Io sono il Papa!

Pope John XXIII

It often happens that I wake up in the night
and begin to think about a serious problem and
decide I must tell the Pope about it. Then I
wake up completely and remember I am the
Pope!

Mi chiamano Mimì, ma il mio nome è Lucia.

Giuseppe Giacosa and **Luigi Illica**
Puccini's *La Bohème*

They call me Mimi, but my name is Lucia.

Morfina questo rozzo sostituto chimico dello stoicismo antico, della rassegnazione cristiana.

Giuseppe Tomasi di Lampedusa
Il Gattopardo

Morphine, this crude chemical substitute for ancient stoicism, for Christian resignation.

Muoiono le città, muoiono i regni:
copre i fasti e le pompe arena ed erba;
e l'uom d'esser mortal par che si sdegni.
Oh nostra mente cupida e superba!

Torquato Tasso
Gerusalemme liberata

Proud cities vanish, states and realms decay,
The world's unstable glories fade away,
Yet mortals dare of certain fate complain,
O impious folly of presuming man.

Natale con i tuoi,
Pasqua con chi vuoi.

Saying

Spend Christmas with the family and Easter with whomever you wish.

Natura il fece, e poi roppe la stampa.

Ludvico Arioso
Orlando Furioso

Nature made him, and then broke the mould.

Ne' giorni tuoi felici ricordati di me.

Pietro Metastasio

In your happy days remember me.

Negli occhi porta la mia donna Amore;
Per che si far gentil ciò ch'ella mira.

Dante
Vita Nuova

In her eyes my lady carries love, and so makes gentle what she looks upon.

Nel mezzo del cammin di nostra vita
Mi ritrovai per una selva oscura,
Che la diritta via era smarrita.

Dante
Divina Commedia, Inferno
opening lines

Midway along the path of this our mortal life,
I found myself in a gloomy wood, gone astray from the right road.

Nella chiesa
Co' santi, ed in taverna co' ghiottoni.

Dante
Divina Commedia, Paradiso

Church is for saints and the tavern for gluttons.

Nessun dorma.

Adami & Simoni
Puccini's *Turandot*

None shall sleep.

Nessun maggior dolore,
Che ricordarsi del tempo felice
Nella miseria.

Dante
Divina Commedia, Inferno

No greater sorrow than to remember the happiness of yesterday in the hour of present misery.

Noi affermiamo che la magnificenza del
mondo si è arricchita di una bellezza
nuova: la bellezza della velocità.

Filippo Tommaso Marinetti
Manifesto del futurismo

We state that the world's magnificence has been blessed by a new kind of beauty: the beauty of speed.

Noi leggiavamo un giorno per diletto
Di Lancialotto, come amor lo stririze;
Soli eraramo e senza alcun sospetto.
Per piú fiate gli occhi ci sospinse
Quella lettura, e scolorocci 'l viso.

Dante
Divina Commedia, Inferno

We read one day for pastime, seated nigh,
Of Lancelot, how love enchain'd him too.
We were alone, quite unsuspiciously.
But oft our eyes met, and our cheeks in hue
All o'er discolour'd by that reading were.

Non c'è piú religione!

Proverb

What have things come to!

Non ne posso piú di stare murato
Nel desiderio senza amore.
Una traccia mostraci di giustizia.
La tua legge qual'è?
Fulmina le mie povere emozioni,
Liberami dall'inquietudine.
Sono stanco di urlare senza voce.

Giuseppe Ungaretti
Sentimento del tempo, Inni, La pietà

I can no longer bear being imprisoned
In desire without love.
Show us a hint of justice.
What is your law?
Blast my poor feelings,
Free me from restlessness.
I am tired of howling voicelessly.

Non nella pena,
Nel delitto è l'infamia.

Vittorio Alfieri

Disgrace is not in the punishment, but in the crime.

Non proviamo piú soddisfazione a com-
piere il nostro dovere, i nostri doveri...
Perché sono doveri troppo vecchi, troppo
vecchi e divenuti troppo facili, senza piú

We no longer feel rewarded by doing our duty, our duties... Because they are such worn out old duties, too old, and they've become so automatic. They no longer have any

significato per la coscienza.

Elio Vittorini
Conversazione in Sicilia

signficance in our consciences.

Non ragioniam di lor, ma guarda e passa.

Dante
Divina Commedia, Inferno

Let us not speak of them, but look, and pass on.

Non si ricordano i giorni, si ricordano gli attimi.

Cesare Pavese
Il mestiere di vivere, July 28, 1940

One doen't remember the days, but rather the fleeting seconds.

Non so se la speranza
Va coll'inganno unita;
So che mantiene in vita
Qualche infelice almen.

Pietro Metastasio

I don't know whether hope should be tied to deceit; but I do know that at least it keeps some unhappy people alive.

Non vuoi capire che la tua coscienza
significa appunto gli altri dentro di te?

Luigi Pirandello
Ciascuno a modo suo

Can't you see that your conscience means, in fact, those others inside you?

O cavallina, cavallina storna,
che portavi colui che non ritorna;
lo so, lo so, che tu l'amavi forte!
Con lui c'eri tu sola alla sua morte.

Giovanni Pascoli
Canti di Castelvecchio, La cavalla storna

O little mare, little grey mare,
Who bore him who will not return;
I know, I know how much you loved him!
You and you alone were with him at his death.

O dignitosa coscienza e netta,
come t'è picciol fallo amaro morso!

Dante
Divina Commedia, Purgatorio

O pure and noble conscience, you in whom each petty fault becomes bitter remorse!

O mio babbino caro.

G. Forzano
Puccini's *Gianni Schicchi*

O my beloved daddy.

O natura, o natura,
perché non rendi poi
quel che prometti allor? perché di tanto
inganni i figli tuoi?

Giacomo Leopardi
Canti, A Silvia

O Nature, Nature, why,
Why do you not give now
The things you promised then, why so deceive
Your children, mortal men?

O notte, o dolce tempo, benché nero,
O ombra del morir, per cui si ferma
Ogni miseria, a l'alma, al cor nemica,
Ultimo degli afflitti e buon rimedio;
Michelangelo Buonarroti
Rime

*O night, o sweet time, although black,
O shadow of death, for whom each affliction,
the enemy of soul and heart, is suspended,
last and best remedy of the wretched.*

Obbedisco.
Giuseppe Garibaldi
dispatch August 9 1866, in reply to General la
Marmora's order to retreat from the Tyrol

I shall obey.

Odio chi non parteggia, odio gli indifferenti.
Antonio Gramsci
Scritti giovanili

*I hate those who do not take sides. I hate people
who are indifferent.*

Ogni medaglia ha il suo rovescio.
Proverb

Every medal has its reverse side. (There are
two sides to every story.)

Ogni movimento rivoluzionario è romanti-
co, per definizione.
Antonio Gramsci
Ordine nuovo

*All revolutionary movements are romantic, by
definition.*

Ognun vede quel che tu pari, pochi
sentono quel che tu sei.
Niccolò Machiavelli
The Prince

*Everyone sees what you seem to be, few realise
what you really are.*

Ognuno sta solo sul cuor della terra
trafitto da un raggio di sole: ed è subito sera.
Salvatore Quasimodo
Ed è subito sera

*Each one stands alone at the heart of the earth,
pierced by a ray of sunlight: and soon it is
evening.*

Oh cieca cupidigia e ira folle,
che sí sproni nella vita corta,
e nell'etterna poi sí mal c'immolle.
Dante
Divina Commedia, Inferno

*Oh, blind cupidity and insane wrath,
spurring us on through our short life on earth,
to steep us then forever in such misery.*

"Or bene," gli disse il bravo, all'orecchio, ma
in tono solenne di comando, "questo matrimonio non s'ha da far, né domani, né mai."
Alessandro Manzoni
I Promessi sposi

*"Look here," said the ruffian in a low but
solemn and commanding tone, "there's not
going to be any marriage, not tomorrow nor
any other day."*

Pagherete caro,
Pagherete tutto.

Slogan of the left

You'll pay dearly,
You'll pay for everything.

Per ben parlar e assai sapere
Non sei stimato senza l'avere.

Alfieri Vittorio
Satire

To be well spoken and wise, it helps not to be
worried about money.

Per essere considerato un classico un film
deve riuscire a far sbadigliare almeno tre
generazioni di spettatori.

Marco Ferreri

To be considered a classic, a film must succeed
in making at least three generations of movie-
goers yawn.

Per me si va nella città dolente,
per me si va nell'etterno dolore,
per me si va tra la perduta gente.

Dante
Divina Commedia, Inferno

Through me lies the way to the sorrowful city;
through me lies the way to eternal sorrow,
through me lies the way among the lost people.

Per tutti la morte ha uno sguardo. Verrà la
morte e avrà i tuoi occhi.

Cesare Pavese
Verrà la morte e avrà i tuoi occhi

Death has its eye on all of us. Death will come
and it will have your eyes.

Perché civile, esser civile, vuol dire proprio
questo: – dentro, neri come corvi; fuori,
bianchi come colombi; in corpo fiele; in
bocca miele.

Luigi Pirandello
L'uomo, la bestia e la virtè

To be civil means precisely this: inside as black
as a crow; outside as white as a dove; in body
rancorous; in speech honeyed.

Perché non tutte le verità sono per tutte le
orecchie, non tutte le menzogne possono
essere riconosciute come tali da un animo
pio.

Umberto Eco
The Name of the Rose

Because not all truths are for all ears, not all
falsehoods can be recognized as such by a pious
soul.

Piccolo mondo antico.

Antonio Fogazzaro
Piccolo mondo antico

A little world of yesteryear

Piove, governo ladro

Proverb

It's raining, and the government's to blame.

Piú d'ogni inganno
D'uomo malvagio l'innocente ha potere.
Giambattista Cinthio Giraldi
Selene

Innocence has more power than all the deceits of an evil man.

Piú tengono a memoria gli uomini le
ingiurie, che i benefici ricevuti.
Francesco Guicciardini

Men's memories are more tenacious of injuries than of benefits they have received.

Pochi, maledetti e subito!
familiar reference to cash transactions

A cursed pittance, and quickly!

Poeti, poeti, ci siamo messi tutte le maschere.
Giuseppe Ungaretti
Un grido e paesaggi, Monologhetto

Poets, poets, we are all wearing masks.

Poiché si domandano cose sì disoneste, voi
sonerete le vostre trombe e noi soneremo
le nostre campane.
Francesco Guicciardini
Storia d'Italia

Since such dishonest things are being asked, you shall blow your horns and we shall ring our bells.

Poiché voi, cittadine infauste mura,
Vidi e conobbi assai, là dove segue
Odio al dolor compagno.
Giacomo Leopardi
La vita solitaria

For I have seen and known you too much, black city walls where pain and hatred follow together.

Possiamo dunque vedere e conoscere
soltanto ciò che di noi è morto. Conoscersi
è morire.
Luigi Pirandello
Novelle per un'anno

[Thus] we can see and know only that part of ourselves which is dead. To know oneself is to die.

Qualunque volta alle universalità degli
uomini non si toglie né roba né onore,
vivono contenti.
Niccolò Machiavelli
The Prince

Provided neither their property nor their honour is touched, the majority of men live content.

Quando Dio non vuole,
ll santo non puole.
Proverb

When God will not, the saint cannot.

Quando discuti con un avversario, prova a metterti nei suoi panni... Ho seguito per qualche tempo questo consiglio dei saggi. Ma i panni dei miei avversari erano cosí sudici che ho concluso: è meglio essere ingiusto qualche volta che provare di nuovo questo schifo che fa svenire.

Antonio Gramsci
Scritti giovanili: "La città futura"

When arguing with an adversary, try putting yourself in his shoes... For a while, I followed this bit of advice from the sage. But my adversary's shoes were so smelly that I concluded it was sometimes better to be unfair than to faint from the stench.

Quando fano il lor nido in America i pettirosi?

Giuseppe Giacosa and **Luigi Illica**
Puccini's *Madame Butterfly*

At what time of year in America do the robins nest?

Quando leggemmo il disiato riso
esser baciato da cotanto amante,
questi, che mai da me non fia diviso,
la bocca mi baciò tutto tremante:
Galeotto fu il libro e chi lo scrisse:
quel giorno piú non vi leggemmo avante.

Dante
Divina Commedia, Inferno

It was when we read about those longed-for lips being kissed by such a famous lover, that this one (who shall never leave my side) then kissed my mouth and trembled as he did. It was the fault of the book and him who wrote it. That day we read no more.

Quando ti chiamano latin lover sei nei guai. Le donne a letto si aspettano da te una performance da Oscar.

Marcello Mastroianni

When they call you a Latin lover you're in trouble. It means that, in bed, women will expect an Oscar performance from you.

Quant'è bella giovinezza
che si fugge tuttavia!
Chi vuol esser lieto, sia:
di doman non c'è certezza.

Lorenzo Medici
*Canti carnascialeschi, Trionfo di
Bacco e Ariane*

*How lovely youth is that ever flies!
Who wishes to be glad, let him be so:
there is no certainty in tomorrow.*

Que prudenti che s'adombrano delle virtú come dévizi predicano sempre che la perfezione sta nel mezzo; e il mezzo lo fissano giusto in quel punto dov'essi sono arrivati, e ci stanno comodi.

Alessandro Manzoni
I promessi sposi

Those prudent folk who shrink from virtue as from vice, forever preaching that perfection lies in the middle; who fix the middle at the exact point where they themselves have arrived, and are comfortably settled.

Quelli che s'innamoran di pratica senza
scienza, son come 'l nocchiere, ch'entra in
naviglio senza timone o bussola, che mai
ha certezza dove si vada.

Leonardo da Vinci
Scritti letterari

*Those who are enamoured of practice without
science are like the pilot who embarks in a ship
without rudder or compass and who is never
certain where he is going.*

Questi sciaurati, che mai non fur vivi.

Dante
Divina Commedia, Inferno

These wretches, who had never truly lived.

Qui giace l'Aretin poeta tosco,
Che disse mal d'ognun fuor che di Dio
Scusandosi col dir, non lo conosco.

attrib. **Giovio Paolo**
epitaph for Pietro Aretino

*The poet Aretino lies below,
Who spoke evil of everyone save God,
And for excuse said: "Him I do not know."*

Qui si fa l'Italia o si muore.

Guiseppe Garibaldi
to Nino Bixio at the Battle of Calatafimi

Either we make Italy here or we die.

Risorgerò nemico ognor piú crudo,
Cenere anco sepolto, e spirito ignudo.

Torquato Tasso
Gerusalemme liberata

*Though in the grave my body buried lies,
still fiercer foeman shall my spirit rise.* (Also
translated as: Still will I rise, a more inveter-
ate foe/And, dead, pursue them from the
shades below.)

Roma di travertino, rifatta di cartone, salu-
ta l'imbianchino, suo prossimo padrone.

Trilussa (Carlo Alberto Salustri)
about Hitler's visit to Rome, 1938

*Rome of travertine, rebuilt in cardboard, greets
the house painter who will be her next master.*

Roma o morte.

"Garibaldini" war cry
by Garibaldi's followers at Aspromonte and
Mentana

Rome or death.

S'i' fossi fuoco, ardereï 'l mondo;
S' i' fossi vento, lo tempestarei;
S' i' fossi acqua, i' l' annegherei;
S' i' fossi Dio, manderei in profondo;
S' i' fossi papa, allor sarei giocondo,
Ché tutt'i cristiani imbrigarei;
S' i' fossi 'mperator, ben lo farei:
A tutti taglierei il capo a tondo.

Cecco Angiolieri

*If I were fire, I'd light the world;
If I were wind, I'd blow it away;
If I were water, I'd sink it;
If I were God, I'd dispatch it to the depths;
If I were Pope, then I'd be merry that I could
meddle with all Christians;
If I were emperor, I'd do that well:
I'd cut everyone's head clean off.*

Saggio guerriero antico
Mai non ferisce in fretta:
Esamina il nemico,
Il suo vantaggio aspetta.
Pietro Metastasio
Adriano in Siria

The wise old soldier is never in haste to strike a blow: he studies the enemy and waits for his advantage.

Sanzionati non sanziano.
Benito Mussolini
when asked if Italy would participate in sanctions against Germany in 1936

Nations who have suffered sanctions do not sanction others.

Se è vero che ci si abitua al dolore, come mai con l'andare degli anni si soffre sempre di piú?
Cesare Pavese
Il mestiere di vivere, November 21, 1937

If it is true that one grows accustomed to pain, why is it that, as the years go by, one suffers even more?

Se non è vero, è ben trovato.
Proverb

If not true, it is very ingenious.

Se un film ha successo, è un affare: se non ha successo, è arte.
Carlo Ponti

If a film is successful, it is commercial; if it isn't, it's art.

Se vogliam che tutto rimanga come è, bisogna che tutto cambi.
Giuseppe Tomasi di Lampedusa
The Leopard

If we want things to stay as they are, things will have to change.

Se vuol ballare, signor Contino,
Se vuol ballare, signor Contino
il chitarrino le suonerò,
il chitarrino le suonerò, si,
le suonerò si, le suonerò.
Lorenzo Da Ponte
Mozart's *Le Nozze di Figaro*

If you want to dance, Count,
If you want to dance, Count,
I will play my small guitar for you,
yes, my small guitar I will play for you,
yes, I will play for you, play for you.

Sempre avanti Savoia!
Margherita, Queen of Italy

Ever onwards, Savoy!

Si dipinge col cervello et non con le mani.
Michelangelo Buonarroti
Lettere

One paints with the brain, not the hands.

Si fa bene a tenere un diario; ed è utile che tanta gente lo sappia.

Giulio Andreotti

One does well to keep a diary; and it is useful that others are aware of it.

Si resiste a star soli finché qualcuno soffre di non averci con sé, mentre la vera solitudine è una cella intollerabile.

Cesare Pavese
Prima che il gallo canti

One can stand being alone as long as one knows that one is missed, but true solitude is like an unbearable cell.

Si sta come
d'autunno
sugli alberi
le foglie.

Giuseppe Ungaretti
L'allegria

One is like autumn's leaves on a tree.

Siccome una giornata bene spesa dá lieto dormire, così una vita bene usata dà lieto morire.

Leonardo Da Vinci
Scritti letterari

As a well-spent day brings happy slumber, so life well-used brings happy death.

Siete voi qui, ser Brunetto?

Dante
Divina Commedia, Inferno
seeing his friend in hell among the Sodomites

Are you here, Master Brunetto?

Simulata! Come avvenne del Palmieri! Hai ben compreso?

Giuseppe Giacosa and **Luigi Illica**
Puccini's *Tosca*

Simulated! As we did with Palmieri! You understand. (Scarpia to his henchman Spoletta, directing him to stage a mock execution.)

Sogni e favole io fingo; e pure in carte mentre favole e sogni orno e disegno, in lor, folle ch'io son, prendo tal parte, che del mal che inventai piango e mi sdegno.

Pietro Metastasio
Nel comporre l'Olimpiade

Dreams and fables I fashion; and even while I sketch and elaborate fables and dreams upon paper, fond as I am, I so enter into them that I weep and am indignant over ills I invented.

Solo e pensoso i piú deserti campi
vo mesurando a passi tardi e lenti,
e gli occhi porto per fuggire intenti
ove vestigio uman la rena stampi.

Francesco Petrarch
Solo e pensoso

Alone and pensive, I pace the most deserted fields with slow hesitant steps, and I am watchful so as to flee from any place where human traces mark the sand.

Soltanto il mare gli brontolava la solita sto- | Only the sea thundered away at him in its
ria lì sotto, in mezzo ai faraglioni, | usual way, down there between the rocks,
perché il mare non ha paese nemmeno lui, | because the sea, too, belongs to none but those
ed è di tutti quelli che lo stanno ad | who stay to listen.
ascoltare.

Giovanni Verga
I malavoglia

Sono poeta. Che cosa faccio? Scrivo. E | *I am a poet. What's my employment? Writing.*
come vivo? Vivo. | *Is that a living? I manage.*

Giuseppe Giacosa and **Luigi Illica**
Puccini's *La Bohème.*

Sorgon cosí tue divino | *Your divine limbs thus rise from the sick bed*
Membra dall'egro talamo, | *and in you beauty is restored. Celestial beauty*
E in te beltà rivive, | *which, alone, gave solace from ills born in*
L'aurea beltà ond'ebbero | *delirious mortal minds.*
Ristoro unico a' mali
Le nate a vaneggiar menti mortali.

Ugo Foscolo
All'amica risanata

Spezzeremo le reni alla Grecia. | *We'll crush Greece.* (Lit. We will break the
kidneys of Greece.)

Benito Mussolini
declaring war on Greece, but
now denoting something which
will fail disastrously

Taci. Sulle soglie | *Hush. On the edge of the wood I do not hear a*
del bosco non odò | *human word you say; but I hear newer words,*
parole che dici | *spoken by far-off drips and leaves.*
umane; ma odò
parole piú nuove
che parlano gocciole e foglie
lontane.

Gabriele D'Annunzio
Alcyone, La pioggia nel pineto

Tanto gentile e tanto onesta pare | *So gentle and so modest doth appear*
la donna mia quand'ella altrui saluta | *My lady when she giveth her salute,*
ch'ogne lingua deven tremando muta | *That every tongue becometh trembling, mute;*
e li occhi no l'ardiscon di guardare. | *Nor do the eyes to look upon her dare.*

Dante
Vita Nuova

Torino piange quando il Prence parte
E Roma esulta quando il Prence arriva.
Firenze, culla della poesia e dell'arte,
Se ne infischia quando giunge e quando
parte.
Anon

Turin weeps when the king departs
And Rome is joyous when the king arrives.
Florence, fount of poetry and art,
Cares not a whit in either case.

Tornando a casa troverete i bambini. Fate
loro una carezza e dite, questa è la carezza
del Papa.
Pope John XXIII

When you go home you will find your little
children. Give them a caress and tell them: this
is from the Pope.

Tre cose cacciano l'uomo di casa:
Fumo, goccia e fimmina arrabiata.
Saying

Three things will make a man flee from home:
smoke, a leaking roof and an angry wife.

Tu, o Iddio, ci vendi tutti li beni per prezzo
di fatica.
Leonardo da Vinci
Scritti letterari

Thou, O God, dost sell unto us all good things
for the price of labour.

Tu proverai si come sa di sale
La pane atrui, e com'e duro calle
Lo scendere e'l salir par l'altrui scale.
Dante
Divina Commedia, Paradiso

You shall learn how bitter is another man's
bread, how steep the stranger's stair.

Tutta la notte Paulo [Uccello] stava nello
scrittoio per trovare i termini della ,
e...quando ella (la moglie) lo chiamava a
dormire, egli le diceva: "Oh che dolce cosa
è questa prospettiva!"
Giorgio Vasari
Lives of the Artists

All night, Paolo [Uccello] used to stay in his
study, trying to work out the vanishing points
of his perspective and, when his wife called him
to bed, he would say, "Oh what a lovely thing
this perspective is!"

Un bel dì, vedremo levarsi un fil di fumo
sull'estremo confin del mare. E poi la nave
appare.
Giuseppe Giacosa and **Luigi Illica**
Puccini's *Madame Butterfly*

One fine day we'll notice a thread of smoke
arising on the sea, on the far horizon. And
then the ship appearing.

Un epigramma è una pistola corta, e
ammazza piú sicuramente di un archibugio.
Curzio Malaparte (Kurt Erich Suckert)
Il battibecco

An epigram is like a short pistol: it is more
likely to kill than an arquebus.

Un vero giornalista spiega benissimo quello che non sa.

Leo Longanesi

A true journalist is one who can explain very well what he doesn't know.

Una delle prime e piú nobili funzioni delle cose poco serie è di gettare un'ombra di diffidenza sulle cose troppo serie.

Umberto Eco
Diario minimo

One of the chief and most noble purposes of frivolity is to cast a shadow of suspicion over anything too serious.

Una diffidenza moderata può esser savia: una diffidenza oltrespinta, non mai.

Silvio Pellico
Le mie prigioni

To be moderately distrustful is wise; to be excessively so is not.

Una puntura di zanzara prude meno, quando sei riuscito a schiacciare la zanzara.

Ugo Ojetti

A mosquito bite itches a lot less after you've squashed the mosquito.

Una volta il rimorso mi seguiva, ora mi precede.

Ennio Flaiano

Regret used to follow me; now it precedes me.

Uno principe, il quale non sia savio per se stesso, non può essere consigliato bene.

Niccolò Macchiavelli
The Prince

A prince who is not wise himself cannot be well advised.

Uomo avvisato è mezzo salvato.

Proverb

A man forewarned is halfway saved.

Va pensiero, sull'ali dorate;
Va ti posa sui clivi, sui colli,
Ove olezzano libere e molli
L'aure dolci del suolo natal!

Temistocle Solera
Verdi's *Nabucco*

Go, O thought, on golden wings: go and land on high and low hills, where the air of our native land gives out a mild, sweet and subtle scent.

Vado verso la vita.

Gabriele D'Annunzio
statement to Parliament when D'Annunzio dramatically abandoned his seat on the right to join the seats of the extreme left

I am headed towards life.

Vaghe stelle dell'Orsa, io non credea
Tornare ancora per uso a contemplarvi
Sul paterno giardino scintillanti,
E ragionar con voi dalle finistre
Di questo albergo ove abitai fanciullo
E delle gioie mie vidi la fine.

Giacomo Leopardi
The Vagabond Path

O you bright stars of the Bear, I did not think that I should come once more, as was my custom, to gaze upon you glittering above my father's garden, or converse with you from the windows of this house, where as a boy I lived, and saw the end of happiness.

Vesti la giubba

Ruggiero Leoncavallo
I Pagliacci

Put on the costume. (On with the motley.)

Vestili come vuoi, fuggiranno sempre.
**Ferdinand IV, Bourbon king of Naples
and Sicily**
to his nephew who had suggested changing
the uniforms of the army

You can dress them however you like and they'll still run away.

Virgini bella, che di sol vestita,
Coronato di stello.

Petrarch
La Ricordanze

Fair virgin, clothed in sunlight, crowned with stars.

Vissi d'arte, vissi d'amore,
Non feci mai male ad anima viva!
Giuseppe Giacosa and **Luigi Illica**
Puccini's *Tosca*

*I lived for art, I lived for love,
I have never harmed a living soul!*

Vittoria nostra, non sarai mutilata.
Gabriele D'Annunzio

Our victory, you shall not be mutilated.

Vivo nel non volere
Del tramontato dopoguerra: amando
Il mondo per odio.

Pier Paolo Pasolini
Le ceneri di Gramsci

I live unwillingly in the postwar twilight, loving a world I hate.

Vogliamo che ognuno sia libero di fare ciò che vuole a patto che ciò non leda la libertà altrui. Per cui assoluta libertà sessuale e modifica totale della mentalità.
1966 editorial in *La Zanzara,* newpaper of the Parini High school in Milan

We want everyone to be free to do what he wants, provided it doesn't interfere with the freedom of others. Thus total sexual freedom and a complete change in mental attitude.

*Voglio partire in perfetto orario... D'ora innanzi ogni cosa deve camminare alla perfezione.

I want to leave precisely on time. From now on, everything must work perfectly.

Benito Mussolini
to a station master

Voi che sapete, che cosa è amor?
Donne, vedete s'io l'ho nel cor.
Donne, vedete s'io l'ho nel cor.
Quello ch'io provo vi ridirò.

You who know these things, what is love?
Ladies, see whether I have it in my heart.
Ladies, see whether I have it in my heart.
And I shall tell you what I feel.

Lorenzo Da Ponte
Le Nozze di Figaro, Act 2

Voler la botte piena e la moglie ubriaca

To want one's cask full and one's wife drunk.
(To have your cake and eat it.)

Saying

*Compare p.218

241

ITALIAN INDEX

SPANISH

The moral of Don Quixote is the strife between temporal and eternal,
between things spiritual and things corporal, between ecstasy and the common life.

Arthur Machen

A batallas de amor campo de pluma.
Luis de Góngora

For the battle of love, a field of feathers.

A las cinco de la tarde.
Eran las cinco en punto de la tarde.
Un niño trajo la blanca sábana
a las cinco de la tarde.
Federico García Lorca
Llanto por Ignacio Sánchez Mejías

At five in the afternoon. It was exactly five in the afternoon. A boy brought the white sheet at five in the afternoon.

A los veinte años reina la voluntad, a los treinta el ingenio, a los cuarenta el juicio.
Baltasar Gracián
Oráculo Manual y Arte de Prudencia

At twenty the will is in command, at thirty the intellect, and at forty the judgement.

A su tiempo nacerá un Newton del placer y un Kant de las ambiciones.
José Ortega y Gasset

In due time pleasure will find its Newton and ambition its Kant.

A una colectividad se le engaña siempre mejor que a un hombre.
Pío Baroja
Memorias de un Hombre de Acción

A group is always more easily deceived than an individual.

A veces el saber verdadero resulta indiferente, y entonces puede inventarse.
Javier Marías
Todas las Almas

When knowledge of the truth proves irrelevant, one is free to invent.

Actualmente yo me definiría como un inofensivo anarquista; es decir, un hombre que quiere un mínimo de gobierno y un máximo de individuo.
Jorge Luis Borges
Soy

Nowadays I would describe myself as an inoffensive anarchist; that is, a man who wants a minimum of government and a maximum of individuality.

Acometer molinos de viento.
Cervantes
Don Quixote

To tilt against windmills.

A los veinte años será pavón, a los treinta león, a los cuarenta camello, a los cincuenta serpiente, a los sesenta perro, a los setenta mona, y a los ochenta nada.

Baltasar Gracián
Oráculo Manual y Arte de Prudencia

At twenty a man will be a peacock, at thirty a lion, at forty a camel, at fifty a serpent, at sixty a dog, at seventy a monkey, and at eighty nothing at all.

Amar una cosa es estar empeñado en que exista; no admitir, en lo que depende de uno, la posibilidad de un universo donde aquel objeto esté ausente.

José Ortega y Gasset

Falling in love even once is an insistence that the beloved exists; a refusal to accept the possibility of a universe without the beloved object.

Aquéste es de los hombres el oficio: tentar el mal, y si es malo el suceso, pedir con humildad perdón del vicio.

Garcilaso de la Vega
Égloga 2

This is man's rôle: to try evil, and, if the outcome be evil, humbly to ask forgiveness for the act of depravity

Bien haya el que inventó el sueño, capa que cubre todos los humanos pensiamentos, manjar que quita la hambre, agua que ahuyenta la sed, fuego que calienta el frío que templa el ardor, y, finalmente, moneda general con que todas las cosas se compran, blanza y peso que iguala al pastor con el rey y al eimple con el discreto.

Cervantes
Don Quixote

Blessings on him who invented sleep, the mantle that covers all human thoughts, the food that satisfies hunger, the drink that quenches thirst, the fire that warms cold, the cold that moderates heat, and, lastly, the common currency that buys all things, the balance and weight that equalizes the shepherd and the king, the simpleton and the sage.

Buscar ante todo la unanimidad me parece tan lóbrego como desear que siempre sea trece y martes.

Fernando Savater

To seek unanimity above all seems as gloomy as to wish that every day should be Friday the thirteenth.

Cada uno es artifice de sa ventura.

Cervantes
Don Quixote

Everyone is the author of his own misfortune.

Cánsare la fortuna de llevar a uno a cuestas tan a larga.

Baltasar Gracián
Oráculo Manual y Arte de Prudencia

Fortune soon tires of carrying us too long on her shoulders.

Casa con dos puertas mala es de guardar.

Proverb

A house with two doors is difficult to guard.

Comenzaba a sospechar que el pesimismo era el precio inevitable que se paga por la lucidez.

Santiago de Mora-Figueroa
Polvora con Aguardiente, Sophie o las Complicaciones de la Guerra

I was beginning to suspect that pessimism is the inevitable price of lucidity.

Con el alma de charol vienen por la carrera.

Federico García Lorca
Romance de la Guardia Civil Española

With their patent-leather souls, they [the Civil Guards] *come along the road.*

Confieso que, a medida que pasan los años, veo con más simpatía a la revuelta que a la revolución.

Octavio Paz

I confess that, as time goes by, I view revolt with more sympathy than revolution.

Considero que es la filosofía la ciencia general del amor.

José Ortega y Gasset

I consider philosophy to be the general science of love.

Contra la moda toda lucha es inútil.

Josep Pla

Fighting against fashion is always in vain.

Creer en Dios es anhelar que lo haya y es además conducirse como si lo hubiera.

Miguel de Unamuno
Del Sentimiento Trágico de la Vida, 1913

To believe in God is to yearn for his existence and, to behave, moreover, as if he did exist.

Crispín: ¡Antes me desprendiera yo de la piel que de un buen vestido! Que nada importa tanto como parecer, según va el mundo, y el vestido es lo que antes parece.

Jacinto Benavente
Los intereses creados

Crispin: I would sooner take off my skin than my good clothes. As this world goes, nothing is so important as appearances, and one's clothes, you must admit, are the first things to appear.

Cristiano y amoroso y caballero,
Parla como un arroyo cristalino.
Así le admiro y quiero.

Ruben Dario
Sonnet to Cervantes

Christian and lover and gentleman, he speaks like a silver torrent. Therefore I admire and cherish him.

Cualquier guerra entre europeos es una guerra civil.

Eugenio D'Ors

Any war between Europeans is a civil war.

Cualquiera sirve para rey; casi nadie para solitario.

Leopoldo Alas Clarín
La Regenta

Anybody may be fit for kingship: not many can be solitary.

¡Cuán preciosa y eficaz es la colaboración involuntaria del enemigo acérrimo para el triunfo de la idea que combate!

Manuel de Falla
Escritos sobre Música y Músicos, I, Introducción a la Música Nueva

How valuable, on the other hand, is the unintentional collaboration of a bitter enemy in the victory of a struggling idea.

Cuando empecé, el cubismo era un análisis de la pintura que era como la descripción de los fenómenos físicos a la Física.

Juan Gris
attrib. D. Khanweiler, *Juan Gris*

When I started, cubism was an analysis of the painting, like the scientific description of physical phenomena.

Cuando hacéis con la violencia derramar las primeras lágrimas a un niño, ya habéis puesto en su espíritu la ira, la tristeza, la envidia, la venganza, la hipocresía.

José Martinez Ruiz Azorín

When you use violence to draw the first tears from a child, you have just put into his soul rage, sadness, envy, vengeance and hypocrisy.

Cuando llegue la inspiración, que me encuentre trabajando.

Pablo Picasso

When inspiration arrives I want it to find me working.

Cuando murió Franco fue una conmoción; no había costumbre.

attrib. **Julio Cerón** by Fernando Jauregui
"Lo que nos Queda de Franco"

When Franco died there was turbulence; we were not used to it.

Cuando un país decide suicidarse a quien no está conforme lo suicidan.

Luis Rosales

When a country decides to commit suicide those who do not agree have suicide imposed upon them.

Cuántas veces nos hallamos con lectores entusiasmados con obras que obviamente no dicen lo que ellos creen entender.

Fernando Lázaro Carreter
¿Qué es la Literatura?

How often we see readers excited by books which obviously do not say what they seem to find in them.

Cuanto son mayores las monarquías, más sujetas están a la mentira.

Diego de Saavedra Fajardo

The bigger the monarchy the bigger the lies.

¡Cuántos debe de haber en el mundo que
huyen de otros porque no se ven a sí mismos!

Lazarillo de Tormes

*How many there are in the world who run
from others because they do not see themselves there.*

Cúrate de la afección de preocuparte cómo
aparezcas a los demás. Cuídate sólo de
cómo aparezcas ante Dios, cuídate de la
idea que de ti Dios tenga.

Miguel de Unamuno
Vida de Don Quijote y Sancho, 1914

*Cure yourself of the disease of worrying
about how you appear to others. Concern
yourself only with how you appear before
God, concern yourself with the idea which
God has of you.*

De sola una vez a incendio
Crece una breve pavesa.

Pedro Calderón de la Barca
El Alcade de Zalamea

*In a single instant a tiny spark can be
fanned into a blaze.*

De todas las reacciones posibles ante la
injuria, la más hábil y económica es el
silencio.

Santiago Ramón y Cajal

*Of all the possible reactions to an injury, the
cleverest and most economical is silence.*

Dedico esta edición a mis enemigos, que
tanto me han ayudado en mi carrera.

Camilo José Cela
*Pascual Duarte de Limpio, Prefacio a una Nuevu
Edición*

*I dedicate this edition to my enemies, who
have helped me so much in my career.*

Dejemos las conclusiones para los imbéciles.

Pio Baroja
Memorias de un Hombre de Acción

Let us leave conclusions to imbeciles.

Desboques del nacionalismo, estupendo
sembrador de estragos.

Pedro Salinas
*La Responsabilidad del Escritor, Reflexiones sobre
la Cultura*

*Nationalism run amok, splendid sower of
destruction.*

Desde entonces conocí que el heroísmo es
casi siempre una forma del pundonor.

Benito Pérez Galdós

*Since then I have learnt that heroism is a
form of pride.*

¡Dios qué buen vassallo, si oviesse buen
señor!

Poema del Mío Cid

*God, what a fine vassal, if only his lord were
as fine.*

Diríase que ciertos espíritus propensos al misticismo, son molestados por las verdades sencillas y patentes.
Santiago Ramón y Cajal
Recuerdos de mi Vida

It could be said that certain spirits with a tendency to mysticism are disturbed by simple and evident truth.

Dueña por primera vez de su destino, Angela Vicario descubrió entonces que el odio y el amor son pasiones recíprocas.
Gabriel García Márquez
Crónica de una Muerte Anunciada

Mistress of her fate for the first time, Angela Vicario then discovered that hate and love are reciprocal passions.

Dulce nombre te dieron; amargos hechos haces.
Fernando de Rojas
about love

Sweet name you were given; bitter actions you commit.

El "¿y si hay?" y el "¿y si no hay?" son las bases de nuestra vida íntima.
Miguel de Unamuno

Is there? Is there not? - these are the bases of our inner life.

El abismo y diferencia mayor entre nuestro sistema y el nazi-fascismo es la característica de católico de régimen que hoy preside los destinos de España.
General Franco
Discurso al Consejo Nacional del Movimiento

The deep and main difference between our system and Nazi-Fascism is the Catholic characteristic of the regime that today presides over Spain's destiny.

El acto sexual es un saludo que cambian dos almas.
Macedonio Fernández
attrib. *J.L. Borges y O. Ferrari, Diálogos, 28*

The sexual act is a greeting exchanged by two souls.

El adulterio lleva mucho trabajo.
Javier Marías
Todas las Almas

Adultery is hard work.

El amor coge al corazón desprevenido; nunca llega a la hora de la cita.
Antonio Gala
El Cementerio de los Pájaros

Love catches the heart unaware; it never arrives at the appointed time.

El amor es como Don Quijote, cuando recobra el juicio es que está para morir.
attrib. **Jacinto Benavente**

Love is like Don Quixote, when it regains sanity it is about to die.

El arte contemporáneo es, o un aprendizaje, o una farsa.

Eugenio D'Ors
Cézanne

Contemporary art is either a learning process or a farce.

El arte es una mentira que nos permite decir la verdad.

Pablo Picasso

Art is a lie which allows us to tell the truth.

El azar es el orden del tiempo.
Guillermo Pérez Villalta

Chance is time's order.

El Caballero de la Triste Figura.
Cervantes
Don Quixote

The Knight of the Doleful Countenance.

El capitalista es un señor que al hablar con vosotros se queda con vuestras cerillas.
Ramón Gómez de la Serna
Greguerías

A capitalist is a man who while talking to you takes your matches.

El ciego se entera mejor de las cosas del mundo, los ojas son unos ilusionados embusteros.
Ramón María del Valle-Inclán
Luces de Bohemia

A blind man actually knows more about the ways of the world because the eyes are only hopeful deceivers.

El conocía que todo estaba muerto en mí, que yo era mi muerto andando entre los muertos.

Luis Cernuda

He recognised that everything in me was dead, that I was dead, walking amongst the dead .

El contable es un señor con el que no se cuenta casi nunca.
Ramón Gómez de la Serna
Greguerías

The accountant is a person you can seldom count on.

El deseo es algo irracional por el cual uno siempre tiene que pagar un alto precio.
Pedro Almodóvar

Desire is something irrational for which one always has to pay a high price.

El deseo es una pregunta cuya respuesta nadie sabe.

Luis Cernuda
No Decía Palabras

Desire is a question to which no-one has an answer.

El día que yo me vaya me llevo la llave de la despensa.

Isabel II

The day I leave I will take with me the key to the pantry.

El discreto encanto de la burguesía.

Luis Buñuel
title of a film

The discreet charm of the bourgeoisie.

El egoísmo es laberíntico.

José Ortega y Gasset

Selfishness is labyrinthine.

El erotismo es la pornografía vestida por Christian Dior.

Luis García Berlanga

Eroticism is pornography in a Dior dress.

El error obliga a rehacer el camino y eso enseña muchas cosas. La duda, no. Entre el error y la duda, opto siempre por el primero.

Juan Benet

Errors force us to retrace the road and that teaches us much. Doubt does not. Faced with error and doubt I always choose the former.

El Estado es necesario. Debe mantenerse. Pero debe mantenerse a raya.

Ramón Pi Torrente

The state is necessary. It must be kept. But it must be kept at bay.

El feminismo, es como tener un enemigo en casa.

Josep Pla
Antifeminismo

Feminism is like having an enemy in one's home.

El hombre de pensamiento descubre la Verdad; pero quien goza de ella y utiliza sus celestiales dones es el hombre de acción.

Benito Pérez Galdos
El Amigo Manso

The man of reflection discovers Truth; but he who enjoys it and makes use of its heavenly gifts is the man of action.

El hombre es un ser escondido en sí mismo.

María Zambrano
Claros del Bosque

Man is a being hidden inside himself.

El hombre, por ser hombre, por tener conciencia, es ya, respecto al burro o a un cangrejo, un animal enfermo. La conciencia es una enfermedad.

Miguel de Unamuno
Del Sentimiento Trágico de la Vida

Man, because he is a man, because he is conscious, is, compared with an ass or a crab, already a diseased animal. Consciousness is a disease.

El hombre, sin saber cómo, se inclina siempre del lado del vencido; el infortunio le parece más bello que la victoria.

José Donoso Cortés
Ensayo sobre el Catolicismo, el Liberalismo y el Socialismo

Man, without knowing how, is drawn to the vanquished side; misfortune seems to him more beautiful than victory.

El humor es, sencillamente, una posición frente a la vida.

Wenceslao Fernández Florez
Discurso de ingreso en la Real Academia Española

Humour is just an attitude to life.

El igualitarismo ni siquiera es una utopía soñada; es una pesadilla imposible.

Gonzalo Fernández de la Mora
La Envidia Igualitaria

Equality is not a Utopian dream; it is an impossible nightmare.

El imperativo de no torturar debe ser categórico, no hipotético.

Ernesto Sábato

The imperative "no torture" must be categorical, not hypothetical.

El ingenio es un duro enemigo de la literatura.

Camilo José Cela
Memorias, Entendimientos y Voluntades. Voy a la Guerra

Cleverness is a powerful enemy of literature.

El jinete se acercaba tocando el tambor del llano. Dentro de la fragua el niño tiene los ojos cerrados.

Federico García Lorca
Romance de la Luna, Luna

Drumming the plain, the horseman is coming. Inside the smithy the child has closed his eyes.

El lector se cansa de reflexiones enojosas sobre lo que a un solo mortal interesa.

Benito Pérez Galdós

The reader grows tired of irritating reflections about what is of interest to just one mortal.

El mar, emblema majestuoso de la vida humana.

Benito Pérez Galdós

The sea, majestic emblem of human life.

El más discreto hablar no es santo como el silencio.

Félix Lope de Vega
La Dama Boba

The wisest speech is less holy than silence.

El mensaje literario remite esencialmente a sí mismo.

Fernando Lázaro Carreter
¿Qué es la Literatura?

The message of literature is essentially about itself.

El mérito para los snobs es hacer siempre descubrimientos. Así han llegado al dadaísmo, al cubismo y a otras estupideces semejantes.

Pío Baroja
Memorias

For snobs merit lies in always making discoveries. That is how they arrived at Dadaism, Cubism and other similar stupidities.

El mundo es un valle de lágrimas y mientras más pronto salís de él mejor.

Pérez Galdós
Miau

The world is but a vale of tears; the sooner we leave it the better.

El objetivo de un buen general no es la lucha, sino la victoria. Ha luchado lo suficiente si alcanza la victoria.

**Fernando Alvarez de Toledo,
Duque de Alba**

A good general's objective is not the fight, but victory. He has fought enough if he achieves victory.

El objetivo final del arte es mostrar los tejidos internos del alma.

attrib. **Manuel Viola**

Art's ultimate objective is to reveal the inward stuff of the soul.

El original es infiel a la traducción.

Jorge Luis Borges
Sobre el "Vathek" de William Beckford

The original is not faithful to the translation.

El pasado de Rusia está vivo y regresa.

Octavio Paz

Russia's past is alive and coming back.

El periodismo es un género literario muy parecido a la novela, y tiene la gran ventaja de que el reportero puede inventar cosas. Y eso el novelista lo tiene totalmente prohibido.

Gabriel García Márquez
speech April 1994. *El País Internacional*

Journalism is a literary genre very similar to that of the novel, but has the great advantage that the reporter can invent things, which is completely forbidden to the novelist.

El placer sexual parece consistir en una súbita descarga de energía nerviosa. La fruicíon estética es una súbita descarga de emociones alusivas. Análogamente es la filosofía como una súbita descarga de intelección.

José Ortega y Gasset
Meditaciones del Quijote

Sexual pleasure seems to consist in a sudden discharge of nervous energy. Aesthetic enjoyment is a sudden discharge of allusive emotions. Similarly, philosophy is like a sudden discharge of intellectual activity.

El poder tiende a ser taciturno.

María Zambrano
España Despierta Soñándose.

Power tends to be taciturn.

El pretexto para todas las guerras: conseguir la paz.

Jacinto Benavente
El Mundo, 19-VIII-1992

The excuse for all wars: to obtain peace.

El privilegio máximo es no tener jefes ni súbditos.

Miguel Ángel Aguilar

The greatest privilege is to have neither bosses nor subordinates.

El progreso comporta – inevitablemente, a lo que se ve – una minimización del hombre.

Miguel Delibes
Un mundo que agoniza

Progress involves – inevitably – a minimisation of man.

El que aquí cuenta lo que que vio y le ocurrió, ni tampoco es su prolongación, ni su sombra, ni su heredero, ni su usurpador.

Javier Marías
Todas las Almas

The person recounting here and now what he saw and what happened to him then is not the same person who saw those things and to whom those things happened; neither is he an extension of that person, his shadow, his heir or his usurper.

El que espera lo mucho espera lo poco.

Gabriel García Márquez
El Coronel no Tiene quien le Escriba

He who expects much can expect little.

El que las sabe las tañe.

Castillejo
Obras Morales. Discurso de la Vida de Corte

He who knows the tunes plays them.

El que lee mucho y anda mucho, va
mucho y sabe mucho.

Cervantes
Don Quixote

*He who reads much and walks much, goes
far and knows much.*

El que no sabe callar, no sabe conservar
amigos.

Diego de Estella
De la Vanidad del Mundo

*He who cannot hold his tongue cannot keep
his friends.*

El que no sabe gonzar de la ventura quando le viene, que no se debe quejar, si se le
pasa.

Cervantes
Don Quixote

*He who cannot enjoy good fortune when it
comes has no right to complain if it passes
him by.*

El que no tiene la cola de paja, no debe
temer el fuego.

Zàvala y Zamora
El Triunfo del Amor y Amistad

*He who has not a tail of straw needs not fear
the fire.*

El rostro feo
Les hice ver del temor.

Juan Ruiz de Allarcón y Mendoza
No hay Mal que por Bien no Venga

I let them see the ugly face of fear.

El sentido común es una constitución que
rige con más eficacia que todas las demás
constituciones.

Angel Ganivet
Los Trabajos de Pío Cid

*Common sense is a constitution which rules
more efficiently than any other.*

El sueño de la razón produce monstruos.

Francisco de Goya
title of a series of etchings

The sleep of reason produces monsters.

El único régimen compatible con la
dignidad del hombre es la democracia.

Ernesto Sábato
*Félix Grande, Elogio de la Libertad, Telegrama
Español, Lema*

*The only regime compatible with human dig-
nity is democracy.*

El valor espera; el miedo va a buscar.

José Bergamín
El Arte de Birlibirloque

Courage waits; fear goes searching.

El verdadero ejercicio intelectual no consiste en seguir modas, sino en encararse con las dificultades de la propia época.

Francisco Ayala
El Escritor en la Sociedad de Masas

Real intellectual activity consists, not in following trends, but rather in facing the difficulties of the time.

El vino conforta el corazon con el calor, y destruye el cerebro con la sequedad.

Ramón Lull
Árbol de los Ejemplos de la Ciencia

Wine comforts the heart with warmth, and destroys the brain by drying it.

El vino es sepultura de la memoria.

Juan Luis Vives
Introducción a la Sabiduría

Wine is the tomb of memory.

El vino tiene dos males: si le echais agua, echaislo a perder; si no lo echais, peirde á vos.

Melchior de Santa Cruz
Floresta Española

Wine has two defects: if you add water, you ruin it; if you do not add water, it ruins you.

El violoncelo es como una mujer que no sólo no envejece con los años sino que se hace más juvenil, más suave, más grácil, más ligera.

Pablo Casals

A cello is like a woman who does not age with the years but becomes younger, softer, more graceful, lighter.

Él presente no existe, es un punto entre la ilusión y la añoranza.

Llorenc Villalonga
Bearn

The present does not exist, it is a point between illusion and nostalgia.

Elocuencia es la previa seguridad de ser escuchado.

Eugenio D'Ors

Eloquence is a guaranteee of being listened to.

En circunstancias especiales, el hecho debe ser más rápido que el pensamiento.

Hernán Cortés
attrib. J. Marías, *España Inteligible*

In certain circumstances action should be quicker than thought.

En cuanto a Alemania, es ésta desde hace algunos años una nación de faquires que se pasan la vida contemplando el ombligo imperial germánico.

Miguel de Unamuno
La Supuesta Anormalidad Española

Germany, for some years now, has been a nation of fakirs who spend their lives contemplating the imperial Germanic navel.

En el folio 416, de su puño y letra y con la tinta roja de boticario, escribió una nota marginal: Dame un prejuicio y moveré el mundo.

Gabriel García Márquez
Crónica de una muerte anunciada

On folio 416, in his own handwriting and with the druggist's red ink, he wrote a marginal note: Give me a prejudice and I will move the world.

En el folio 382 del sumario escribió otra sentencia marginal con tinta roja. La fatalidad nos hace invisibles.

Gabriel García Márquez
Crónica de una Muerte Anunciada

On folio 382 of the brief, he wrote another marginal pronouncement in red ink: Fate makes us invisible.

En España la mejor manera de guardar un secreto es escribir un libro.

Manuel Azaña

The best way of keeping a secret in Spain is to write a book.

En este país en que siempre estamos clamando por la libertad, no siempre se perdona la libertad.

Gonzalo Torrente Ballester

In this country where we are always claiming liberty, a liberty is not always forgiven.

En este tipo de historia es difícil encontrar el primero de los actos.

attrib. **Che Guevera** by Paco Ignacio
"El año que Estuvimos en Ninguna Parte"

In this kind of story it is very difficult to find the first act.

En la boca del discreto lo público es secreto.

Proverb

In the mouth of a discreet person even that which is notorious remains a secret.

En la copa de Otoño un vago vino queda en que han de deshojarse, Primavera, tus rosas.

Rubén Darío
Versos de Otoño

In autumn's cup lingers a cloudy wine into which spring's roses must shed their petals.

En nuestro mortal estambre,
Lo que adelgaza es el hambre.

Félix Lope de Vega
Los Mialgros del Desprecio

*Hunger it is that puts to proof
The fineness of our mortal woof.*

En Oriente la mujer no suele ver al hombre antes de casarse. En Occidente, después.
Alvaro de Laiglesia

In the Orient the woman does not see the man before marriage. In the West, after it.

En política, como en gramática hay que distinguir los sustantivos de los adjetivos. Hitler era un sustantivo. Mussolini sólo era un adjetivo. Hitler era una amenaza. Mussolini era sangriento. Juntos eran una amenaza sangrienta.
Salvador de Madariaga

In politics as in grammar, one should be able to tell the substantives from the adjectives. Hitler was a substantive; Mussolini only an adjective. Hitler was menacing. Mussolini was bloody. Together a bloody menace.

En realidad el presente es muy poca cosa: casi todo fue.
Juan Benet
Volverás a Región

The present is really very small: almost everything has already happened.

En un ánimo constante
Siempre se halla igual semblante
Para el bien y el mal.
Pedro Calderón de La Barca
El Príncipe Constate

A constant spirit always shows the same face to good and bad alike.

En un lugar de la Mancha, de cuyo nombre no quiero accordarme, no há mucho tiempo que vivia un hidalgo de los de lanza en astillero, adargo antigua, rocin flaco, y galgo corredor.
Cervantes
Don Quijote , opening lines

In a village of La Mancha, the name of which I won't try to recall, there lived, not long ago, one of those gentlemen, who usually keep a lance upon a rack, an old shield, a lean horse and a greyhound for coursing.

En una hora no se ganó Zamora.
Fernando de Rojas
La Celestina

Zamora was not taken in an hour.

En vano a la puerta llama
Quien dentro la flecha tiene.
Jerónimo de Villaizan
Sufrir Mas por Querer Mas

*In vain the outward wound to heal,
And leave the arrow head within.*

Error funesto es decir que hay que comprender la música para gozar de ella. La música no se hace, ni debe jamás hacerse para que se comprenda, sino para que se sienta.
Manuel de Falla
Escritos sobre Música y Músicos

It is a huge mistake to say that one has to understand music before one can enjoy it. Music is not made, and should never be made, to be understood but to be felt.

Es la cortesía la principal parte de la cultura.

Baltasar Gracián
Oráculo Manual y Arte de Prudencia

Politeness is the chief ingredient of culture.

Es mejor ser la viuda de un héroe que la mujer de un cobarde.

Dolores Ibarruri

It is better to be a hero's widow than a coward's wife.

Es preferible morir de pie que vivir de rodillas.

Dolores Ibarruri
Discurso, Paris

It is better to die on your feet than to live on your knees.

Es propio de la lisonja
Olvidar al que está lejos.

Antonio Hurtado de Mendoza
El Marido Hace Mujer

It is the nature of flattery to forget the absent.

¿Es toda acción humana, como estimas ahora, fruto de imitación y de inconsciencia?

Luis Cernuda
Como Quien Espera el Alba. La Familia en La Realidad y el Deseo

Is every human action, as you now think, the fruit of imitation and thoughtlessness?

España es una nación de teólogos armados.

Marcelino Menéndez Pelayo
Imaginarios, 2, I. El Cardenal Cisneros

Spain is a nation of armed theologians.

Esta lucha con un enemigo a quien se comprende es la verdadera tolerancia, la actitud propia de toda alma robusta.

José Ortega y Gasset
Meditaciones del Quijote, Lector

This struggle with an enemy who is understood is true tolerance, the proper attitude of every robust soul.

Estos años asistimos al gigantesco espectáculo de innumerables vidas humanas que marchan perdidas en el laberinto de sí mismas por no tener a que entregarse.

José Ortega y Gasset
La Rebelión de las Masas

These days we are witnessing the vast spectacle of innumerable human lives wandering lost in the labyrinth of their own being because they have nothing to which they can devote themselves.

França és una grácia; Anglaterra és una forca; Alemanya és una técnica.

Eugenio D'Ors
Glossari, VII-1914

France is grace; England is force; Germany is method.

Gobernar es resistir.
Ramón María Narváez

To govern is to resist.

Habéis contraido una gravísima responsabilidad legalizando el Partido Comunista:
la historia os pedirá cuentas.
Fraga Iribarne
attrib. L. Calvo Sotelo, *Memoria Viva de la
Transición*

*You have assumed a huge responsibility in
legalising the Communist Party; history will
ask you to justify it.*

Haga como yo, no se meta en política.
General Franco

*Do the same as me, do not get involved in
politics.*

Hasta los bodegones tienen ideología.
Manuel Vásquez Montalbán
Cambio 16, 26 febrero 1996

Even still life paintings have an ideology.

Hay días tan húmedos que los tenedores
padecen el reumatismo.
Ramón Gómez de la Serna
Greguerías

*There are days so damp that even forks suffer
from rheumatism.*

Hay que hacer políticamente normal lo
que al nivel de la calle es normal.
Adolfo Suárez González
*Discurso en las Cortes defendiendo
la Ley para la Reforma política*

*What is normal in the street must be
made politically normal.*

Hay que tener razón, pero no a destiempo.
Antonio Buero Vallejo
Diálogo Secreto

*One must be right but not at the wrong
time.*

Hay quien llora lágrimas del color de la ira.
Vicente Aleixandre
Pasión de la tierra

*There are people who cry wrath-coloured
tears.*

Hay tres clases de ingratos: los que callan
el favor, los que lo cobran y los que lo
vengan.

Santiago Ramón y Cajal

*There are three types of ungrateful people:
those who hide a favour, those who charge
for it and those who take revenge for it.*

Hay una línea de Verlaine que no volveré
a recordar
Hay una calle próxima que está vedada
a mis pasos,

*There is a line of Verlaine I shall not recall
again,
There is a nearby street forbidden to my step,
There is a mirror that has seen me for the*

Hay un espejo que me ha visto per última vez,
Hay una puerta que he cerrado hasta el fin del mundo.
Entre los libros de mi biblioteca (estoy viéndolos)
Hay alguno que ya nunca abriré.
Este verano cumpliré cincuenta años;
La muerte nos desgasta incesante.

Jorge Luis Borges
Antología Personal, Límites

last time,
There is a door I have shut until the end of the world.
Among the books in my library (I have them before me)
There are some I shall never reopen.
This summer I complete my fiftieth year:
Death constantly diminishes us.

He conocido lo que ignoran los griegos: la incertidumbre.

Jorge Luis Borges
Ficciones, Tlön, Uqbar, Orbis Tertius. La Lotería en Babilonia

I have known what the Greeks did not know: uncertainty.

Hombres necios que acusáis a la mujer sin razón, sin ver que sois la ocasión de lo mismo que culpáis.

Sor Juana Inés de la Cruz
"Sátira Filosófica"

You foolish and unreasoning men who cast all blame on women, not seeing that you yourselves are the cause of these very faults.

Hoy en día los ejércitos se toman muy en serio eso de que el primer deber de un militar no es morir por su patria sino procurar que el enemigo muera por la suya.

Santiago de Mora-Figueroa

Nowadays armies take very seriously the proposition that a soldier's first duty is not to die for his country but to ensure that the enemy dies for his.

Hoy la Nave del contento
Con viento en popa de gusto,
Donde jamas hay disgusto.

Félix Lope de Vega
Hoy la Nave del Deleite

Today the ship of contentment set sail with a favourable wind for a country where there are no troubles.

Hoy la he visto..., la he visto y me ha mirado...
!Hoy creo en Dios!

Gustavo Adolfo Bécquer
Rimas

Today I saw her, and she smiled at me.
Today I believe in God.

Hablo en español a Dios, en italiano a las mujeres, en francés a los hombres y en alemán a mi caballo.

attrib. **Carlos I**

I speak in Spanish to God, in Italian to women, in French to men and in German to my horse.

Juventud, divio tesoro, ya te vas para no volver! Cuando quiero llorar, no lloro, y a veces lloro sin querer.

Rubén Darío
Canción de Otoño en Primavera

Youth, divine treasure, you will not come back again! When I want to cry I do not cry, and sometimes I cry pretending not to cry.

L'arena se tornó sangriento lago,
La llanura con muertos, aspereza;
Cayó en unos vigor, cayó denuedo,
Más en otros desmayo y torpe miedo.

Fernando De Herrera
Canción por la Perdida del Rei Don Sebastián

The battlefield became a bloody lake, the plain harsh with corpses; there fell the brave and the bold, there too the cowardly and the frightened.

La admiración es bien recibida aunque venga de los tontos.

Palacio Valdés

Admiration is always welcome even when it comes from stupid people.

La caça es arte e sabiduria de guerrear e de vencer.

Alfonso el Sabio
Las Siete Partidas

Hunting is the art and science of warfare and of conquest.

La casualidad es la décima musa.
Enrique Jardiel Poncela
Máximas Mínimas

Chance is the tenth muse.

La ciencia, el arte, la justicia, la cortesía,
la religión son órbitas de la realidad que
no invaden bárbaramente nuestra persona
como hace el hambre o el frío; sólo existen
para quien tiene voluntad de alles.

José Ortega y Gasset

Science, art, justice, manners, religion are orbits of reality which do not overwhelm our persons in a brutal way as hunger or cold does; they exist only for him who wishes them to exist.

La codicia en las manos de la suerte
Se arroja al mar, la ira a las espadas,
Y la ambición se ríe de la muerte.

Andrés Fernández de Andrada
Epístola Moral

Greed seeking fortune braves the ocean, anger throws itself on the swords of the enemy, and ambition laughs at death.

La constancia de la veleta es cambiar.

José Bergamín
Prosas Previas, Aforística Persistente

A weathercock's constancy lies in change.

La cultura es una forma de la memoria.
Guillermo Díaz-Plaja
Ensayos sobre Comunicación Cultural,
Mensaje Oral y Texto Excrito, I, Oralitura

Culture is a form of memory.

La democracia es la transposición de lo cuantitativo: que lo que quieren los más se convierta en lo mejor.
Enrique Tierno Galván

Democracy is the transposition of quantity into quality: that which the majority want becomes the best.

La dictadura es el sistema de gobierno en lo que no está prohibido es obligatorio.
Enrique Jardiel Poncela

Dictatorship is the system of government in which what is not forbidden is compulsory.

La encuentro [la ciencia] analítica, pretenciosa, superficial; en gran medida porque no tiene en cuenta los sueños, el azar, la risa, los sentimientos y las paradojas – aquello que yo más amo.
Luis Buñuel

I find it [science] analytic, pretentious, superficial; largely because it does not take into account dreams, fate, laughter, feelings and paradoxes - those things which I love most.

La experiencia no consiste en lo que se ha vivido, sino en lo que se ha reflexionado.
José María de Pereda

Experience is not what you have lived but what you have reflected on.

La filosofía es idealmente lo contrario de la noticia, de la erudición.
José Ortega y Gasset

Ideally, philosophy is the opposite of information or erudition.

La fórmula de la vejez digna es la soledad sin resquemor.
José Luis Sampedro
El País, 5 febrero 1996

Solitude without resentment is the formula for a dignified old age.

La gasolina es el incienso de la civilización.
Ramón Gómez de la Serna
Greguerías

Petrol is the incense of civilisation.

La generalidad de los hombres nadamos en el océano de la vulgaridad.
Pío Baroja
Las Inquietudes de Shanti Andía

Most of us swim in the ocean of the commonplace.

La historia es una rama de la literatura.
Pío Baroja
Memorias

History is a branch of literature.

La historia me absolverá.
Fidel Castro
during his trial by the Court of Justice, 1953

History will absolve me.

La ingratitud humana no tiene límites
Gabriel García Márquez
El Coronel no Tiene Quien le Escriba

There are no limits to human ingratitude.

La justicia de rey es la paz de su pueblo.
Ramón Lull
Árbol de los Ejemplos de la Ciencia (Proverbios)

The justice of the king is the peace of his people.

La libertad no hace felices a los hombres,
los hace sencillamente hombres.
Manuel Azaña

Freedom does not make men happy, it simply makes them men.

La literatura no puede reflejar todo lo
negro de la vida. La razón principal es que
la Literatura escoge y la vida no escoge.
Pío Baroja
Memorias

Literature cannot reflect all the darkness of life. The main reason for this is that Literature selects and life does not.

La modestia es la virtud de los que no
tienen otra.
Alvaro de Laiglesia

Modesty is the virtue of those who have no other.

La moral, por muy concienzuda que sea,
rara vez supera sus propios términos
municipales. No hay una moral universal.
Sólo hay morales municipales.
Francisco Umbral
Memorias de un Niño de Derechas

Morality, no matter how thorough it might be, rarely reaches beyond its own municipal limits. There is no universal morality, only a municipal one.

La mucha luz es como la mucha sombra:
no deja ver.
Octavio Paz
"La mirada anterior", Prólogo a C. Castaneda, Las enseñanzas de Don Juan

Too much light is like too much darkness: you cannot see.

La necesidad desecha la tardanza.
Fernando de Rojas
La Celestina

Necessity rejects delay.

La patria nos bendice y el patriotismo
nos condena.
Luis Rosales

The fatherland blesses us and patriotism condemns us.

La paz entre estas dos potencias, razón y sentimiento, se hace imposible, y hay que vivir de su guerra. Y hacer de ésta, de la guerra misma, condición de nuestra vida espiritual.
Miguel de Unamuno

Between these two powers, reason and feeling, there can never be peace, and we must live with their war. We must make this war the condition of our spiritual life.

La peor soledad que hay es el darse cuenta de que la gente es idiota.
Gonzalo Torrente Ballester

The worst solitude is realising that people are idiots.

La pluma corta más que espadas enfiladas.
Antonio Pérez
Aforismos

The pen cuts deeper than a sharpened sword.

La poesía es el punto de intersección entre el poder divino y la voluntad humana.
Octavio Paz

Poetry is the intersection between divine power and human will.

La poesía no es nada sino tiempo, ritmo perpetuamente creador.
Octavio Paz
El Arco y la Lira

Poetry is nothing but time, perpetually creative rhythm.

La poesía tiene su honradez y yo he querido siempre ser honrado.
José Martí
Versos libres, Mis versos

Poetry has its own honesty and I have always wanted to be honest.

La política no es más que el conjunto de las razones para obedecer y de las razones para sublevarse.
Fernando Savater
Política para Amador

Politics are nothing more than a group of reasons to obey and of reasons to rebel.

La quinta columna.
General Emilio Mola

The fifth column. (The Nationalist General Mola said that he had four columns ready to attack Madrid, and a fifth column of sympathisers waiting for him inside the city.)

La religión nunca debe olvidarse porque entonces los pecados perderían su gracia.
Reynaldo Arenas

Religion should never be forgotten, otherwise sins would stop being fun.

La rosa sería soberbia sino hubiese nacido entre espinas.

Ramón Lull
Árbol de los Ejemplos de la Ciencia (Proverbios)

The rose would have been proud if it had not been born amongst thorns.

La verdad, si no es entera, se convierte en aliada de lo falso.

Javier Sádaba

Truth, if not complete, becomes the friend of falisity.

La victoria en la guerra sólo se consigue cuando se hace ganar también a los vencidos.

Fraga Iribarne

Victory in war can be achieved only when one allows the vanquished to win as well.

La vida es como el café o las castañas en otoño. Siempre huele mejor de lo que sabe.

Maruja Torres

Life is like coffee or chestnuts in autumn. The smell is better than the taste.

La vida es siempre personal, circunstancial, intransferible y responsable.

José Ortega y Gasset
Estructura de "Nuestro" Mundo

Life is always personal, circumstantial, untransferable and responsible.

La vida es trivial. ¡Afortunadamente!

Antonio Buero Vallejo
El Tragaluz

Life is trivial. Fortunately!

La vida es una película mal montada.

Fernando Trueba
Diario 16, 27-X1-92

Life is a badly edited film.

La vida no se nos ha dado para ser felices, sino para merecer serlo.

Palacio Valdés

Life has not been given us to be happy but to deserve to be.

Las almas enamordas y enfermas son tal vez las que tejen los más hermosos sueños de la ilusión.

Ramón María del Valle-Inclán
Sonata de Otoño

Souls that are sick and in love are perhaps more prone than others to dream dreams and weave illusions.

Las convicciones políticas son como la virginidad: una vez perdidas no vuelven a recobrarse.

Francesc Pi I Margall

Political convictions are like virginity: once lost they cannot be recovered.

Las diferencias entre el idioma hablado o escrito y los otros – plásticos o musicales – son muy profundas, pero no tanto que nos hagan olvidar que todos son, esencialmente, lenguaje: sistemas expresivos dotados de poder significativo.

Octavio Paz
El Arco y la Lira

The differences between spoken or written language and the other kinds - plastic or musical - are very profound, but not enough to make us forget that essentially they are all languages: systems of expression which possess a significant power.

Las mismas cosas tienen, en distintos días, distintos modos de acontecer y lo que ocurrió bajo la lluvia, sólo bajo la lluvia puede ser contado.

Rafael Sánchez Ferlosio

The same things happen differently on different days, and what happened in the rain, can be told only in the rain.

Las mujeres gobiernan América porque América es una tierra en que los jóvenes no quieren crecer.

Salvador de Madariaga
The Perpetual Pessimist

Women govern America because America is a land of boys who refuse to grow up.

Las novelas no las han escrito más que los que son incapaces de vivirlas.

Alejandro Casona
Tres Perfectas Casadas

The only people who write novels are those incapable of living them.

Las palabras son horcas donde a trozos cuelgo la razón.

Salvador Espritu
Les hores, Perqué un dia torni la cançó a Sinera

Words are gallows where I hang reason in pieces.

Las palabras, vestido de los conceptos.
Antonio Pérez
Aforismos

Words, the raiment of thought.

Las perplejidades que no sin alguna sober-bia se llaman metafísica.

Jorge Luis Borges
Elogio de la sombra, Prólogo

The perplexities that, not without some arrogance, are called metaphysics.

Le expliqué que el mundo es una sinfonía, pero que Dios toca de oído.

Ernesto Sábato
Quique Estaba Sombrío

I explained that the world is a symphony, but God plays by ear.

Liberal es aquel que piensa que su país es de todos, incluso de quienes piensan que es sólo de ellos.

Camilo José Cela
Entrevista, Montserrat Roig, Los Hechiceros de la Palabra, Camilo José Cela, un lobo manso

A liberal is one who thinks his country belongs to everyone, even to those who think it belongs only to them.

Lo bello nace de la muerte de lo útil: lo útil se convierte en bello cuando ha caducado su utilidad.

José Enrique Rodó
letter to Miguel de Unamuno, 1903

What is beautiful has its origin in the death of what is useful; what is useful becomes beautiful when it has outlived its usefulness.

Lo esencial en la obra de un creador sale de alguna obsesión de su infancia.

Ernesto Sábato
Abaddón el exterminador, Cavilaciones, un diálogo

What is essential in the work of an artist comes from his childhood obsessions.

Lo grave de que la muerte se acerque no es la propia muerte con lo que traiga o no traiga, sino que ya no se podrá fantasear con lo que ha de venir.

Javier Marías
Todas las almas

The worst thing about the approach of death isn't death itself and what it may or may not bring, it's the fact that one can no longer fantasise about the future.

Lo importante no es escuchar lo que se dice, sino averiguar lo que se piensa.

José Donoso Cortés

The important thing is not listening to what is said but discerning what is thought.

Lo importante y raro
No es entender de todo,
Sino ser discreto en algo.

Charles Yriarte
Fábulas Literarias

*That which first and rarest is
Is not to seek all things to know,
But sense in certain things to show.*

Lo mejor de la santidad son las tentaciones.
Ramón María del Valle-Inclán

The best thing about sanctity is the temptation.

Lo mismo podermos ver a gente que viene a ofrecerme la corona sobre un cojín, que a la Guardia Civil con orden de arrestarme.

Juan Carlos
El Rey, Conversaciones con D. Juan Carlos I de España, de José Luis de Villalonga

We may see people offering me the crown on a cushion or else the civil guard coming to arrest me.

Lo propio pierde quien lo ajeno busca.
Alvarez de Toledo
La Burromaquia. Rebuzno Primero

His own he loses who the wealth of others seeks.

Lo que poseemos nos posee.
Fernando Savater

What we own owns us.

Lo que puedo contar no tiene interés, y lo que tiene interés no puedo contarlo.
Sabino Fernández Campo, Conde de Latores

What I can tell is not interesting, and what is interesting I cannot tell you.

Lope de Aguirre: No olviden mis hijos que la conciencia del peligro es ya la mitad de la seguridad y de la salvación.
Ramón J Sender

Lope de Aguirre: My children, you must not forget that being aware of danger is halfway towards security and salvation.

Los creyentes no sirven más que para mártires.
Camilo José Cela
Memorias, entendimientos y voluntades. Claudio Coellio

Believers are useful only as martyrs.

Los errores tienen numerosas vidas.
Salvador de Madariaga
Ingleses, Franceses, Españoles

Mistakes have numerous lives.

Los fanatismos que más debemos temer son aquellos que pueden confundirse con la tolerancia.
Fernando Arrabal
La Torre Herida por el Rayo

The fanaticism we should most fear is that which can be mistaken for tolerance.

Los intelectuales siempre están donde hay un canapé.
Javier Sádaba

You can always find intellectuals wherever there are canapés.

Los jueces se rigen por la legalidad; los políticos por la oportunidad.
Juan Alberto Belloch
El País Internacional, 1994

Judges are guided by the law, politicians by expediency.

Los niños son mendigos por intuición.
Wenceslao Fernándex Flórez
El Malvado Carabel

Children are instinctive beggars.

Los ojos tristes, de llorar cansados,
Alzando al cielo, su clemencia imploro;
Mas vuelven luego al encendido lloro,
Que el grave peso no les sufre alzados.
Juan Menéndez Valdés
El Despecho

Worn out with weeping, I raise my sad gaze to heaven, imploring its mercy; but then I begin to weep still more, so that my heavy sorrow prevents my looking upward any longer.

Los príncipes nacieron poderosos pero no enseñados.
Diego de Saavedra Fajardo
Idea de un Príncipe político cristiano

Princes were born powerful but not trained.

Los que amigos se fazen, ante que bien se conozcan, ligeramente guardan despues la amistad de entrellos.
Alfonso el Sabio
Las Siete Partidas

Those who make friends before they know each other well afterwards hold their friendship lightly.

Los siglos que en sus hojas cuenta el roble,
Arbol los cuenta sordo, tronco jugo.
Quien mas ve, quien mas oye, menos dura.
Luis de Góngora
Sonetos Varios

*The years of which the oak leaves chatter,
The trunk and sap do darkly tell;
They who see and hear most freely,
Do on earth most briefly dwell.*

Los suspiros son aire y van al aire.
Las lágrimas son agua y van al mar.
Dime, mujer: cuando el amor se olvida,
¿sabes tú a dónde va?
Gustavo Adolfo Bécquer
Rimas

*Sighs are air, to air returning,
Tears are water, to the sea,
But when love has been forgotten,
Tell me, woman, where goes he?*

Luchando, cuerpo a cuerpo, con la muerte,
al borde del abismo estoy clamando a
Dios. Y su silencio, retumbando, ahoga mi
voz en el vacío inerte.
Blas de Otero
Ángel Fieramente Humano, Hombre

Fighting hand-to-hand with death, at the edge of the abyss I am crying out to God. And his silence, booming, drowns my voice in the lifeless vacuum

¡Malditos treinta años!
Funesta edad de amargos desengaños.
José de Espronceda
El Diablo Mundo

Accursed the age of thirty years, with all our fond illusions dead.

Malo es tener pensado ni previsto nada en la vida.

Jacinto Benavente y Martínez
Rosas de Otoño

It is bad to plan or foresee anything in life.

Más calla
Quien mas siente.

Guillén de Castro
Las Mocedades del Cid

He says least who feels the most.

Más largo
Que una noche de diciembre
Para un hombre mal casado.

Luis de Góngora
Romances Burlescos

Longer than a winter's night for a man who is unhappily married

---

Más sabe el corazón que la cabeza.

Ramón de Campoamor
Los Grandes Problemas

More than the head, the heart doth know.

Más triunfos, más coronas dió al prudente
Que supo retirarse, la fortuna,
Que al que esperó obstinada y locamente.

Andrés Fernández de Andrada
Epístola Moral

Fortune has given more victories and prizes to those who knew when to withdraw than to those who obstinately and insanely waited in hope.

Más vale ir al presidio para toda la vida que no denunciar a un hombre.

Pío Baroja
La Dama Errante

It is better to go to prison for life than to denounce someone.

Más vale que digan aquí huyó, que aquí murió.

Proverb

It is better they should say "Here he ran away" than "Here he died".

Materializar en la realidad una metáfora es lograr el poema perfecto.

Luis Racionero
Raimon, la Alquimia de la Locura

To materialise a metaphor is to achieve a perfect poem.

Me desconcierta tanto pensar que Dios existe, como pensar que no existe. Entonces prefiero no pensar en eso.

Gabriel García Márquez
La hojarasca

I get just as upset thinking that God exists as thinking that he doesn't. That's why I'd rather not think about it.

Me interesan las cosas ajenas, porque las mías no tienen remedio.

Ramiro de Maeztu
Autobiography

I am interested in other peoples' affairs because mine have no solution.

Mi concepto de la novela: decir las cosas por insinuación.

Gabriel Miró
Nota autobiográfica

My concept of the novel: to say things by insinuation.

Mi primo Francisco y yo estamos de acuerdo: los dos queremos Milán.

Carlos I
attrib. B. Granián

My cousin Francis and I are in perfect accord - he wants Milan and so do I.

Mi punto fuerte es, creo yo, ser un hombre normal. Completamente normal. No hay sitio para los genios en nuestra actual situación.

Adolfo Suárez González
Declaraciones al Süddeutsche Zeitung, 1V-1977

My strongest point, I believe, is being a normal man. Completely normal. There is no room for geniuses in our present situation.

Morir cuerdo, y vivir loco.

Cervantes
Don Quijote's epitaph

To die in wisdom having lived in folly.

Morir es una costumbre
Que sabe tener la gente.

Jorge Luis Borges
Elogio de la Sombra

Dying is a well-known custom.

Mucho más grande que no admirar nada es no despreciar nada.

Leopoldo Alas Clarín
La Regenta

Far grander than not admiring anything is not to despise anything.

Muchos van por lana, y vuelven trasquilados.

Cervantes
Don Quijote

Many who go for wool come back shorn.

Mujeres al borde de un ataque de nervios.
Pedro Almodóvar
title of a film

Women on the verge of a nervous break-down.

Nada da idea de la vejez prematura de un hombre hecho y derecho como su sumi-sión incondicional a la juventud de los otros.
Gregorio Marañón
Ensayos liberales

Nothing indicates the premature old age of an honest and true man more than his unconditional submission to others' youth.

Nada prende tan pronto de unas almas en otras como esta simpatía de la risa.
Jacinto Benavente
Los Intereses Creados

Nothing is so contagious as the sympathy of a smile.

Necesitamos de la historia íntegra para ver si logramos escapar de ella, no recaer en ella.
José Ortega y Gasset
La Rebelión de las Masas

We need the whole of history in order to see if we can escape from it and not fall back into it.

Ni un solo momento, viejo hermoso Walt Whitman, he dejado de ver tu barba llena de mariposas.
Federico García Lorca
Oda a Walt Whitman

Not for a moment, beautiful aged Walt Whitman, have I failed to see your beard full of butterflies.

No cederemos ni un átomo de nuestro honor.
Fidel Castro

We shall not yield one atom of our honour.

No eran sino molinos de viento, y no lo podía ignorar sino quien llevase otros tan-tos en la cabeza.
Cervantes
Don Quijote

There were only windmills, and no one could doubt it save a man who carried similar windmills in his head.

No es la miel para la boca del asno.
Cervantes
Don Quijote

Honey is not for the ass's mouth.

No está lejos de su acuerdo
El loco que conoce su locura.
Ruiz de Alarcón
La Amistad Castigada

The madman who knows his madness is not far from sanity.

No hace el numen el que lo dora, sino el que lo adora.

Gracián
Oráculo Manual

Divinity is created not by adorning, but by adoring, it.

No hay dolor más grande que el dolor de ser vivo, Ni mayor pesadumbre que la vida consciente.

Rubén Darío
Lo Fatal

There is no greater sorrow than that of being alive; no greater burden than conscious existence.

No hay en Occidente pueblo más gregario que el catalán a la hora de elegir su residencia: a donde va uno a vivir, allí quieren ir los demás. Donde sea, era el lema, pero todos juntos.

Eduardo Mendoza
La Ciudad de los Prodigios

There is no people in the Western world more gregarious than the Catalans: where one Catalan goes to live, the others want to go too. "Anywhere at all", was the motto, "but all together".

No hay mal que no se oyga bien,
Ni bien que no se oyga mal.

Fernández de León
Venir el Amor al Mundo

There is no evil of which good is not heard, no good of which some do not think ill.

No, no quiero ese mundo. Me aturde, me marea y me confunde. Sus hombres y sus cosas revolotean zumbando en torno de mi espíritu y me impiden soñar; son como nube de langosta que me vela mis luceros.

Miguel de Unamuno
Después de una Conversación

No, I don't love this world. It perplexes me, makes me feel sick and confuses me. Its men and its things flutter and buzz arounnd my spirit and prevent me from dreaming; they are like a cloud of locusts blocking out my stars.

¡No pasaran!

Dolores Ibarruri
Nationalist troops subsequently chanted
"¡Hemos pasado!", "We passed".

They shall not pass!

No puedo perdonar a mis enemigos, porque los he matado a todos.

Ramón María Narváez

I cannot forgive my enemies because I have killed them all.

No quiero que se vierta una sola gota de sangre española por mi persona.

Alfonso XIII

I do not want one drop of Spanish blood to be spilled on my account.

No se mueren de amor
Las mujeres de hoy en día.

José de Espronceda
El Estudiante de Salamanca

Women nowadays do not die for love.

No sentía mis pies. Quise cogerlos
en mi mano, y no hallé mis manos:
quise gritar, y no hallé mi voz. La
niebla me envolvía.

Luis Cernuda
Los Placeres Prohibidos

I couldn't feel my feet. I wanted to take hold of them with my hand, but I couldn't find my hands: I wanted to shout, and I didn't find my voice. Mist enveloped me.

No son muchos los hombres que tienen
una idea medianamente adecuada de lo
que es la mujer. Para ello hace falta un
interés complejo y casi todos los intereses
que los hombres experimentan por las
mujeres son demasiado simples.

Julián Marías
Todas las Almas

Not many men have even a moderately right idea of what a woman is. It requires a complicated degree of interest, and almost all the interest which men have in women is too basic.

No soporto al artista cuya principal moti-
vación sea la provocación. Creo que los
grandes provocadores lo son sin pro-
ponérselo.

Pedro Almodóvar

I cannot stand an artist whose main motivation is to provoke. I believe the great provokers are those who did not mean to be so provocative.

No suelen ser nuestras ideas las que nos
hacen optimistas o pesimistas, sino que es
nuestro optimismo o nuestro pesimismo, de
origen fisiológico o patalógico quizás ... el
que hace nuestras ideas.

Miguel de Unamuno
Del Sentimiento Trágico de la Vida

It is not normally our ideas which make us optimists or pessimists, but our optimism or pessimism, perhaps of physiological or pathological origin, which forms our ideas.

No todo lo grande es bueno: más todo lo
bueno es grande.

Melchor de Santa Cruz
Floresta Española

Not everything great is good; but everything good is great.

No valen de nada los criterios cronológicos
para evocar el tiempo pasado.

Carmen Martín Gaite
La Prima Magdalena

Chronological criteria are worthless in evoking past times.

Nuestra finalidad al fomentar una insurrección, es la de salvar a la Europa Occidental de la amenaza del comunismo.
General Franco

Our aim in promoting insurrection is to save Western Europe from the menace of Communism.

Nunca más.
Ernesto Sábato
title of the report about the *Desaparecidos* (missing people) in Argentina

Never again.

Nunca un triunfo ha sido tan amargo ni una derrota tan dulce.
Alfonso Guerra
El País, 5 de marzo 1996,
after the defeat of the socialist government in the 1996 elections

Never has a victory been so bitter nor a defeat sweeter.

Odiar a alguien es sentir irritación por su simple existencia.
José Ortega y Gasset
Estudios sobre el Amor

To hate someone is to feel irritated by his mere existence.

Opinión, ninguna gana;
pues la que más se recata,
si no os admite, es ingrata,
y si os admite, es liviana.
Sor Juana Inés de la Cruz
"Satira Filosófica"

No one can gain your good opinion; for she who modestly withdraws and refuses to admit you is ungrateful, yet if she does admit you, she is too easily won.

Paciencia y barajar.
Cervantes
Don Quijote

Patience and shuffle the cards.

Para destruir las malas prácticas, la ley es mucho menos útil que los esfuerzos individuales.
Ángel Ganivet
Idearium Español

For getting rid of bad behaviour the law is much less useful than the effort of individuals.

Para el triunfo sobra el talento mientras que para la felicidad ni basta.
Camilo José Cela
Diario 16, 14-II-1992

Talent is more than enough for success, but for happiness it is not enough.

Para mí sola nació Don Quijote, y yo para él.
Cervantes

For me alone was Don Quixote born, and I for him.

Para ver una cosa hay que comprenderla. Si viéramos realmente el universo, tal vez lo comprenderíamos.
Jorge Luis Borges
El Libro de Arena

One must understand a thing to see it. If we really saw the world, perhaps we would understand it.

Pensar es el afán de captar mediante ideas la realidad.
José Ortega y Gasset
La Deshumanización del Arte, 1925

Thinking is the urge to achieve reality through ideas.

Pintar un cuadro es o muy sencillo o imposible.
Salvador Dalí

Painting a picture is either very easy or impossible.

Pinto las cosas como las pienso, no como las veo.
Pablo Picasso

I paint not what I see but what I feel.

Pobre México, tan lejos de Dios y tan cerca de los Estados Unidos.
Porfirio Díaz

Poor Mexico, so far from God and so near to the United States.

Poca cosa es la vida si no piafa en ella un afán formidable de ampliar sus fronteras. Se vive en la proporción en que se ansía vivir más.
José Ortega y Gasset
la Deshumanización del Arte

Life is a petty thing unless there pounds within it an enormous desire to extend its boundaries. We live to the extent that we yearn to live more.

"Pocos," respondio Don Quijote.
Cervantes
Don Quixote

"Few," replied Don Quixote (when asked if there were no modest poets).

¡Por una mirada un mundo;
por una sonrisa, un cielo;
por un beso... ! yo no sé
qué te diera por un beso!
Gustavo Adolfo Bécquer
Rimas

For one look...I would give my world,
For one smile...I would give all my heaven,
For one kiss...I do not know what I would give for one kiss.

Porque en noches como ésta la tuve entre
mis brazos,
mi alma no se contenta con haberla
perdido.
Aunque ésta sea el último dolor que ella
me causa,
y estos sean los últimos versos que yo le
escribo.
Pablo Neruda

*Because through nights like this I held her in
my arms, my soul is not content to have lost
her, though this be the last pain that she
causes me and these are the last verses that I
write her.*

Prefiero el profesional, aunque sea
mediocre, a un aficionado brillante.
Francisco Umbral
*Entrevista, Montserrat Roig, Los Hechiceros
de la Palabra, Paco Umbral y su sombra*

*I prefer a mediocre professional to a
brilliant amateur.*

Publicamos para no pasarnos la
vida corrigiendo los borradores.
Alfonso Reyes

*We publish so we do not have to spend our
lives correcting the drafts.*

Puedo escribir los versos más tristes esta
noche.
Escribir, por ejemplo: "La noche está
estrellada,
y tiritan, azules, los astros, a lo lejos".
El viento de la noche gira en el cielo y canta.
Puedo escribir los versos más tristes esta
noche.
Yo la quise, y a veces ella también me
quiso.
Pablo Neruda
*Viente Poemasde Amor y una Canción
Desesperada*

*Tonight I can write the saddest lines.Write,
for example, "The night is starry and the
stars are blue and shiver in the distance"
The night wind revolves in the sky and
sings. Tonight I can write the saddest lines. I
loved her, and sometimes she loved me too.*

Pues bien, mi señor don Miguel, también
usted se morirá, también usted, y se
volverá a la nada de que salió ... ¡Dios
dejará de soñarle!
Miguel de Unamuno
Niebla, 1914

*Well then, my lord don Miguel, you also
will die, and return to nothingness from
whence you came ... God will stop dreaming
of you!*

Pues la palabra blanda nos concede
Lo que la dura pocas veces puede.
Castellanos
Varones Ilustres de Indias

*Gentle words may oft obtain
What the hard ones fail to gain.*

281

Que el cielo exista, aunque mi lugar sea el infierno.

Jorge Luis Borges
Ficciones, Tlön, Uqbar, Orbis Tertius. La Biblioteca de Babel

Let heaven exist, even if my place be hell.

Que es como pimienta el oro
Que al que más come más pica.

Ruiz de Alarcón
El Desdichado en Fingir

Gold is like pepper. The more you eat the more it pricks you.

Que hay cosas que no parecen
Tan mal hechas, como dichas.

Calderón
Los Cabellos de Absalon

There are some things that seem not so ill when done as when said.

¿Qué es la vida? Una ilusión,
Una sombra, una ficción...
Que toda la vida es sueño,
Y los sueños sueños son.

Calderón

What is life? An illusion, a shadow, a fiction...for the whole of life is a dream, and dreams themselves are but dreams.

"¿Qué es poesía?" – dices mientras clavas
en mi pupila tu pupila azul.
"¿Qué es poesía?" Y tú me lo preguntas?
Poesía...eres tú.

Gustavo Adolfo Bécquer
Rimas

*"What is poetry?" you ask as you hold my eyes with your eyes of blue.
What is poetry? Well, since you ask me, it is you.*

Quien quiera enseñarnos una verdad que
no nos la diga: simplemente que aluda a
ella con un leve gesto, gesto que inicie en
el aire una ideal trayectoria, deslizándonos
por la cual lleguemos nosotros mismos a
los pies de la nueva verdad.

José Ortega y Gasset
Meditación preliminar, 4, Trasmundos

He who wishes to teach us a truth should not tell it to us, but simply suggest it with a brief gesture which starts trajectory of ideas in the air, along which we glide until we find ourselves at the feet of the new truth.

Quien teme la muerte no goza la vida.

Proverb

He who fears death cannot enjoy life

Quiso cantar, cantar para olvidar su vida
verdadera de mentiras y recordar su mentirosa vida de verdades.

Octavio Paz
Condición de Nube, Epitafio para un Poeta

He tried to sing, singing so as to forget his true life of lies and to remember his lying life of truths.

Religión es la caballería.	*Knight-errantry is religion.*
Cervantes *Don Quijote*	
¡Santificadas sean las cosas! ¡Amadlas, amadlas!	*Blessed be things! Love them, love them!*
José Ortega y Gasset *Meditaciones del Quijote*	
Ser humano exige ver lo perecedero y el mismo pereciemiento como elementos de nuestra propia condición.	*Being human requires us to see what is perishable and the perishing itself as elements of our own condition.*
Enrique Tierno Galván	
Ser liberal es, precisamente, estas dos cosas: primero, estar dispuesto a enterderse con el que piensa de otro modo, y segundo, no admitir jamás que el fin justifica los medios, sino que, por el contrario, son los medios los que justifican el fin. El liberalismo es, pues, una conducta y, por lo tanto, es mucho más que una política.	*Being a liberal means two things; firstly, being ready to talk to people with different ideas, and, secondly, never to admit that the end justifies the means, but, on the contrary, that the means are what justify the end. Liberalism is a mode of behaviour and, therefore, much more than politics.*
Gregorio Marañón *Ensayos liberales*	
Si Dios me hubiese consultado sobre el sistema del universo, le habría dado unas cuantas ideas.	*If God had consulted me about the creation of the universe, I could have provided some useful ideas.*
Alfonso el Sabio	
Si es o no invención moderna, vive Dios, que no lo sé! Pero delicada fué la invención de la taberna!	*Whether or not it was a modern invention, by God I cannot tell! But the invention of the tavern was indeed a dainty thought!*
Baltasar del Alcazar	
Si queréis entablar verdadera un inglés, no le habléis nunca; !sobre todo! no le dejéis jamás que os cuente sus intimidades, porque nunca habrá de perdonárselo.	*If you want to have a real friendship with an Englishman, never talk; especially never let him tell you his intimate thoughts because he will never forgive himself.*
Ramiro de Maeztu *Autobiography*	
Si uno es Che Guevara, actúa sobre el poder; si es Einstein, sobre la tecnología;	*If one is Che Guevara, one will work on power; if Einstein, on technology, if Jesus on*

si es Jesucristo, sobre los valores. En el primer caso se suele acabar fusilado, en el segundo Premio Nobel, en el tercero crucificado.

Luis Racionero

values. In the first case, one usually gets shot, in the second a Nobel prize, in the third crucified.

¡Silencio!...¡Silencio!
Ante la muerte sólo vale el silencio.

León Felipe
¡Oh, este viejo y roto violin!, öngeles

Silence!...Silence! Before death only silence counts.

Sin los escritores, aun los actos más laudables son de un día.

José Martínez Ruiz Azorín
De un atranseúnte 16-VI-1914

Without writers, even the most praiseworthy acts last only a day.

Solo temo a mis enemigos cuando empiezan a tener razón.

attrib. **Jacinto Benavente**

I fear my enemies only when they start being right.

Sólo hay una diferencia entre un loco y yo. Yo no estoy loco.

Salvador Dalí

There is only one difference between a madman and me. I am not mad.

Sólo la luna sospecha la verdad. Y es que el hombre no existe.

Vicente Aleixandre
Mundo a Solas

Only the moon suspects the truth. Which is that mankind does not exist.

Sólo la virtud tiene argumentos poderosos contra el pesimismo.

Leopoldo Alas Clarín
La Regenta, I. Cavilaciones

Only virtue has powerful arguments against pessimism.

Soy ateo gracias a Dios.

Luis Buñuel

I am an atheist, thank God.

Soy el desperado, la palabra sin ecos, el que lo perdió todo, y el que todo lo tuvo.

Pablo Neruda

I am the one without hope, the word without echoes, he who lost everything and he who had everything

Soy, mas, estoy. Respiro. Lo profundo es el aire. La realidad me inventa, soy su leyenda. ¡Salve!

Jorge Guillén
Cántico. Más Allá

I exist, more than that, I'm alive. I'm breathing. Deep is the air. Reality invents me, I am its legend. Hail!

Soy reacio a escribir mis memorias, pues
uno queda bien a costa de los demás.
Felipe González
Cambio 16, 4 marzo 1996

*I am reluctant to write my memoirs because
one always gets credit at the expense of
others.*

Soy, tácitos amigos, el que sabe
Que no hay otra venganza que el olvido.
Jorge Luis Borges
Soy

*I am, my silent friends, the one who knows
there is no revenge except forgetfulness.*

Tan ciego estoy a mi mortal enredo que no
te oso llamar, Señor, de miedo de que
querrás sacarme de pecado.
Francisco Gómez de Quevedo y Villegas
Heráclito ristiano

*So blind am I to my mortal entanglement
that I dare not call upon thee, Lord, for fear
that thou wouldst take me away from my
sin.*

Tengo memoria, que es el talento de los
tontos.
Francisco Umbral

I have memory, which is the idiots' talent.

Toda crítica es oposición es contrarevolu-
cionaria.
Fidel Castro
Socialism or death. The New Yorker

*All criticism is opposition, and therefore
counterrevolutionary.*

Todo deseo tiene un objeto y éste es siempre oscuro. No hay deseos inocentes.
attrib. **Luis Buñuel**

*Every desire has an object and it will always
be a shady one. There are no innocent
desires.*

Todo lo vital es irracional, y todo lo
racional es antivital, porque la razón es
esencialmente escéptica.
Miguel de Unamuno
Del Sentimiento Trágico de la Vida

*All that is vital is irrational, and all that is
rational is anti-vital, for reason is essentially
sceptical.*

Todo te lo tragaste, como la lejanía
Como el mar, como el tiempo.
Todo en ti fue naufragio!
Pablo Neruda

*You swallowed everything, like distance, like
the sea, like time. In you everything sank!*

Todos creen que tener talento es cuestión
de suerte; nadie piensa que la suerte
pueda ser cuestión de talento.
Jacinto Benavente

*Everybody thinks that having talent is a
matter of luck; nobody thinks that luck could
be a matter of talent.*

Todos los hombres que no tienen nada que decir hablan a gritos.

Enrique Jardiel Poncela
Máximas Mínimas

Every man who has nothing to say shouts.

Todos sueñan lo que son,
Aunque ninguno lo entiende.

Pedro Calderón de La Barca
La Vida es Sueño

Everyone in the world dreams what he is, although none realises it.

Todos tenemos un momento de oro en que se nos concede la felicidad. Luego unos se quedan con el momento y otros con el oro.

Antonio Gala
La Vieja Señorita del Paraíso, Primera Parte

Everybody has a golden moment where happiness is granted to us. Then some take the moment and others the gold.

¡Tu historia!, ¡qué naufragia en mar profundo!
¡Pero no importa, porque ella es corta, pasa, y la muerte es larga, larga como el amor!

Miguel de Unamuno
En Gredos

Your [i.e. Spain's] history; what a shipwreck in the ocean's deep! But it is of no importance, for history is short and it passes, whereas death is long - long as love!

Un ángulo me basta entre mis lares,
Un libro y un amigo, un sueño breve,
Que no perturben deudas ni pesares.

Andrés Fernández de Andrada
Epístola Moral

For me it is sufficient to have a corner by the hearth, a book and a friend, and a nap undisturbed by debts or grief.

Un arte para minorías sólo puede lograrse en medida considerable y ser un gran arte cuando sea el arte de una sociedad regida por esas minorías; en una sociedad dominada por las masas, si acaso puede haber un gran arte, no será sino un arte popular.

Francisco Ayala
El escritor y el cine, Mitología del cinema

An art for minorities can only be properly achieved and be great art when it becomes the art of a society ruled by those minorities; in a society dominated by the masses, if great art is possible, it will be nothing more than popular art.

Un hijo es una pregunta que le hacemos al destino.

José María Pemán

One's child is a question that we ask of destiny.

Un hombre tonto no es capaz de hacer en ningún momento de su vida los disparates que hacen a veces las naciones, dirigidas por centenares de hombres de talento.

Benito Pérez Galdós

Never in his life could an idiot do such foolish things as are sometimes done by nations governed by hundreds of talented people.

Un pintor es un hombre que pinta lo que vende. Un artista, en cambio, es un hombre que vende lo que pinta.

Pablo Picasso

A painter is a man who paints what he sells. An artist, on the contrary, is a man who sells what he paints.

Un problema deja de serlo si no tiene solución.

Eduardo Mendoza
La Verdad sobre el Caso Savolta

A problem ceases to be a problem if it has no solution.

Un riguroso pedagogo es algo más terrible que un terrible demagogo.

Ramón Gómez de la Serna
Gollerías, Un Legoz Pedagogo

A strict pedagogue is more terrible than a terrible demagogue.

Un sólo minuto de reconciliación tiene más mérito que toda una vida de amistad.

Gabriel García Márquez
Cien Años de Soledad

A single minute of reconciliation is worth more than a lifetime of friendship.

Uno buena mentira hay que contarla por etapas, como toda narración bien compuesta.

Gonzalo Torrente Ballester

A good lie must be told in chapters like a well composed story.

Una cosa es estar en el Gobierno y otra es gobernar.

Antonio Maura

To be in the Government is one thing, to govern is another.

Una de las virtudes por las cuales prefiero las naciones protestantes a las de tradición católica es su cuidado de la ética.

Jorge Luis Borges
Elogio de la Sombra, Prólogo

One of the virtues for which I prefer Protestant nations to those of the Catholic tradition is their concern for ethics.

Una fe que no duda es una fe muerta.

Miguel de Unamuno
La Agonía del Cristianismo

A faith which does not doubt is a dead faith.

Una novela es el escape de una angustia por la válvula de la fantasía.

Wenceslao Fernández Florez
Discurso de Ingreso en la Real Academia Española

A novel is the escape of anguish through the valve of fantasy.

Una sola palabra puede bastar para
enterrar a un hombre.

A single word can be enough to bury a man.

Luis Rosales
El Mundo Sideral es la Esperanza

Uno no es más que lo acerca de uno
creen los demás.

One is only what others think of us.

Gonzalo Torrente Ballester

Vencer no es convencer.

To conquer is not to convince.

Miguel de Unamuno
speech at Salamanca University, 1936

Verde que te quiero verde.
Verde viento. Verde ramas.
El barco sobre el mar
y el caballo en la montaña.

Green how I love you green. Green wind.
Green boughs. The ship on the sea and the
horse on the mountain.

Federico García Lorca
Romance Sonámbulo

Viajar produce el mismo efecto que a
un enfermo cambiar de posición.

Travel produces the same effect as changing
the posture of a sick person.

Josep Pla
La Bicicleta

Vuélvete, paloma,
Que el ciervo vulnerado
Por el otero asoma,
Al aire de tu vuelo, y fresco toma.

Turn back, my dove, that the wounded deer
may reappear on the hillside and, in the
breeze of your wings, find new solace.

St John of the Cross
Canciones Entre el Alma y el Esposo

Y aun si mi hijo fuera hereje, yo mismo
traería la leña para quemarle.

If my son was a heretic, I would myself
bring the logs to burn him.

Felipe II

¡Y Dios no te dé paz y sí gloria!

May God give you not peace but glory!

Miguel de Unamuno
Conclusión

Y es cosa manifesta
Que no es de estima lo que poco questa.

And there is one thing clear,
Naught we esteem save that which cost us
dear.

Cervantes
Don Quijote

Y mientras miserablemente se están los otros abrasando en sed insaciable del no durable mando, tendido yo a la sombra esté cantando.

Fray Luis de León
Vida Retirada

And while others are miserably parched with an unquenchable thirst for power which does not last, let me sing this song in the shade.

Y una constate mujer
Que es el mayor imposible.

Tirso de Molina
El Amor y el Amistad

A constant woman - the greatest impossibility!

Yo creo que no debemos respetar nunca las ideas contrarias a las que profesamos. Debemos, si, respetar a las personas que las sustenten, pero nada más.

Manuel de Falla
Escritos sobre Música y Músicos, I, Introducción a la Música Nueva

I think we should never respect ideas opposed to our own. We should, of course, respect the people who profess them, but nothing more.

Yo nací un día que Dios estuvo enfermo.

César Vallejo

I was born on a day God was ill.

Yo no busco, encuentro.

Pablo Picasso

I do not search, I find.

Yo no cambio mi bautismo de cristiano por la sonrisa de un cínico griego. Yo espero ser eterno por mis pecados.

Ramón María del Valle-Inclán
El Marques de Bradomín. Luces de Bohemia

I'll not change my Christian baptism for the smile of a cynical Greek. I expect to be eternal because of my sins.

Yo no la quiero, es cierto, pero cuánto la quise.
Mi voz buscaba el viento para tocar su oído.
De otro. Será de otro. Como antes de mis besos.
Su voz, su cuerpo claro. Sus ojos infinitos.
Ya no la quiero, es cierto, pero tal vez la quiero.
Es tan corto el amor, y es tan largo el olvido.

Pablo Neruda

I no longer love her, that's certain, but how I loved her. My voice tried to find the wind to touch her hearing. Another's. She will be another's. As she was before my kisses. Her voice, her bright body. Her infinite eyes. I no longer love her, that's certain, but maybe I love her. Love is so short, forgetting is so long.

Yo no quería servir a nadie, si acaso a todos.

Gloria Fuertes
Obras Incompletas, Prólogo

I did not want to serve anybody, maybe everybody.

Yo no quiero que el sistema
democrático de convivencia sea,
una vez más, un paréntesis en la
historia de España.

Adolfo Suárez González
Intervención en TVE anunciando su dimisión

*I do not want the democratic system to be
once again a parenthesis in the history of
Spain.*

Yo pinto como si fuera andando por la
calle. Recojo una perla o un mendrugo de
pan; es eso lo que doy, lo que recojo; cuando me coloco delante de un lienzo, no sé
nunca lo que voy a hacer; y yo soy el
primer sorprendido de lo que sale.

Joan Miró
Federico Delclaux, El Silencio Creador, Sencillez

*I paint as if I was walking in the street. I
pick up a pearl or a crust of bread; what I
pick up, I give; I never know what I am
going to do when I place myself in front of a
canvas; and I am the first one shocked by
what comes out.*

Yo que anhelé ser otro, ser un hombre
de sentencias, de libros, de dictámenes,
a cielo abierto yaceré entre ciénagas;
pero me endiosa el pecho inexplicable
un júbilo secreto. Al fin me encuentro
con mi destino hispanoamericano.

Jorge Luis Borges
Antología personal, Poema conjetural

*I who longed to be something else, a man of
opinions, books, judgment, will lie in the
midst of marshes under the open sky. And
yet a secret joy inexplicably exalts me. I have
met my destiny, my final Latin American
destiny.*

Yo soy un hombre sincero
De donde crece la palma,
Y antes de morirme quiero
Echar mis versos del alma.

José Martí
Versos Sencillos

*I am a sincere man from the land of the palm
tree, and before dying I want to share these
poems from my soul.*

Yo soy yo y mi circunstancia, y si no
la salvo a ella no me salvo yo.

José Ortega y Gasset

*I am myself plus my situation; if I do not
save it, I cannot save myself.*

Yo vivo en paz con los hombres y en guerra con mis entrañas.

Antonio Machado

*I live in peace with men and at war with my
innards.*

SPANISH INDEX

ENGLISH INDEX

295

297

vanquished: allows the v. to win as well 269
Varus: V. give me back my legions 43
vase: A worthless v. doesn't get broken 21
  It was intended to be a v. 4
vassal: what a fine v. 251
vegetarian: society of the future will be v. 156
vendetta: better than starting a v. 209
vengeance: envy, v. and hypocrisy 250
  risking our v. to pospone it 56
Venus: it is V. herself seized of her prey 58
Verlaine: a line of V. I shall not recall 263
verse: anger prompts a v. 37
verses: these are the last v. that I write her 281
vice: most obvious v. of human nature 80
  There is only one v. 69
  V. is the evil we do 93
vices: fashionable v. pass for virtues 79
victor: If I am not the v. by tomorrow 190
victories: Who speaks of v. 146
victory: A v. is not a v. 58
  Never has a v. been so bitter 279
  objective is not the fight, but v. 256
  Our v., you shall not be mutilated 240
  V. in war can be achieved 269
Vienna: V. is nothing 141
violence: When you use v. to draw 250
violins: sobs of the v. of autumn 97
vipers: V. breed v. 87
Virgilian: The V. lottery 38
virgin: Fair v., clothed in sunlight 240
virginity: Political convictions are like v. 269
virtue: Be strong in v. 20
  Modesty is the v. 267
  Only v. has powerful argumemnts 284
  this is v.'s task 39
  v. lies in the blood 136
vital: All that is v. is irrational 285
voice: A v. and nothing more 45
  my v. stuck in my throat 29
  the v. of the people is the v. of God 24
vulgar: try to speak in a v. tongue 97
vulgarity: V. will call itself freedom 136

W

Wagner: W has some beautiful moments 99
waiting: I was nearly kept w. 71
  W. is still an occupation 204
wander: And we must w., w. 186
  You who w. the wide world 139
wandering: for him who is tired of w. 193
  human lives w. lost 262
  The years of w. 187
wanted: It's what you w. 121
war: Any w. between Europeans 249
  desires peace should prepare for w. 34
  Every w. contains all earlier w 172
  for a man who has w. in his heart 207
  He who would live of w. 192
  Help - after the w. 32
  history of class w. 145
  I was in the world of w. 155
  if it does not put an end to w. 58
  In w. three-quarters turns on morale 53
  It is easier to make w. than peace 67
  magnificent, but it is not w. 56
  The situation before w. began 39
  There's no safety in w. 27
  w. the condition of our spiritual life 268
  W. always finds a way 141
  W. is too serious a matter 83
  W. is nothing else but 141
  W. on the palaces 160
  who doesn't want peace shall have w. 207
warfare: the art and science of w. 265
wars: The excuse for all w. 257

wars *(cont.)*:
  world does not live by w. 184
war-school: From the w. of life 133
wasps: Do not reach into a w. nest 163
wasteful: It is w. to use more things 14
watch: the w...on the Rhine 175
Waterloo: W! W! melancholy plain 121
waters: Clear, fresh and sweet w. 209
ways: To stand upon the old w. 38
weakness: between strength and w. 145
wealth: by spending the w. of others 226
wealth: contentment surpasses w. 64
  God gave me w. 63
  he equalled the w. of kings 35
  He who seeks w. in a day 209
  Life's w. is in its memories 223
  Poverty amidst great w. 21
  rich man speaks approvingly of w. 92
  the w. of others seeks 272
  The w. of centuries has been reduced 223
  w. and worldly honour 171
  W., acquire 19
weariness: W. of life 40
weathercock: w.'s constancy lies in change 265
weathervane: My head feels like a w. 141
weed: Wine, the w. and women 205
weeds: W. always flourish 99
weep: but are embarrassed to w. there 61
  fear of having to w. at it 73
weeping: Worn out with w. 273
weights: the system of w. and measures 112
welfare: contribute to the w. of society 116
whimpering: w. humility 144
whip: Do not forget the w. 152
whisper: W. as you go past 206
whispered: care about what's w. here 207
Whitman: beautiful aged Walt W. 276
whole: It is the w., not the detail 136
whore: Truth is similar to a...w. 177
wicked: How demanding is it to be w. 191
wickedness: punish the w. of men 68
widow: better to be a hero's w. 262
wife: a leaking roof and an angry w. 238
  and one's w. drunk 241
  than a constant w. 262
  took a w., and died 157
will: divine power and human w. 268
  by the w. of the people 54
  independing of my w. 151
  It is God's w. 56
  The general w. rules in society 87
willing: God w. 9
wills: Whoever w. the end, w. also 190
win: password is w. And w. we will 223
  To w. without danger 53
  trying to w. too much 104
wind: the w. whistles, and the waves 167
  the w. that blew through them 187
  The w. is the only free thing 143
windmills: w. in his head 276
  to tilt at w. 247
winds: unleash the w. across open fields 165
wine: a pure and noble w. 57
  but he enjoys drinking their w. 154
  lingers a cloudy w. 260
  often warmed by w. 24
  the hostess is beautiful the w. is good 106
  The w. is poured 93
  Under the influence of w. 17
  W. comforts with heart 259
  W. has two defects 259
  W. is the tomb of memory 259
  W. should have flavour 64
  W., the weed and women 205
  Without food and w. love grows cold 37

wings: Go, O thought on golden w. 239
  If I had w. I would fly to them 152
winning: not so much w. as taking part 80
wisdom: w. there is is to know oneself 223
  Here is w. 56
  how little w. the world is governed 25
  more than all the w. in this world 153
  professing a w. which was no w. 31
  the collective w. of his ancestors 142
  the first step of w. 143
  W. does not come free 189
wise: A w. and prudent king 90
wise: A w. man has no dealings 118
  A word is enough for the w. 43
  A word to the w. is enough 9
  The w. man distrusts everything 62
  to be well spoken and w. 231
  To love and be w. 4
wisely: who goes slowly goes w. 208
withdraw: those who knew when to w. 274
without: W. which, not 38
witnesses: behaving without w. 84
  from the mouths of two w. 153
witticism: The w. you think of only 77
woe: W. to the conquered 18
wolf: be damned, o ancient w. 226
woman: loved w. who is not interested 68
  a w. who can gladden 189
  A cello is like a w. 259
  A constant w. 289
  Angel of the family is the w. 219
  because of a w. 103
  disputes which weren't started by a w. 27
  Good fortune is a loose w. 136
  Look for the w. 59
  my pleasure lay in a beautiful w. 161
  the love of a good w. 184
  The leader...was a w. 10
  to be a w. is so fascinating 214
  W., always fickle
  W. is fickle 222
  W. was God's second blunder 137
  Beware w.'s waywardness 166
  moderately right idea of what a w. is 278
  You are going to a w. 152
women: Free w. are not w. 95
  leave pretty w. to men 88
  play at being in love with w. 96
  That's what all w. do 210
  The company of women 143
  The w. come to see the show 38
  w. never notice what is done 82
  w. want to make mistakes 190
  W. are beautiful 134
  W. govern America 270
  W. nowadays do not die for love 278
  W. of today are overthrowing 95
  W. on the verge of a nervous breakdown 276
  Wine, the weed and w. 205
wonder: W. is belief's favourite child 194
wonder-realm: the w. of Night 137
wondrous: W. to relate 23
woods: We will go no more to the w. 102
wool: who go for w. come back shorn 275
word: A single w. can be enough to bury 288
  A w. once spoken flies 36
  A w. to the wise is enough 9
  A w. is enough for the wise 43
  A w. once uttered 25
  die for the sake of an empty w. 176
  I do not hear a human w. 237
words: because they live without w. 164
  Gentle w. may oft obtain 281
  if only I could get the w. 28
  O w., what crimes are committed 102

INDEX OF AUTHORS